The
Future
of the
Self

Also by Walter Truett Anderson

Evolution Isn't What It Used to Be
The Truth About the Truth
Reality Isn't What It Used to Be
To Govern Evolution

The Future of the Self

Inventing the Postmodern Person

Walter Truett Anderson

Jeremy P. Tarcher/Putnam
a member of
PENGUIN PUTNAM INC.
New York

Most Tarcher/Putnam books are available at special quantity discounts for bulk purchases for sales promotions, premiums, fund-raising, and educational needs. Special books or book excerpts also can be created to fit specific needs. For details, write or telephone Putnam Special Markets, 200 Madison Ave., New York, NY 10016; (212) 951-8891.

Jeremy P. Tarcher/Putnam
a member of
Penguin Putnam Inc.
200 Madison Avenue
New York, NY 10016
http://www.putnam.com

Library of Congress Cataloging-in-Publication Data

Anderson, Walter, date.
    The future of the self : inventing the postmodern person / Walter Truett Anderson.
       p.   cm.
    ISBN 0-87477-881-6 (alk. paper)
    1. Self (Philosophy)—Controversial literature.   I. Title.
BD438.5.A63 1997   97-19571 CIP
126—dc21

BOOK DESIGN BY LEE FUKUI

Printed in the United States of America
10 9 8 7 6 5 4 3 2 1
This book is printed on acid-free paper. ∞

To understand is to invent.
JEAN PIAGET

Contents

Do not ask me who I am and do not expect me to remain the same. Leave it to the bureaucrats to see that our papers are in order.

MICHEL FOUCAULT

Introduction: Everybody's Identity Crisis

All human societies are built upon a lie, the lie of self—the conceit that we know what a human being is and can satisfactorily describe one with the customary names, roles, and badges of identity that are the currency of all our lives. This fundamental premise of all social orders is not necessarily an evil lie. It can certainly become evil, as it does when societies wander into the extremes of fascism or racism, but it can also be practical, reassuring, helpful, even noble—as it was when Socrates proposed the "noble lie" of telling the warriors of his ideal republic that they had actually been reared within the womb of their native land, so that they would defend it as they would their own biological mothers. In any case it is a lie, or what contemporary scholars call a social construction of reality.

Having accepted the lie—which we all must, and all do—we live out our lives as the selves we believe ourselves to be. And all day, every day, we speak the language of self. We talk of selfishness and unselfishness, and watch out for self-centered people. We hear about self-actualization, self-confidence, self-control, self-denial, self-defense, self-destruction, self-determination, self-esteem, self-gratification, self-improvement, self-indulgence, self-knowledge, self-pity, self-righteousness. And of course we think about ourselves all the time. Who doesn't? The shelves of the bookstores are crammed with self-help books of all persuasions. Yet it is a curious fact of life that we rarely if ever really question the meaning of the word "self." We don't often turn around and take a hard look at the concept that is underneath all our concern about selfishness and unselfishness.

Nothing in the world seems—at least at first glance—more obvious, real, and commonsensical than the idea of the self. I am I, and you are you. The self is what's in here, and the not-self is what's out there. Nothing seems more obvious, yet nothing turns out to be more elusive when you try to examine it directly. We think of the self as a whole, but see it only in fragments. We think of it as somehow distinct from its surroundings, but never experience it apart from an environment. We think of it as a thing that endures, at least for a lifetime, but from moment to moment the self is never quite the same. "In the same rivers we step and we do not step," goes one of the oldest recorded comments on the subject: "We are and we are not."

This book is an invitation to think about self. And it's more than that. It is also an urgent plea for you to consider this subject, however elusive it might seem; to wrestle with it deeply. We need to do that for three reasons: one, because the subject is of the greatest importance to every one of us; two, because we really can't get very far in any of our self-help or self-improvement efforts without giving at least a little thought to the question of what, exactly, is the self we want to help or improve; and three, because the self—as we have come to understand it and to take it for granted in the modern world—is an endangered species, quite possibly destined for extinction sooner than any of us would expect. So if you're interested in self-development and personal growth—and who isn't?—you are going to need some different skills, some different information, a different map of the social world than you would have needed a few decades ago.

The idea of self is important because it is at the heart of so much of what we do and what we think, both as individuals and as a society:

It is at the heart of psychology and psychotherapy, which are institutionalized attempts to understand and maintain the modern self;

it is at the heart of politics, because identification with any cause, community, nation, or ideology is just that, *identification*—a way of answering the question of who and what you are; and

it is at the heart of religion, because every faith seeks some connection between the self and the universe. That's the matter of "ultimate concern" that Paul Tillich believed to be the essence of all spirituality.

In any of these fields of endeavor, we have a much greater chance of success if we develop a little more awareness of the different kinds of ideas about the self—at the very least a knowledge that there *are* different ideas. Failing to do so is like looking for all the answers in a single book, without ever knowing there is a whole library available.

Considering how central the idea of self is to every aspect of our lives, it is obviously an event of enormous historical importance when a society's fundamental idea of self changes dramatically. And that is happening now. The ground is shifting beneath us all.

Every civilization creates its own concept of the self. The modern self-concept defines each of us as an individual, with a distinct identity (from the Latin *idens*, meaning the same) that remains the same wherever one goes. This idea served its purpose reasonably well, but it rapidly erodes in the postmodern world as different aspects of it are undermined by different currents of thought and action. Michel Foucault's flat-out rejection of identity—his denial of its importance—was an unusually explicit challenge. Other challenges are more modest, less eager to take on one of our deepest, most fundamental assumptions in such a direct way. Most of them only tug away mischievously at some *part* of the modern self. Moralists of various persuasions do battle against what they see as an excess of selfish individualism, want us to sacrifice some of our autonomy and go back to being more community-bonded. Some environmentalists want us to stop being "anthropocentric" (that is, to stop looking at nature solely in terms of human purposes) and become more connected to the Earth. Psychologists are converging from several directions on the idea of the unitary self as a model of mental health, and saying instead that the healthy person is more a posse than a Lone Ranger. Medical science is rewriting the rule book on biological identity as people exchange organs, skin, blood, and bone marrow, and get used to new techniques of reproduction, such as artificial insemination and surrogacy, that blur the lines of parenthood. Anthropologists, historians, artists, and postmodern philosophers keep telling us that the self is *constructed*—assembled and reassembled in different ways by individuals and societies. The information/communications revolution creates a vast and mysterious electronic landscape of new relationships, roles, identities, networks, and communities, while it undermines that cherished luxury of the modern self—privacy. The globalization of economics and politics sends people scurrying about the planet; pulling up roots; trampling boundaries; letting go of old certainties of place, nationality, social role, and class. And meanwhile ancient esoteric traditions, now thriving far from their original Oriental hangouts and disseminating their teachings through the mass media, mysteriously suggest, as they have for millennia, that we are *something else*, that this identity we cling to and strive for is not really what we are at all.

Put all these together and you have what amounts to a global identity crisis.

I realize that the idea of a fundamental shift in our social concept of self will seem difficult or abstract to some readers, and I will try in the following chapters to bring it down to earth. We'll start with a brief tour through history to examine some evidence of different ideas about the self that have been held by people in the past, and then look into the world of psychology, where, not surprisingly—since self is the psychologist's stock in trade—the current change is being most clearly described and the issues most heatedly argued. Along the way we'll visit other arenas within which modern ideas of identity are being

challenged and other ways of experiencing life are being invented—
cognitive science, medicine, cyberspace, global politics.

A word about words: You will hear many different voices in this
book, because it reports on many conversations that are now going on
around the world. And different people use the same words to mean
different things. I plan to use the terms "human being" and "self" in
very specific ways, and those uses are central to everything in this
book. By "human being" I mean all that you are—biological and
psychological, conscious and unconscious. By "self" I mean the
person that you construct with words and with the help of the people
around you. The human being is always changing, has no clear
boundaries, and cannot be described fully. The self craves stability, has
a strong sense of boundaries, and maintains its existence through a
continuous act of description. Your self takes over your consciousness
so that you come to equate it with the human being that you are. You
describe your self by using language to identify with various things—
your nationality, your profession, your place in the family. People have
always identified, at least since they had language, but in the contemporary world, identifying becomes a precarious business: Nationalities
change, professions become obsolete, families collapse. Sometimes we
lack anything to identify with; sometimes we have more identities than
we know what to do with.

In this book we will consider two slightly different ways of answering the question of how we may move through the identity crisis. I'll
call these the multiple-self answer and the no-self answer.

The multiple-self answer, as we'll see, is being widely chosen and
acted upon already. You can find it in intellectual circles, where
thinkers of many disciplines are arguing that the modern era's concept
of self—the one most of us in the Western world have accepted
unquestioningly and built our lives upon—is now being replaced by a
postmodern concept in which the self is seen as decentered, multidimensional, changeable. And you can find it on the streets, where
many people, with or without any particular theories in their heads,
are finding it necessary to construct multiple instead of single selves, to
let go of identities, to change radically in the course of their lives.

These self-transformation efforts are often stressful, sometimes bizarre, frequently unsuccessful. But they all are attempts to adapt to the circumstances of the contemporary world; they conform to what biologists call the "law of requisite variety," meaning that an organism, if it is to survive, must be at least as complex as its environment.[1]

The no-self answer proposes that the identity crisis of our time presents a precious opportunity for an even more radical reunderstanding of self, so that in a sense you abandon it entirely and develop in its place a deeper sense of the human being. This idea is central to the esoteric spiritual traditions of Asia, but I will argue that it is a logical and sane notion—more so than the one we now take to be common sense—and can be approached without benefit of incense, gurus, trips to the mysterious East, psychedelic drugs, or any of the other accoutrements of what we think of as spirituality.

So I suppose this could be labeled a self-help book, since it presumes to offer some guidelines for living happily and effectively in today's world. But it is really more of a multiple-self-help book and, toward the end, a no-self-help book. And I will consider my work well worth the effort if everyone who reads it becomes, if only slightly, a different self as a result.

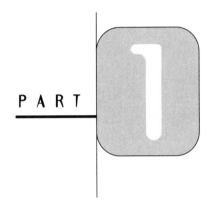

PART 1

Constructing
and
Deconstructing
the
Modern
Self

So we naturally come to think that we have selves the way we have heads or arms, and inner depths the way we have hearts and livers, as a matter of hard, interpretation-free fact.

CHARLES TAYLOR[1]

The Western conception of the person as a bounded, unique, more or less integrated motivational and cognitive universe . . . is, however incorrigible it may seem to us, a rather peculiar idea within the context of the world's cultures.

CLIFFORD GEERTZ[2]

Now, as everyone knows, it has only been in the last two centuries that the majority of people in civilized countries have claimed the privilege of being individuals.

SAUL BELLOW[3]

A Brief History of the Self

How did you get to be the way you are? If the modern self is an invention, who invented it?

No scholar has yet written the definitive history of the modern self, but we know now that it does have a history—and a geography. Although all human beings construct a self, most people in the past were probably not individual selves in the modern Western sense, and people in some parts of the world probably are not now. That is, they do not experience themselves as clearly bounded, but rather as seamlessly embedded in their tribes and their ecosystems; they do not think of themselves as unique, but rather as more or less identical to others of their kind; and they do not think of themselves as neatly integrated, but rather as invaded by strange spirits and forces that may pull them in many different directions.

They also don't think *about* their concept of self any more than we do—in fact, probably a whole lot less. The exploration of such a subject—the one in which we are engaged here—is both the curse and blessing of those of us who live in the urbanizing, globalizing, high-technology, postmodern world. Lots of people have other kinds

3

of experiences and assume that those experiences represent the way human life has always been and always will be. Yet some of those unquestioned, commonsense notions of what constitutes a self may seem, as anthropologist Clifford Geertz put it, "more than a little odd" from our point of view. During his years of intensive study of the lives of people in places such as Java, Bali, and Morocco, he found self-concepts far different from our own reality:

> [People] may be conceived to dart about nervously at night shaped like fireflies. Essential elements of their psyches, like hatred, may be thought to be lodged in granular black bodies within their livers, discoverable upon autopsy. They may share their fates with *doppleganger* beasts, so that when the beast sickens or dies they sicken or die too.[4]

Charles Taylor, whose *Sources of the Self* comes closest to being the definitive history, observed along similar lines:

> We can probably be confident that at one level human beings of all times and places have shared a very similar sense of "me" and "mine." In those days when a Paleolithic hunting group was closing in on a mammoth, when the plan went awry and the beast was lunging toward hunter A, something similar to the thought, "Now I'm for it" crossed A's mind. And when at the last moment, the terrifying animal lunged to the left and crushed B instead, a sense of relief mingled with grief for poor B was what A experienced. In other words, the members of the group must have had very much the same sense that we would in their place. . . . But alongside these strands of continuity, which would probably make even our remote ancestors comprehensible to us, there are baffling contrasts when we try to understand human agency in its moral and spiritual

dimension. This is driven home to us in our puzzle-
ment at the three souls of the Buriats in northern
Siberia.[5]

The Buriats apparently believe that every person has three souls,
one of which can leave the body and remain outside it for some time.
Realities change, selves change.

The modern Western concept of self has been in the making for
thousands of years, and there's no way we can ever know precisely
what life was like for people before that concept took hold. But ancient
people did, sometimes, leave stories about their life experiences, and
those give us a glimpse of radically different beings who lived in a
radically different world.

The Self as Playground of the Gods

Consider the early Greeks, in the distant ages before the period of
classical Athens, at the morning of recorded Western history. We have
surviving messages from their time: the Homeric stories of the Trojan
War and the adventures of Ulysses. Although those great fables are
certainly not treatises on personal identity, they do reveal much about
how people of that era saw the world: a place occupied by human
beings, who did various things, and by gods—powerful, mysterious,
capricious—who did various things to (and with) human beings. And
human beings weren't quite the same as you and I.

Some scholars have pointed out that there really isn't a word in the
works of Homer that translates neatly into "mind." Thoughts and
feelings seem to have happened in and around people, sometimes in
locations that can be identified with body parts—such as the lungs and
heart—and sometimes they really can't be located anywhere at all.[6]

In the 1970s psychologist Julian Jaynes offered the startling
thesis that people of the Homeric era did not possess a personal
consciousness that we would recognize as such. He argued that the
style of thinking we call consciousness does not blossom sponta-

neously out of the human brain, but rather is a learned process, the result of a social invention that began to take form only about 3,000 years ago—some time *after* the Trojan War. He came to his conclusions mainly through studying the literature of the ancient Greeks, in particular the Iliad, which stands as one of the immortal classics of Western literature—part legend, part history, part poetry. Jaynes proposed that we see it also as a psychological study, a case history, an honest documentation of how people lived and thought. How did they?

Well, they seem to have heard voices a lot. They had frequent experiences of the sort that today we would call auditory hallucinations but which they took to be communications from the gods, and obeyed as such. "The characters of the Iliad do not sit down and think out what to do," Jaynes wrote. "They have no conscious minds such as we say we have, and certainly no introspections."[7] Instead of introspections, instead of any of the terms that stand for will, psychic conflict, plans, reasons, thoughts, motives, we find gods telling people what to do and how to feel, freely manipulating them as though they were icons in some cosmic computer game. And we find people taking no personal responsibility for their acts. Thus, when the war is nearly over and Achilles reminds King Agamemnon of how he robbed him of his mistress, the king replies, "Not I was the cause of this act, but Zeus, and my portion, and the Erinyes who walk in darkness: they it was in the assembly put wild *ate* upon me on that day when I arbitrarily took Achilles' prize from him, so what could I do? Gods always have their way." Jaynes commented, "And that this was no particular fiction of Agamemnon's to evade responsibility is clear in that this explanation is fully accepted by Achilles, for Achilles also is obedient to his gods. Scholars who in commenting on this passage say that Agamemnon's behavior has become 'alien to his ego,' do not go nearly far enough. For the question is indeed, what is the psychology of the Iliadic hero? And I am saying that he did not have any ego whatever."[8]

Jaynes's theory is not an easy one to accept, and a lot of people don't. But whether or not we buy it in full, I think we have to go along with him so far as to assume that the author of the Iliad (whoever he, she, or they actually were) *meant what he said*. The poet was not kidding around. His description of how people felt, why they did what they did, is as worthy of being taken seriously as is the work of any contemporary novelist who uses Freudian language to describe her characters' motivations. It deserves to be read as an honest statement about how people of the Homeric era understood the world and human life. Equally worthy of being taken seriously are the countless other people, religions, and civilizations who have operated on the belief that the voices of gods spoke within the human mind and could be *heard*, and who knew the gods as alien agents that were forces in personal behavior as powerful as the inner agents—ego, superego, id—are assumed to be by modern psychoanalysts. And if you operate on the basis of such a belief, you do not have the kind of self-concept so memorably expressed by the nineteenth-century poet William Ernest Henley, at a time when both the British Empire and the modern self were riding high:

> *It matters not how strait the gate,*
> *How charged with punishments the scroll,*
> *I am the master of my fate;*
> *I am the captain of my soul.*[9]

Something—during the three-thousand-year span that separates Homer from Henley—had changed, and changed enormously. Of course we can't go back in time and enter people's minds and *feel* that change taking place, but we can examine the works of philosophers who were trying to understand what, exactly, is a human being.

The River and the Statue

We have other messages from the distant pre-Socratic Greek past, and they also hint at ideas of self far different from Henley's stiff-upper-lip, steady-as-she-goes image. Perhaps the most fascinating of all these are the works of the philosopher Heraclitus. Written around 500 B.C.—three or four centuries after Homer—they suggest a radically unstable sense of self, devoid of certainty and permanence—certainly not the bounded, unique, more or less integrated character structure that Geertz described as the essence of modernity. The fragments of Heraclitus have much in common with the ideas Gautama Buddha was proclaiming in another part of the world at about the same time:

> *In the same rivers we step*
> *and we do not step,*
> *we are and we are not.*[10]

Was this the accepted, conventional idea of the self for Greeks of Heraclitus' time? Probably not. Probably it represented a minority view, as such ideas tend to wherever they are expressed. Some scholars even doubt that the passage stated above was written by Heraclitus. It may have been the version written by Cratylus, a lesser-known philosopher who is said to have been so infatuated with the idea of continual change that he told Heraclitus you can't even step in the same river *once*.[11] But whoever wrote it, the fact that it was written informs us that a much different concept—of a sort we would be more likely to describe as mystical or Oriental—was being expressed in Greece before the time of Socrates. Had it prevailed as the mainstream view, I doubt very much that you and I today would be living with the same set of assumptions about personal identity that we take to be commonsense reality. Modern societies view identities as real and persistent. And for such practical purposes I am, Heraclitus notwithstanding, the same person as the seventeen-year-old kid who got a Social Security card so he could go to work in Leo Bernacchi's grocery store.

If you go back to Socrates, Plato, and Aristotle—who lived a century or so after Heraclitus—you can see in their works parts of the modern self being born. Socrates (in the dialogues recorded by Plato) built his philosophical system upon the doctrine of eternal

Ideas or Forms, which had a supernatural existence somewhere apart from human consciousness yet were the true realities, of which all things seen and felt in the ordinary world were only reflections. So according to the Socratic-Platonic doctrine, the famous river would continue to be (at least as long as it still had water in it) not only the same river but an earthly manifestation of such an Idea—of essential, eternal, transcendent River-ness. And for Socrates the individual self, as the embodiment of an immortal soul, was more than the ethereal consciousness of the moment. A human self had its own moral life. A human self experienced conflict between the baser desires of the body and the higher aspirations of the reasoning intelligence, which was described by Socrates as a *personal, inner* struggle for integration and self-control, not just more fun and games among the Olympian superstars with the human mind as the playground.

The gods and goddesses were still around as offstage presences in the Socratic dialogues, but they were undergoing a sort of metamorphosis—turning into mythic embodiments of Ideas, abstractions whose significance you might hear Joseph Campbell explaining to Bill Moyers on television. And at the same time a new concept of the human being was being forged, one that saw people as active, rational agents of ethical behavior. "Perhaps on the basis of his own highly developed sense of individual selfhood and self-control," commented Richard Tarnas, "Socrates brought to the Greek mind a new awareness of the central significance of the soul, establishing it for the first time as the seat of the individual waking consciousness and of the moral and intellectual character."[12]

The seat of the individual waking consciousness . . . The notion of the soul was not new, had been present in Greek mythology and philosophy since the unrecorded past. Even Heraclitus had talked about souls. Some Greeks believed in the ancient concept of transmigration—what we usually call reincarnation—in which a soul might wander eternally from one person or animal to another, unable to remember, except on rare occasions, what he or she had been before. This understanding of the soul changes in Socratic thought, and we get a soul recognizable to modern believers of several different faiths—an immortal yet *personal* moral agent that retains its identity in the afterlife. The soul is a self, as clearly described in *Phaedo*, the account of Socrates' last reflections before he drank the fatal cup of hemlock. Talking through the night with a little group of grieving friends who had come to visit him in prison, Socrates reassured them that the soul survives after death and that, if the person has succeeded in attaining virtue and wisdom while alive, his soul will ascend to the "real earth" and live happily in communion with the gods. Socrates was jailed in part because he had been accused of undermining religion, but in fact his view of human existence was profoundly religious—and at the same time an important contribution to modern individualism. According to Socrates, the personal soul had not only an identity, but an immortal one, with a cosmic career. There was plenty of ego in Socratic virtue, as there is in Judeo-Christian morality.

The traditional gods and goddesses retreated farther into the background in the thinking of Plato's student Aristotle, whose quest for knowledge had a more secular, scientific spirit. Aristotle put a different spin on the eternal Forms, which began to resemble scientific categories whose reality was *not* separate from and superior to the things in which they were embodied.[13] Aristotle's idea took another step in the direction of modern selfhood, because it located the observing individual consciousness in a *real world* of material things that could be studied and understood in themselves—that weren't just pale reflections of Ideas, as Socrates had described them—and it powerfully affirmed the human ability to comprehend this real world through rational thought.

In the work of Aristotle we glimpse something that begins to look even more like the modern mind—reasoning, questioning, aware of its own boundedness and stability. However, important pieces of the modern, individualistic self were still missing: Greek philosophy did not, for example, have a concept of individual rights; there is no evidence that Greeks were particularly concerned about personal privacy in their daily lives; and many centuries were yet to pass before Rene Descartes would come along and put the waking consciousness firmly inside the head—where of course all right-thinking people now know it to be. But the foundation was in place. The person that emerged from the golden philosophical decades of Socrates, Plato, and Aristotle was no longer hearing the voices of gods like the Homeric heroes, and was not the evanescent wraith of Heraclitus, either. She had a permanent identity, and he could call his soul his own.

Philosophical systems are not always about self explicitly, but the subject is always there. Your worldview and your self-concept are always connected, and when one changes so does the other. The Greeks succeeded in expressing ideas about both that have stood like statues in the Western mind for thousands of years, and have been taken for granted by countless people as unquestioned reality. The ideas about truth were summarized by Isaiah Berlin:

> The view that the truth is one and undivided, and the same for all men everywhere at all times, whether one finds it in the pronouncements of sacred books, traditional wisdom, the authority of churches, democratic majorities, observation and experiments conducted by qualified experts, or the convictions of simple folk uncorrupted by civilization—this view, in one form or another, is central to Western thought, which stems from Plato and his disciples.[14]

Thus in this view, somebody either knows truth or finds it out, and truth is applicable to everybody for all time. It is this agreement concerning truth that makes differences of belief so fiercely important. It is what has historically given a flaming gut-level urgency to conflicts among religions, and later to conflicts between religion and science, and later still to conflicts among political ideologies. These conflicts have mattered so deeply because they were not seen as mere differences of opinion in a you-do-your-thing-I'll-do-mine kind of world. The disagreements on doctrine mattered because people agreed on the basic nature of truth. They knew it was "out there"—they assumed that somebody had the absolute truth and that everybody else was really wrong and quite possibly in serious trouble with God because of it. For the Greeks, that much was known with certainty. And most people knew, with the same certainty, that they had an identity that would be theirs at least for a lifetime and perhaps for all time.

I doubt that many people today appreciate the power of the Platonic concept of abstract Ideas—or recognize how much we are still in the grip of them. I don't know anybody who calls himself or herself a Platonist, but I often find myself in conversations with people who refer to abstract ideas—democracy, community, masculinity, femininity, justice, love—as though they were real things, with an existence of their own apart from the ways we understand and experience them in our lives. In that regard, the Greek gods still rule us.

The Mask of the Actor

French sociologist Marcel Mauss, another scholar who attempted to document the emergence of the modern Western self, thought that the Romans made an important contribution with their concept of the person. This concept, which was central to the Roman legal system as it developed and was passed on to the various societies that evolved out of the Empire, seems to have emphasized a sense of the self as façade, as the external being that is presented to the world and recognized by others. It apparently had its roots in ancient clan ceremonies—both drama and religious ritual—that had made heavy use of masks. The Latin *persona* comes from *per/sonare*, meaning the mask through which (*per*) the voice of the actor sounds. In Roman law the word "*persona*" took on an important meaning, central to the Roman view of self and society: It signified the individual whose family, status, and privileges were officially recognized. The system of family names—*nomen, praenomon,* and *cognomen*—was firmly laid down by the Senate, and the words "*cognomen*" (family name) and "*imago*" (the ancestral death-masks that were displayed in the houses of Roman families) were closely linked. These names established the person as an individual, a self, a free citizen. Personhood seems to have been conceived as an almost-tangible *thing*, something some people had and some people didn't have. Slaves were denied a *persona*, according to Mauss: "*Servus non habet personam*. He has no personality. He does not own his body; he has no ancestors, no name, no *cognomen*, no goods of his own."[15] Although the Roman *persona* was essentially a legal concept, Mauss believes it later became the basis of a growing *moral* sense of self as well, under the influence of Stoic philosophers such as Marcus Aurelius, and was further developed by the Christians into an idea of the person as a metaphysical entity with an immortal soul.

The Roman Empire was officially polytheistic, and many Romans who turned to philosophy were drawn more to the Stoics than to the Platonists. The strongest link we can find between the disciples of Plato and the modern mind is in the work of Augustine, who converted the Platonic ideas into the thoughts of God, and who made a sharp distinction between the inner and the outer person. For Augustine the soul lay inward, and the outward body was essentially the same as that of animals. "Do not go outward," he advised; "return within yourself. In the inward man dwells truth."[16] It is not surprising that many people see Augustine as the forerunner of Descartes, with his view of a nonmaterial mind that looked out through material eyes at a material, even mechanical, world. The assumption that consciousness is inside us is one of the most important assumptions of the Western self—so important, in fact, that we rarely think of it as an assumption—and Augustine's work stands as a marker for that growing inwardness.

The project of constructing the modern self doesn't appear to have made much progress throughout the medieval era. People in the Middle Ages may have had a belief in personal salvation and a sense of inward consciousness, but surely they did not assume, as moderns do, that they were or should be or ever could be in the drivers' seats of their own lives. Personal identity, whatever it may have been, was deeply rooted within the confines of the feudal system, which had rigid definitions of class and role that changed slowly, admitted of very little social mobility, and entertained no concept of an individual apart from that system. It didn't have much of an image of any other way of life, either, at least until the Crusades—those looney but ultimately world-changing adventures—put many people on the move and ultimately brought to every little inbred village the news of distance and difference. The religious worldview of the times was a powerful factor in the way people understood the self—and it didn't encourage them to believe their personal selves counted for much. As Roy Baumeister—another scholarly detective searching for the origins of the modern self—put it:

> A main reason for the relative indifference to individuality was the firm medieval faith in Christianity, which regarded life on earth as imitative or derivative of the ultimate, otherworldly realities. In fact, the particulars of individual human experience were not very important. What mattered was the broad cosmic drama of faith and salvation. The life of a particular person was only a good or poor approximation of the archetypal patterns of heavenly or biblical events. The individual self was significant only as an example of the general struggle between good and evil, virtue and vice, faith and heresy, honor and disgrace.[17]

Although it may well have seemed at the time that nothing changed or even *could* change, the Western world went through a tremendous transformation over the next few centuries—spectacular upheavals in government, philosophy, religion, science. Not only did new worldviews emerge, but so did a new world, as the voyages of Columbus and other explorers discovered continents and previously unknown civilizations. And clearly human consciousness of self changed as well.

One sign of such change was an increasing concern for personal privacy. The history of everyday life has become an important and valuable intellectual activity in recent years—turning our attention to homelier aspects of past ages—and those histories depict medieval lifestyles that most moderns would find distinctly uncomfortable:

> People crowded together cheek by jowl, living in pro-miscuity, sometimes in the midst of a mob. In feudal residences there was no room for individual solitude, except perhaps in the moment of death. When people ventured outside the domestic enclosure, they did so in groups. No journey could be made by fewer than two people, and if it happened that they were not related, they bound themselves by rites of brotherhood, creating an artificial family that lasted as long as the journey required.[18]

"In fact," declared Philippe Aries, one of the leading practitioners of this kind of history, "until the end of the seventeenth century, nobody was ever left alone."[19] Some hints of change can be seen in architecture: People began to build houses with rooms reserved as bedrooms, and with corridors so that each room could be reached without having to pass through others. Another change was the gradual replacement of live-in servants by domestics who did not sleep in the same house—or the same room—with their employers.[20] In such small, often scarcely noticed transitions, a revolution took place—a progression from the time when privacy simply did not exist as either an ideal or a part of everyday life, to the present time when it is regarded as a deep human need and a political right.

Other historians direct our attention to the emergence of auto-biography as a new literary form that expressed two of the main features of individualism: (1) placing value on the unique characteristics and particular experiences of each person, and (2) believing that each person has a special unique potentiality or destiny that may or may not be fulfilled.[21]

One of the most famous autobiographers of all time was Ben-venuto Cellini. Theodore Zeldin, in his *Intimate History of Human-ity*, wrote of this immortal artist and oversized Renaissance ego:

Having become a world-famous jeweller and sculptor, he believed he had found a method for avoiding self-doubt. He advised everybody to write their autobiography, not in order to understand themselves, but, more simply, to assert their individuality. He went so far as to kill people who he thought were obstructing the flowering of his genius, and boasted of the beautifully made daggers he used.[22]

Another historical clue to the evolutionary transition, according to Baumeister, is given by the increasing attention paid in literature and philosophy to deception. This might not sound like a sign of progress, but it is closely related to the idea of privacy. Just as people had private spaces in their homes, they insisted on having private spaces in their selves that were not necessarily identical to their public façades. "People began to regard the self as a hidden entity that might or might not be reflected in outward acts. The belief in a real self that is hidden, that is not directly or clearly shown in one's public behavior, can be regarded as a first step toward making identity a problem."[23] The literary critic Lionel Trilling found the sixteenth century to be "preoccupied to an extreme degree with dissimulation, feigning and pretense."[24] He talked about the various disguises and mistaken identities among characters in Shakespeare's plays, and about Machiavelli's infamous cookbook on how to be a tricky statesman.

Actually, Machiavelli contributed more to modern individualism than his ideas about chicanery in leadership; he also expounded on the subject of the two great driving forces in human affairs that he called *virtu* and *fortuna* — *virtu* being personal initiative, drive (Italian *chutzpah*), and *fortuna* being the impersonal powers of fate. So for Machiavelli at least half of life was what you made of it yourself. That was a lot more than would have been granted by most medieval theologians, but it was barely enough for many of his Renaissance contemporaries who were intoxicated with the idea of a person's life as his own creation, a work of art. That seems to have been the way Cellini looked at things, and it is also the exuberant vision of Pico della

Mirandola's *Oration on the Dignity of Man*, in which God tells Adam that "you, being your own free maker and artificer, may fashion yourself into whatever form you choose."

"I Think, Therefore I Am"

According to some accounts, the modern self was born in a room with a stove—a private space—in a little house in southern Germany, early in the seventeenth century. That happened during the winter in which Rene Descartes holed up and commenced thinking his way down to the very core of reality.

It was a modern kind of project. He was in search of certainty, and prepared to doubt everything, including all that he had been taught, until he could find some basis for it. The premodern person, warmly contained within the tribe or the village, had no such need to embark on such a search for certainty, and no such reason to doubt the accumulated wisdom of ancestors and contemporaries. But Descartes lived in a time of great political, religious, and philosophical turbulence. Old orders and old beliefs were literally collapsing around him. The Thirty Years' War filled most of his adult life. He served in two different armies in the course of it. The war itself was a complex tangle of princely ambitions and religious disputes following the Reformation. It was also—although of course this was not recognized at the time—the death throes of the old feudal system that had ordered European life for centuries. It ended, finally, with the Peace of Westphalia, which legitimized the emergence of the modern age's preeminent political institutions and definers of identity—the sovereign nation-states.

Another source of turbulence in Descartes' time, one that rumbled on even longer than the war, was the dispute over Nicolaus Copernicus' heliocentric theory of the solar system. Copernicus' theory had been published in 1543, but the massive backlash against it—both from church authorities, who saw it as a devilish contradiction of religious doctrine, and from rival astronomers, who saw it as a ridiculous departure from scientific truth—was slow to get started and was still going strong while Descartes was growing up. Descartes' contemporary Galileo was in the thick of that upheaval, looking through his telescope and discovering a solar system—indeed, a universe—unlike anything that had been imagined before.

During that winter in Bavaria, Descartes mentally listed all the things it was possible to doubt and came down to the one fact that he could trust. It was not the reality of the physical world—that could be doubted. It was not his own body—that could be only a dream. But the "I" who was doing the doubting, his own self-awareness—it was beyond doubt. He thought, therefore he existed. That much was certain. Upon this foundation, upon this confidence in a rational and integrated self, prepared to question all his society's received truths, he built his edifice of thought. Modern science rests in part upon that Cartesian foundation, as does the modern sense of a critical consciousness that can stand back from the world and study it.

Descartes located the human subject at the center of the knowable world, and also located a center of the human subject—an observer of the world, seated inside the brain. This was the pineal gland—the central processor of all sensory experience, and also the passageway from the physical brain to the nonphysical mind. It's hardly surprising that so many people give Descartes credit for inventing the modern self and that so many people today use him as the reference point to describe contrasting views of how the mind works. Tarnas described Descartes' work as "the prototypical declaration of the modern self, established as a fully separate, self-defining entity, for whom its own rational self-awareness was absolutely primary—doubting everything except itself, setting itself in opposition not only to traditional authorities but to the world as subject against object, as a thinking, observing, measuring, manipulating being, fully distinct from an objective God and an external nature."[25]

After Descartes, the self became a major topic for philosophers such as David Hume, Immanuel Kant, and John Locke. There was much disagreement about the subject—and for good reason, because in some ways the Cartesian self wasn't really such a simple and logical idea. David Hume, the Scottish skeptic, sometimes sounded like Heraclitus (or a postmodern psychologist) in pointing out the paradoxes. In his view the self is the mind and its contents, and since these are always changing it hardly makes sense to think of a permanent identity. "What then," he asked, "gives us so great a propension . . . to suppose ourselves possest of an invariable and uninterrupted existence thro' the whole course of our lives?" He concluded that "the identity, which we ascribe to the mind of man, is only a fictitious one."[26] But Hume was a minority voice on this issue; other thinkers were managing to override the paradoxes. Kant, for example, did so by positing a pure, real "noumenal self" that was distinct from the changeable "phenomenal self" of conscious experience. This was now a modern discourse, and despite Hume's dissent, it was busily engaged in inventing the modern self, consolidating it out of various ideas that had emerged over several centuries of historical experience. The philosophers might have been less troubled if they had understood that it was a fiction, a social construction of reality. They thought they were *discovering* the truth about the self rather than *making* a truth that would serve the political and scientific agendas of the modern era.

Locke was a part of this project, and one of the most prominent among the line of philosophers—which included Hobbes, Rousseau, and Voltaire—who gave the modern self its most valuable possession: rights. Rights, which had been scarcely visible in the medieval worldview, became an increasingly powerful force in political life—proclaimed in manifestos such as the French declaration of the Rights of Man and the American Declaration of Independence. The parallels between Locke's writing and the Declaration rhetoric of Thomas Jefferson are striking. In the *Second Treatise of Government*, Locke wrote:

> Man being born, as has been proved, with a title to perfect freedom and an uncontrolled enjoyment of all the rights and privileges of the law of nature, equally with any other man or number of men in the world, hath

> by nature a power . . . to preserve his property, that is,
> his life, liberty and estate. . . .

The Declaration of Independence states:

> We hold these truths to be self-evident, that all men are
> created equal; that they are endowed by their Creator
> with certain inalienable rights; that among these are life,
> liberty, and the pursuit of happiness.

Locke wrote:

> [M]en unite into societies that they may have the united
> strength of the whole society to secure and defend their
> properties . . .

Jefferson's version was:

> That to secure these rights, governments are instituted
> among men, deriving their just powers from the consent
> of the governed . . .

Rights thus became a piece of the property of the self, God-given,
inalienable, as much a part of the human organism as our hearts or
livers. The concept of rights owes something to the ancient Roman
legal system, but as it exploded into the consciousness of eighteenth-
century Europeans, it was a distinctly modern creation. And although
there is some discussion nowadays about group rights, it has tended to
be an individualistic creation: The owner of rights is the citizen, the
individual self. Governments are created for the purpose of protecting
rights, and can—in the view of libertarians—all too easily become the
enemies of these rights.

All of these developments mark the transition from the late medieval to the early modern. They are inventions whose inventors did not
think of them that way: privacy, nationalism, the concept of a central

observer within the brain, the idea of an individual life as the product of personal choices, and the belief that every person is the possessor of rights. These all are fundamental elements of the way you and I think of ourselves, and they all are being threatened now by the transition into a postmodern era.

Modernity is a post-traditional order, in which the question, 'How shall I live?' has to be answered in day-to-day decisions about how to behave, what to wear and what to eat—and many other things—as well as interpreted within the temporal unfolding of self-identity.

ANTHONY GIDDENS[1]

The other-directed person is cosmopolitan. For him the border between the familiar and the strange—a border clearly marked in the societies depending on tradition-orientation—has broken down.

DAVID REISMAN[2]

2

Twilight of the Modern Self

When did the modern Western self—sculpted out of centuries of historical experience, imagined by towering philosophers such as Socrates, Descartes, and Locke—begin to slip from its pedestal? Certainly, as I look back upon my own childhood and youth in the 1940s and 1950s, the basic assumptions about personal identity seem in retrospect to have been holding up fairly well. In church I learned about my duties as caretaker of an immortal (and personal) soul which would be eternally rewarded or punished after I died, depending on how well I'd succeeded in controlling my naughty impulses. I knew I had rights—I remember telling my third-grade teacher that I had a right to hit the kid who sat in the desk ahead of me, in retaliation for some earlier transgression on his part. When I grew up and studied psychology—which had displaced philosophy as the authoritative source of wisdom about human nature—I had my choice between two ideas of the self: There was the ascendant Skinnerian one, favored by scientists, which paid no attention to inner conflict and viewed the person as a single unit of behavior, a sort of glorified laboratory rat that acted in response to events in the external environment; and then there was the older Freudian version, more influential in the arts and psychotherapy, with its secular but rather Socratic view of inner conflict and its goal of the strong and healthy ego. The message seemed to be that either I was already a unitary, integrated psychological entity or I had damn well better grow up and become one.

So the center seemed to be holding. The view of the person as a bounded, unique, more or less integrated cognitive universe was still the social consensus, the official definition of sanity and identity. But the times were a-changin' in those mid-century years, even though we did not yet have Bob Dylan to sing about it.

Some of the changes—and hints of changes yet to come—were described in David Reisman's landmark book *The Lonely Crowd*. Reisman and his colleagues—studying trends in "social character" in post-World War II America—reported that a deep psychological transition was under way. They noted a decline in the numbers of "inner-directed" individualists, the hardy types who stayed the course of personal values and goals, and a corresponding increase in "other-directed" conformists, who seemed to lack that internal gyroscope and were more inclined to adapt to their immediate social surroundings—or, as we might say today, go with the flow and answer the "how shall I live?" question by looking at how other people lived, the way an insecure dinner guest might sneak a peek at somebody else before deciding which fork to pick up.

Reisman divided all human beings into three categories: tradition-directed, inner-directed, and other-directed. The premodern tradition-directed person lived in a relatively stable social surrounding in which there was no fundamental question about what was true, what was right, and who you were. The inner-directed type, according to Reisman, began to emerge in the Western world at about the time the medieval feudal societies were breaking down—the time of Descartes. Such a person might have to interact with other people who held to different realities, but was able to do so because he or she had a strong, permanent social identity based on internalized beliefs that functioned like an internal gyroscope. The other-directeds, making their way in what was in the process of becoming what we would now call a postmodern, pluralistic, information society, had not swallowed whole the beliefs of their ancestors and consequently had to search continually for guidance as to how to be—and whom to be. Their control equipment, Reisman said, was more like radar than a gyroscope.

These emerging other-directed people of the 1940s and '50s were still modern individuals, but not quite the "rugged individualists" celebrated in American myth. The main difference from the inner-directeds—a difference that would be much more apparent in the next generation—was a shift from ancestors to contemporaries as the main source of approval and direction. People were finding a different way of orienting themselves as they constructed (and occasionally reconstructed) their values and beliefs and personal identities:

> *What is common to all other-directeds is that their contemporaries are the source of direction for the individual—either those known to him or those with whom he is indirectly acquainted, through friends and through the mass media. This source is of course "internalized" in the sense that dependence on it for guidance in life is implanted early. The goals toward which the other-directed person strives shift with that guidance: it is only the process of striving itself and the process of paying close attention to the signals from others that remain unaltered throughout life.*[3]

These other-directed individuals lived with constant tension—torn by the need to maintain a stable identity yet be in step with the times. Being in step meant revising everything from clothing styles to political opinions in response to their peers. Reisman said social conformity itself, "keeping up with the Joneses," was nothing new or different: that could be found in other societies, and history had ample evidence of ancient people—generally the elites, of course—whose lives had been driven by the fads and fashions of the moment. What was different was the enormous growth in the numbers of the fashion-conscious. Style had ceased to be an exclusive preoccupation of the upper classes—even the poor and uneducated were becoming parts of a new mass-based and continually changing popular culture. A major driver of this development was the ever-growing reach of the communications media, which carried the news about what was in and out of style at the moment. The whole society was becoming other-directed—a lonely crowd of socially sensitive people, eager to conform, yet always in some doubt as to what exactly it was that they were to conform to:

> The other-directed person is cosmopolitan. For him the border between the familiar and the strange—a border clearly marked in the societies depending on tradition-orientation—has broken down. As the family continuously absorbs the strange and so reshapes itself, so the strange becomes familiar. While the inner-directed person could be "at home abroad" by virtue of his relative insensitivity to others, the other-directed person is, in a sense, at home everywhere and nowhere, capable of a superficial intimacy with and response to everyone.[4]

And there was yet a deeper problem, born of the growing urge of the other-directed to conform not only outwardly but also inwardly: "The other-directed person, though he has his eye very much on the Joneses, aims to keep up with them not so much in external details as in the quality of his inner experience."[5] It's not surprising that psychologists were beginning to talk about anxiety as a major problem of modern life. Rollo May (in a book published the same year as *The Lonely Crowd*) described the time as an "age of anxiety."[6]

T. S. Eliot, the poet laureate of mid-century, high, modernist culture, caught the essence of the conformist's anxiety in *The Love Song of J. Alfred Prufrock*, whose fretful protagonist anguishes about doing something that might appear foolish (*Shall I part my hair behind? Do I dare to eat a peach?*), suffers the ennui of inauthentic life (*There will be time, there will be time / To prepare a face to meet the faces that you meet*), laments his sense of purposelessness (*I should have been a pair of ragged claws / Scuttling across the floors of silent seas*), and walks in fear of making a statement that he believes true only to have it rejected (*If one, settling a pillow by her head, / Should say: "That is not what I meant at all. / That is not it, at all.*).[7]

Three Faces of the Modern Self

Reisman and other thinkers of the post–World War II years did good work. They showed Western societies being transformed into popular-culture mass societies, with the communications media becoming a force in shaping values, beliefs, and personal identities. They noted that this brought unprecedented personal freedom but that it came with a price—anxiety, the ailment of people with so much freedom of choice that they were chronically worried about perhaps making the *wrong* choice, saying the wrong thing, behaving according to the wrong set of social rules. The anxious person believed that she should have a permanent and integrated self but needed constant verification of her identity from others—and, in an increasingly pluralistic society, didn't always get it.

That picture of mid-twentieth-century life is still in some ways valid. The concept of the integrated and permanent self remains the ideal—if only rarely the lived experience—for most people. Yet, as we'll see in the following chapters, even the concept is in trouble. Recent decades have brought a vigorous movement away from the classical idea of truth, away from the modern idea of the integrated self. Postmodernity challenges the view that the truth is—as Isaiah Berlin put it—one and undivided, the same for all men everywhere at all times. The newer view regards any truth as socially constructed, contingent, inseparable from the peculiar needs and preferences of certain people in a certain time and place. This notion has many implications—it leaves no value, custom, belief, or eternal verity totally untouched. Among the casualties is the Western concept of self, which begins to look like just another socially constructed reality. This was the viewpoint from which Michel Foucault testily told a questioner to forget about asking him who he was or expecting him to remain the same. He was trying to be taken as a human being and not a self.

These are fragmented times. Multiple discourses, as the post-modernists like to say. There are even different ways of believing in absolute truth and the unified self. We now have, in our highly pluralistic society, not just a split between modernists and postmodernists, but four distinct communities of belief: the neo-Romantic, the social-traditional, the scientific-rational, and the postmodern.[8] I suppose if I had to draw cartoons characterizing (or caricaturing) these four types, I would show the neo-Romantic as an androgynous figure in Birkenstocks meditating in the woods; the social-traditionalist as a respectably dressed Midwestern couple on their way to church; and the scientific-rationalist as a white-coated researcher in a laboratory. I'm not sure how I would draw a postmodernist (we'll get to them in the next chapter), but probably I would imitate the collage style of David Hockney—an eclectic pastiche of images and styles.

The first three communities of belief agree on accepting the traditional concept of truth, but disagree fundamentally on how it is found. The neo-Romantic finds the truth in harmony with nature, or by exploring the inner self through spiritual practices or psychedelic drugs. The social-traditionalist finds the truth in his or her cultural heritage. The scientific-rationalist finds it through methodical, disciplined inquiry. All three of these different communities of belief hold to the modern image of the personal self as a bounded, unique, more or less integrated motivational and cognitive universe. They believe that there is a True Self, to put it more simply. But they differ profoundly in how they go about living out that belief.

Today's neo-Romantics, a sizable subculture in Europe, the Americas, and some parts of Asia, have strong roots in the Romanticism of the eighteenth and nineteenth centuries. Those earlier Romantics were definitely moderns, heirs of the Renaissance and the Enlightenment, yet deeply alienated from what they perceived as the evils of modernization—particularly mechanization and urbanization—and powerfully nostalgic for the past. Romanticism is sometimes historically described as a reaction against the rationalist side of the Enlightenment, with its faith in progress. As one historian of the Romantic movement put it, "It was not self-evident that three centuries of new birth, new learning, new continents, new science, new humanist ideology—the fruits of science shared by all—has actually enhanced the dignity and value of human life."[9] Skeptical of the direction progress was taking, critical of the outward manifestations of modern society, the Romantics looked toward the past, to solitude and poetry. Most of all they looked to nature, which was taken to be the ultimate source of truth, and which could be located either deep within the soul or in wilderness. Often the heroes of their literature were passionate storm-tossed wanderers, at odds with the times. And the True Self of the Romantic was (and is) the inner self—natural, savage, yet inherently good.

Nineteenth-century Romanticism never really went away, and it revived exuberantly in the 1960s amid a burst of psychedelia, hippies, protest movements, primitivism, wild music and dancing, and a rediscovery of the natural environment. Today it coexists in reasonable comfort with mainstream Western secular society. It has an ideal of a different kind of inner-directed self not carrying around the respectable ideas of parents and society, but rather internally guided by the wisdom of one's own nature. Consider, for example, the basic principles that Abraham Maslow, one of the founding fathers of humanistic psychology, was proposing in the 1960s:

> We have, each of us, an essential biologically based inner nature, which is to some degree "natural," intrinsic, given, and, in a certain limited sense, unchangeable, or, at least, unchanging. . . . Each person's inner nature is in part unique to himself and in part species-wide. . . . This inner nature . . . seems not to be intrinsically evil, but rather either neutral or positively "good." What we call evil behavior appears most often to be a secondary reaction to frustration of this intrinsic nature. . . . Since this inner nature is good or neutral rather than bad, it is

best to bring it out and to encourage it rather than to
suppress it. If it is permitted to guide our life, we grow
healthy, fruitful, and happy.[10]

The follower of this line of thought is confident that she possesses a
true inner self and that it can be discovered and enabled to flower—in
meditation or by communing with nature—and that society as a whole is
either ignorant of this inner self or actively organized to repress it.

For the social-traditionalists—who remain a large, healthy, powerful, and active segment of the modern world, even though they may be
an endangered species in the long run—it is precisely within that
society, within its norms and roles and ways of behaving, that the true
self is to be found. The healthy identity is rooted in community,
country, church, family, and occupation, and the self is defined in
those terms—as neighbor, American, Christian, Jew, mother, father,
worker, doctor, lawyer, etc. Apart from those, you are nobody and lost.
Thus Phyllis Schlafly, archenemy of women's liberation, warned of the
dangers of wandering from the time-honored female path:

Marriage and motherhood, of course, have their trials
and tribulations. But what lifestyle doesn't? If you look
upon your home as a cage, you will find yourself just as
imprisoned in an office or a factory. The flight from the
home is a flight from yourself, from responsibility, from
the nature of woman, in pursuit of false hopes and fading
illusions.[11]

The scientific-rationalist mentality is in sharp contrast to the neo-
Romantic. For the good rationalist the self is a subject amenable to
scientific research, and introspection is deeply suspect because it
cannot be objective. In a way, the rationalist's answer to the question of
how to find your true self is almost the precise opposite of the
Romantic's. Instead of looking inside, you look outside—go to the
experts, take a battery of tests, and get the *facts* about what kind of a
person you are. It is understood that every person possesses certain

characteristics that consistently express themselves in behavior and can be objectively studied—even measured and quantified—by other people who possess accurate knowledge of how to do that. It is understood also that there is a certain range of normal characteristics and behaviors, and various abnormal ones outside of that range. Abnormalities can be treated in therapy, and, as Sheila McNamee's study of the social role of therapy noted:

> Although there are multiple possibilities for therapeutic treatment available to us today, most of these treatments are based on the assumption that one treatment is or could be the correct one [at least within a particular population]. This belief is a by-product of modernist thought where the emphasis on progress issues us toward a utopian goal of "knowing" how best to understand and operate in the world.[12]

Even the great explorers of the unconscious regions of the self, Freud and Jung, were rationalists who described their work as science and offered their theories as accurate maps of the parts of ourselves we do not know.

Romantic selves, traditional selves, rational selves—and probably other kinds of selves as well, if we look long and hard enough. All are holdouts—ways of clinging to the modern sense of identity and of resisting the fierce tide of ideas and events that is sweeping it away.

The modern self was—is—one of the noblest creations of the human mind, and one of the most inspiring achievements of evolution on this planet. It was a construction of thought that freed people from the tyrannies of popes and kings, expanded the horizons of life, opened the mind to the vast possibilities of science. It was a great evolutionary achievement, but evolution moves quickly these days, and we begin to wonder now if the jailbreaking thoughts of past centuries did not create yet another kind of prison for the human spirit.

An open slate emerges on which persons may inscribe, erase, and rewrite their identities as the ever-shifting, ever-expanding, and incoherent network of relationships invites or permits.

KENNETH J. GERGEN[1]

What we call the self—one's inclusive sense [or symbolization] of one's own being—is enormously sensitive to the flow of history.

ROBERT JAY LIFTON[2]

Today, it is the speaking subject who declared God dead one hundred years ago whose very existence is now being called into question.

PAUL KUGLER[3]

3

From Modern Self to Postmodern Selves

Despite all the factionalism in the world of psychology, most theorists and therapists have tended to accept the modern self as both a description of human consciousness and a model of mental health. Western ideas about human development have been enormously influenced by Erik Erikson's account of how a person ideally grows, gets through his identity crises, avoids the perils of "identity diffusion," and becomes a stable adult with "an assured sense of inner continuity and social sameness which will bridge what he was as a child and what he is about to become, and will reconcile his conception of himself and his community's recognition of him."

Psychology is, after all, an agent of the social order, and the civilizing agenda of societies has always been to develop responsible human beings who can bring their wildly divergent urges and voices and energies under control and take up their roles in the community's economic and social and political lives. Stable societies need stable people. A limited society—which is the only kind there is—needs limited people.

So the problems of patients are often seen as failures to develop

this "inner continuity and social sameness," and the therapeutic prescription is likely to be: Integrate your wayward drives and descriptions into a coherent whole. Even Carl Jung, who had proclaimed that
"the so-called unity of consciousness is an illusion," based his therapy
on the goal of developing a mature, "individuated" personal self.[4]
Robert Assagioli, who made an extensive study of the "subpersonalities" that reside within us all, nevertheless created a therapy
of "psychosynthesis," which meant locating the "true self" and building around it a personality that would be "coherent, organized, and
unified."[5] And so it went. Although the terminologies, the maps of the
mind, the therapeutic approaches varied enormously, the general
message tended to be the same: Get your act together; be consistent,
integrated, authentic, whole.

But that consensus has unraveled. Many psychologists now claim
that the way to health and happiness in today's decentralized, pluralistic world is to *be* decentralized and pluralistic. Kenneth Gergen, one of
the leading spokesmen for this point of view, summed it up some years
ago in the title of his article: "The Healthy, Happy Human Being
Wears Many Masks."[6] This new postmodern psychology is in part a
response to the times—if stable societies need stable people, then fast-
changing societies need fast-changing ones—and also a search for a
new image of our possibilities, a more expansive vision of the human
being than any society's roles have yet made room for. It moves us
toward an understanding of people as open systems—ever seeking
new contacts, prepared to take in new information, willing to move
boundaries, unafraid of change.

To get an idea of what postmodern psychology is about, let's
briefly review what some psychologists of that persuasion have been
saying recently about selfhood. I'll do this by exploring three terms
that turn up frequently in such dialogues: multiphrenia, protean, and
decentered. Each of these words gives a bit of the flavor of postmodern
psychology, and each invites us—in fact dares us—to think fundamentally new and different thoughts about who and what we are.

The Challenge of Postmodern Psychology

There is no central doctrine, acknowledged leader, or organizational headquarters for postmodern psychology and probably never will be. One of the leading thinkers about psychology's role in the postmodern world, Steinar Kvale of Aarhus University in Denmark, said, "The very concept of a unitary discipline is at odds with postmodern thought."[7] But even though the field of postmodern psychology is, to say the least, pluralistic, we can approach the essence of it easily enough with the help of two propositions that most of its spokesmen and spokeswomen subscribe to. The first, not too controversial in itself, is that identity is a social product and that people in different kinds of societies have quite different kinds of identity-forming experiences. The second, and more likely to provoke argument, is that most of us today live in "postmodern" societies in which it is difficult—if not impossible—to create and maintain a single, stable, personal identity.

So, the argument goes, in premodern traditional societies—of the sort that once existed everywhere in the world and still remain in a few remote places—people may have had many problems, but at least they usually had the security of living within a single culture. They knew what was true, because everyone in their tribe or village shared the same values and beliefs; they knew with the same certainty who and what they were, because every interaction through the day's activities or through a lifetime recognized and reaffirmed their names, family connections, and social roles.

But in modern or modernizing societies, people lived in much wider social spaces and were much more likely to hear about—or to come into direct contact with—other people with quite different values and beliefs. They also had to deal with other kinds of subdivisions within their own societies, such as the separation between the public and private spheres of life. This "pluralization of life-worlds," as Peter Berger calls it, was always stressful, and it always provoked responses.[8] People found it necessary to develop psychological tools for maintaining their faith in the rightness of their own ways, for remaining in some respects closed systems even in a much wider and more complex environment. One such device was the one Reisman (and before him Freud) described—the "internalization" of a culture so strongly that the individual carried it about within himself and continued to follow its rules and affirm its values and beliefs even when far away and surrounded by strangers, who thought and behaved differently. This kind of inner-directedness might easily be taken for arrogance, ignorance, or insensitivity, but at least it did have a certain survival value. It came in particularly handy for explorers, anthropologists, missionaries, and empire builders.

The British Empire produced some of the world's finest specimens of inner-directed people who were unwaveringly British wherever they went. This was widely admired, widely resented—and widely lampooned by humorists. I have a copy of a classic *New Yorker* cartoon that shows a safari scene, three impeccably black-tie-clad gentlemen dining at a candlelit table in front of their tent, while another, in khakis and pith helmet, sits off alone some distance away, eating from a plate balanced on his lap. "Rotten shame that cheetah making off with Sir Roger's dinner jacket," says one of those at the table.[9] It was English literature that gave us, in Joseph Conrad's *Heart of Darkness*, an immortal portrayal of what might lay in store for the civilized man who went native: the unfortunate Mr. Kurtz who descended too far into the jungle and gave himself up to savagery—savagery so unspeakable that the author kept it outside the narrative, leaving the reader to guess at what primitive depravities Kurtz may have indulged in—and at the end could die whispering only, "the horror."

And the modern era provided a myriad of "external" institutions—such as organized religions, political ideologies, high cultures of art and literature—to help people form and maintain certain beliefs about the world. You could always be pretty sure of who and what you were if you stayed within the life of the Catholic Church or if you were inscribed in the rolls of a political movement. Drama and stories provided not only entertainment but portrayals of how ladies and gentlemen behaved—useful models for the rest of us. The modern era also had, according to the much-quoted analysis of the French philosopher Jean-François Lyotard, historical "metanarratives," such as the West's story of progress, which framed the larger events of life in a way everybody could accept and understand. Each of those, in different ways, furnished people with ready-made answers to the ancient questions of who they were and what was true.

In the postmodern world—meaning the advanced industrial countries from roughly the late 1960s onward, and increasingly the rest of the world as well—the modern era's strategies for reality construction and identity formation don't seem to be working as well as they used to. Most of us, say the postmodern psychologists, are not strongly inner-directed, and few of us succeed in wrapping around ourselves a community of belief that completely shields us from strange and conflicting messages. We live in virtually endless contact with otherness. In traveling, or simply by opening our eyes and ears to the communications media, we are bombarded daily by different values, different beliefs, different realities.[10]

Postmodern thought, influenced by the work of Ludwig Wittgenstein and other twentieth-century philosophers, places great emphasis on the role of language in human life. Whereas earlier generations had tended to regard language as a "transparent" medium that *describes* the real world, postmodernists see it as an active medium that *creates* the real world. We live in language. So when postmodern social theorists talk of "the social construction of reality," they are likely to be drawing attention to the ways we use language to give meaning and value to the objects around us. And when postmodern psychologists talk about "the construction of the self," they are drawing attention to the ways we use language—speech, writing, internal chatter—to maintain our sense of who and what we are.

"Multiphrenia" is the term one of the leading postmodernists, Kenneth Gergen of Swarthmore College, invented to describe the "populating of the self, the acquisition of multiple and disparate potentials for being" that is the lot of people who live in our time.[11] Multiphrenia is the consciousness of all of us who are, as he put it, "saturated" with messages that flow into our minds from the daily experiences of a mobile, multicultural, media-rich civilization, and whose sense of personal identity may well be as transient as the image in a kaleidoscope. Gergen said, "Emerging technologies saturate us with the voices of humankind—both harmonious and alien. As we absorb their varied rhymes and reasons, they become part of us and we of them. Social saturation furnishes us with a multiplicity of incoherent and unrelated languages of the self. For everything that we 'know to be true' about ourselves, other voices within respond with doubt and even derision. This fragmentation of self-conceptions corresponds to a multiplicity of incoherent and disconnected relationships. These relationships pull us in myriad directions, inviting us to play such a variety of roles that the very concept of an 'authentic self' with knowable characteristics recedes from view." In the postmodern world as Gergen described it, you just don't get to be a single and consistent somebody because you don't have a social environment in which all your interactions and relationships, all the voices that you hear and the images reflected back to you by others, unanimously support a consistent view of who and what you are.

Many forces help to make up this new world. Here I'll mention four of them:

1. THE MOBILITY OF PEOPLE. Once, remaining in the same place was the norm for most people, and migration was a deviation. Now, the demographers tell us, migration is the norm. People are on the move in unprecedented numbers, in all directions and for many reasons. The moves are rural to urban, urban to rural, within regions, between countries. People move because they are pulled by hopes and economic opportunities, or because they are pushed by famine, disaster, and war. They move temporarily, and they move permanently— and the movements are occurring all over the world, at all levels of economy and society. And as people move they do not simply abandon their old homes and their old social networks for new ones. More and more are becoming "multilocality people" who have links to more than one place, more than one community. These may be high-flying

international jet-setters, or they may be itinerant laborers and domestic servants who work in distant foreign countries but send money to—and sometimes return to—their original homes.

2. THE MOBILITY OF SYMBOLS. Words and visual images are the raw material out of which our realities are made, and they are zipping around the world as never before, transported by radio, television, telephone, and of course through the newer networks of cyberspace.

3. CULTURAL PLURALISM. Many parts of the world that were once ethnically and culturally homogenous are now cosmopolitan, with large—in many cases permanent—colonies of residents from other lands.

4. CULTURAL CHANGE. We now assume in the West that whatever we do, whether we go anywhere or not, conditions will change. Values and beliefs and lifestyles change; sometimes whole political orders collapse around us. There is much social mobility, with newcomers gaining access to wealth, status, and power. Some of the early sociologists of knowledge theorized that people who live in societies with high "vertical" social mobility are less likely to be inner-directed, and thus more likely to be changed by the "horizontal mobility" of travel. Social rigidity, according to Karl Mannheim, increases the binding force of a society's constructions of reality and makes it easier for individuals to view other cultures as merely primitive or wrong; social fluidity tends to make people more relativistic, likely to be open to other values and beliefs when they go abroad.[12]

For whatever reason, most of us, instead of carrying around a solidly internalized set of values and beliefs that we hold on to unless we get brainwashed or lose our dinner jackets, are attuned to the cultural signals around us, and we change as the messages change.

In some ways the postmodern analysis runs fairly close to the one that had been offered to the world by David Reisman in *The Lonely Crowd* a couple of decades before—and which Gergen describes in *The Saturated Self* as "a modernist evaluation of . . . the early emanations of the postmodern mentality."[13] But although Gergen appears to agree generally with Reisman's description of how Western society was changing, he takes issue with the conformist bashing that had been evident in the earlier work and which became a major sport among social scientists and media pundits throughout the 1950s and early 1960s—the nostalgic elevation of the inner-directed individual, the man with "the courage of his convictions," to the status of a model of mental health and moral probity. Multiphrenia, as Gergen described it, is part problem and part solution. It is indeed the mind of the hassled and harried, torn in all directions by conflicting commitments, yet it is also potentially the key to a more spacious and supple way of being, a richer inner and outer life. He cited research that directly contradicts Riesman's and showed other-directed people to be more psychologically healthy in several respects—"more positive in their attitudes toward others, less shy, less upset by inconsistencies, superior in remembering information about others, more emotionally expressive, and more influential"—than their cousins with the famous inner gyroscopes.[14]

At this point it should be obvious how much is at stake here, how much more than a mere fine point of psychological theory. We are not only talking about a new model of mental health—no small matter in itself—but also questioning some major assumptions about human morality and social behavior. We are considering a drastically different way of evaluating your life and mine, and the lives of the people we know. We are participating in a mental revolution as the one that took place when the Greeks ceased to believe that their personal lives were directed from Mount Olympus.

The Shape Changers

Robert Jay Lifton, whose thinking is closely akin to Gergen's but who comes at the subject from a slightly different direction and with a slightly different emphasis, presented a somewhat different perspective on this revolution. Lifton reported some years before that he had, in his psychiatric work, identified a new type of person he called "the protean self." The protean person is unafraid to change, goes willingly through many metamorphoses in the course of a life. These may be stressful to the person who is going through them, and bewildering to others, but they are not simply signs of pathology or weakness. Furthermore, said Lifton, this pattern extends to all areas of the person's experience. It may include changing political opinions and sexual behavior, changing ideas and ways of expressing them, changing ways of organizing one's life.

Lifton's first contribution to the literature of psychology—and his first exploration of the protean self, although not yet under that label—had come much earlier. That was his groundbreaking study of brainwashing as it was practiced on political prisoners during the time of the Cultural Revolution in China.[15] One of the most common arguments against postmodern psychology is the charge that it describes only the problems of postmodern intellectuals and others like them in the contemporary Western world and has little or nothing to say about humanity in general. But what Lifton documented was a profound *changeability* in human consciousness—something universal, to be found in all people: When people are manipulated with sufficient skill and ruthlessness, they can literally "change their minds" not only about what's true—what is right and wrong politically—but also about who they are. This was exploited by the brainwashers—as it had been by various inquisitors and propagandists before them—but it was not invented by them. It was inherent in the nature of human consciousness. It was also, I suspect, what most human cultural institutions—from the rituals of traditional societies to the ideologies of the modern world—had been designed to keep under control so that people stayed on track, secure in their identities and their beliefs.

When I first encountered Lifton's ideas about the protean self, in a work published in 1970, I got the impression that he was talking mainly about conversions over time.[16] But in a more comprehensive work on the subject published in the '90s, he said that although the protean person might indeed change sequentially—trading in one personal style, personality, role, or belief system for another—proteanism could also be simultaneous, "in the multiplicity of varied, even antithetical images and ideas held at any one time by the self, each of which it may be more or less ready to act upon. . . ."[17]

Although Lifton's ideas are radically different from those of mainstream modern psychology, we should note where he draws the line, because it points up another difference—this one within the rather unregimented ranks of postmodern psychologists:

> I must separate myself . . . from those observers, post-modern or otherwise, who equate multiplicity and fluidity with disappearance of the self, with a complete absence of coherence among its various elements. I would claim the opposite: proteanism involves a quest for authenticity and meaning, a form-seeking assertion of self. . . . The protean self seeks to be both fluid and grounded, however tenuous that combination.[18]

The Death of the Self

Other postmodern psychologists—the ones Lifton doesn't agree with—are calling into question the idea of *any* self as a stable, continuing entity apart from its own fleeting descriptions of itself. This "decentered" view is particularly popular among poststructuralist French intellectuals, and it usually takes the form of denying that the speaking subject—the "I" of our personal consciousness—really exists at all. For the psychoanalyst Jacques Lacan, the subject is not the speaker of language but its creation. "I am not a poet, but a poem," he has written. This view of the subject as the product of its own discourse is expressed in a different way by Jacques Derrida and the deconstructionists. For more politically oriented intellectuals such as Louis Althusser and Michel Foucault, the subject is still a fiction, but a fiction imposed upon us by external power agendas: A solid, centered, identifiable self can be more easily controlled or punished, is more capable of feeling guilt. It is hardly surprising that Foucault, who has rivaled Franz Kafka in his descriptions of society's fiendish cleverness at finding ways to deprive individuals of their privacy and freedom, is the most determined to reject anybody's effort to know who he is or expect him to remain the same.

So for these latter-day Heraclitans, the self—at least that part of it that you experience as the subjective "I"—is its own description of itself in the present tense. Who you are is neither more nor less than who you are in the process of *telling yourself*—or others—that you are.

Paul Kugler, a contemporary Jungian, said:

> Today, it is the speaking subject who declared God dead one hundred years ago whose very existence is now being called into question. No longer is the speaking subject unquestionably assumed to be the source of language and speech, existence and truth, autonomy and freedom, unity and wholeness, identity and individuality. The transcendence of Descartes' "cogito" is no longer so certain. The speaking subject appears to be not a referent beyond the first person pronoun, but, rather, a fragmented entity produced by the act of speaking. Each time the first person pronoun is uttered it projects a different entity, a different perspective and identity. It is positioned in a different location.[19]

This is about as far as you can get from the concept of the integrated self that dominated Western society until only a couple of decades ago—and that still dominates commonsense assumptions about personal identity. It goes so far, in fact, that it comes very close to the no-self of Oriental mysticism.

The Case of the Invisible Elephant

The multiphrenic self, the protean self, the decentered self—each of these terms is an attempt to describe the quality of life in our times, the kinds of people we have become. Each analysis is persuasive in its way, but yet each points to somewhat different features, like the famous blind men feeling the elephant. The first stresses our multiplicity, the second our changeability, the third the elusiveness of our own subjective consciousness.

Of all the concepts of postmodern psychology, the declaration that there is nothing more to the self than its description *of itself* in the moment seems to be the hardest for us to grasp. People with whom I have discussed this matter find it especially troublesome for many reasons—not the least of which being that it pushes them toward not only thinking differently about life, but also *feeling* differently about it. Most don't have much trouble accepting multiphrenia and protean selves as descriptions of how people live today—and I find a surprising number who regard that as a good thing despite the obvious difficulties involved. But if you go far enough into testing—in your own consciousness—the proposition that your subjective sense of yourself is your present description of it, you are likely to experience something akin to what psychologists call an altered state of consciousness. Some people find the experience pleasant, bringing a certain sense of relief. Others report feelings of vertigo, confusion, even panic. Some say it feels like dying.

Ernest Becker wrote about the denial of death, about the fear of not-being, which, he said, we do everything possible to avoid, but which "haunts the human animal like nothing else."[20] It is hard enough to admit that we will die sometime in the future: Who is prepared to realize that we are, in a very real sense, dying every second as we let go of the consciousness of the second before? Of course we can console ourselves with the fact that we are being born every second as well, but that seems a touch Pollyannaish and not nearly as comforting as the delusion that what we are now has a certain permanence, is what we have been and will be—the delusion of the modern self.

There are positive ways of dealing with this ever-present death, overcoming the denial of it, making it a source of wisdom and even of joy. In fact there are many such ways, including psychotherapy and various pursuits called spiritual practice. They come in different forms, but all require that you take the denial seriously, respect it. And this is something that, it seems to me, many of the postmodern theorists fail to do. Enthusiastically proclaiming the death of the self, they reveal a singular lack of compassion for real people who feel that their selves *are* dying and who don't like it a damn bit.

In Search of Limits

Often in discussions of postmodern psychology, when words like "multiphrenic" and "protean" begin to fill the air, somebody asks about limits. Are there not limits—imposed upon us by such old favorites as heredity and environment—on how many personalities we are able to entertain within one individual consciousness? Aren't there limits on how frequently we can change our roles, opinions, beliefs, lifestyles, or personal characteristics? Aren't there limits on how radically we can ever depart from our customary identities?

The answer to those questions is yes and no:

Yes, there are limits. Genes give us the shapes of our bodies, as well as brains, which come with certain built-in predispositions— things we are driven to do and things we just can't do. And our life experiences do leave their marks on us internally and externally. To some extent the Freudians are right in their insistence that we spend much of our adult lives reprocessing our childhoods. The slate is not completely clean. Lifton's research on brainwashing showed not just that people can be forced to make astonishing changes in what they believe to be true about the world and even whom they believe themselves to be, but also that people are capable of resisting such pressures—although not all with equal success.

But no, we really don't know what the limits are. The question is far from being settled in any scientific sense, and even farther from being settled in most people's opinions. The contemporary postmodern world is a colossal circus of people pushing the limits in all directions—changing identities, appearances, genders, social roles, even consciousness in ways that most people in the past would never have believed possible. We will examine specific instances of this kind of limit-pushing in this book, because it is only in the experiences of real people, not in any body of abstract theory, that we can see what the limits are, or at least what they are now.

Historically the strongest limits—and the most visible and numerous—have been the social ones: the Thou Shalt Nots, the norms, the recognized roles, the traditions, the rituals, the authority systems, the demands of others that we be consistent selves. These are the limits that are losing much of their power now and are being tested and questioned everywhere.

Getting Through the Identity Crisis

There is a lot of debate in the psychology world about the postmodernists and their ideas. This argument isn't about whether or not contemporary life tends to cause a fragmentation of the self. It does, and everybody knows it. The debate is about how bad this situation is, whether it is inherently pathological, and about how people ought to cope with it. In the spring of 1994 and again in the spring of 1995, *American Psychologist* ran a series of articles on these issues, with Kenneth Gergen speaking for the postmodernists, and Brewster Smith of the University of California at Santa Cruz as the leading critic.

Smith was inclined to stress the downers of postmodern life: "the prevalent cynicism about politics, indeed, about most social institutions; the shallowness of the mass media and the chaos of contemporary attempts at high art and literature; the inescapable climate of sensationalism focused on sex and violence; the unnegotiable clash between fundamentalism and absolutism on the one hand and nihilistic relativism on the other; the uncertainty about all standards, whether they concern knowledge, art, or morals—or the utter rejection of standards; and the fin de siecle sense of drift and doom."[21]

Gergen, on a more optimistic note, insisted that the postmodern world is perilous but also promising, that it "does not militate against practices of research or moral deliberation. Rather it invites us to place them in broader cultural and historical context. By striking our banners of truth and morality, we might live less aggressively, more tolerantly, and even more creatively with others in the world."[22]

As for coping, it really comes down to two basic alternatives. The first is to make your own life—and perhaps society as a whole—less multiphrenic. The second is to get good at multiphrenia.

Brewster Smith spoke for the first alternative, and his prescription was one that is now extremely popular: Become a member of a community, less individualistic, and more committed to society. He cited with approval the popularity of *Habits of the Heart*, by Berkeley sociologist Robert Bellah et al., which describes Western society as a place of "individualism grown cancerous" and makes a strong case for a "morally coherent life" based on a sense of citizenship and social responsibility.[23] He mentioned, also favorably, the manifesto on "communitarianism" that had been the work of another sociologist, Amitai Etzioni, and has since attained the status of an organized social movement advocating the need for deeper roots in civic life.[24]

It's amazing how strongly the fashion has shifted—about 180 degrees from the celebration of inner-directed individualism, the condemnation of conformity, that was mainstream thinking among liberal intellectuals only a few decades ago. Today the same kind of people condemn individualism and celebrate life in the bosom of a community, a kind of life that can be lived only by conforming to the community's norms and values.

Gergen is much less inclined to view the postmodern situation with alarm or to characterize the multiphrenic state of mind as a form of mental illness. Although he devoted a lot of space in *The Saturated Self* to descriptions of the perils, discontents, confusions, and stresses of life in the postmodern world, his personal position appears to be that it offers great opportunities:

> If one's identity is properly managed, the rewards can be substantial—the devotion of one's intimates, happy children, professional success, the achievement of community goals, personal popularity, and so on. All are possible if one avoids looking back to locate a true and enduring self, and simply acts to full potential in the moment at hand. Simultaneously, the somber hues of multiphrenia—the sense of superficiality, the guilt at not measuring up to multiple criteria—give way to an optimistic sense of enormous possibility.[25]

There's a lot to be said in favor of the communitarian case as an exhortation to better citizenship, but it offers no real solution to the personal problem—the lack of a single social setting that can help us to define a single and consistent identity. Life has changed in fundamental ways for most people, and no amount of moralizing can recreate the idyll of intimate and familiar connection to a single town or neighborhood. We all are becoming multicommunity people, inhabiting multiple and ever-changing life-worlds. We need a different understanding of self and society, and that presents us with new problems. Sometimes conflicts between the demands of different communities—such as professional community and that of the family and neighborhood—wreak havoc with marriages. Sometimes people can't decide which community they most want to be a part of, and spend their time and energy shopping among churches, self-help groups, and other societies in search of that true and completely satisfying home. Often communities become possessive and make strident demands upon their members for more time, loyalty, energy, or money. People need to learn new skills, become adept at prioritizing the claims made on them by different communities—which also compete to define who and what we are.

As we have inherited it, the notion of a "self" does not appear to fit women's experience. . . . A question then arises: Do only men, and not women, have a self?

JEAN BAKER MILLER[1]

A vast and unprecedented transformation has already taken place, a change that few institutions, in the West or anywhere else, have begun to assimilate, a change that no one fully understands. That change is inside the heads of women—not only inside the heads of Western women, who have been among the first to feel it, but inside the heads of women elsewhere in the world too.

PAMELA MCCORDUCK AND
NANCY RAMSEY[2]

Women have always lived discontinuous and contingent lives, but men today are newly vulnerable, which turns women's traditional adaptations into a resource.

MARY CATHERINE BATESON[3]

4

The Selves and Stories of Women

To the list of three key concepts of postmodern psychology that I have mentioned—multiphrenic, protean, and decentered—we need to add a fourth: relational. This idea comes from feminist theory, but it has something to say to—and about—everybody. It helps us understand that real people in today's world are not faced with a simple choice between being lonely individualists or rooted members of a single community.

The basic proposition is that women tend to be more context-dependent or relationally oriented than men, and that most of modern Western psychology has come from the male armchair. The women say this male-oriented view places far too much emphasis on the individual, tends to describe the growth of the self as a process of inner integration and separation from others—"becoming one's own man," as Daniel Levinson put it.[4] They say that this perspective defines character solely in terms of drives, which reside somewhere inside the individual and express themselves regardless of where a man is, what he's doing, or whom he's with. Psychologist Janet Surrey writes:

Our conception of the self-in-relation involves the recognition that, for women, the primary experience of self is relational, that is, the self is organized and developed in the context of important relationships. To understand this basic assumption, it is helpful to use as a contrast some current assumptions about male [often generalized to human] development. . . . High value is placed on autonomy, self-reliance, independence, self-actualization, "listening to and following" one's unique dream, destiny and fulfillment. . . . Our theory suggests, instead, that for women a different—and relational—pathway is primary and continuous, although its centrality may have been "hidden" and unacknowledged.[5]

I don't think Western psychology and psychotherapy were ever *quite* as heavily individualistic as some of the critics have charged. The indictment above fits the boosters of inner-directedness much better than it does such psychologists as Harry Stack Sullivan. Sullivan, a divergent but respected voice in Western psychology, always insisted that a personality "can never be isolated from the complex of interpersonal relations in which the person lives and has his being."[6] But there definitely was a tendency, especially among psychologists of a more scientific-rationalist bent, to think of characteristics, values, and ways of behaving as properties of the individual rather than as expressions of the situation and the moment; and if you look back at some of the celebrations of the inner-directed person, you get a distinct impression that the rugged individualists being celebrated are male. This bias is what the women in psychology set out to change—and in the process, they are also changing our ideas of male selves as well. Ideas like Sullivan's are being revived, therapists of all persuasions are saying that any understanding of a person must be based on context as well as character—and context means not community in the abstract, but the actual social environments in which we live, work, and play. The idea of the self-in-relation joins the other postmodern themes that are attempting to get us all to look at our lives in a new mirror.

Women as Proteans and Multiphrenics

The conditions of postmodern life require us to construct not just one self-image but many. Sometimes we need more than one at the same time in order to relate adequately to the multifaceted situations in which we find ourselves; and sometimes we have to abandon familiar identities and self-images and fashion new ones to deal with changes in the world. Women, often particularly sensitive to social cues and exquisitely capable of adjusting to their environments, may create new and strikingly different selves; the lives of women, as they struggle to conform to the expectations of parents, the fantasies of men, and the ludicrous vagaries of style, call forth some heroically protean efforts.

Consider the experience of Dorinne Kondo, a young American anthropologist who went off to Japan to do fieldwork on kinship and economics. Being of Japanese descent, she was often taken for a native—but then those encounters would turn awkward and sometimes unpleasant when it became apparent that she had an imperfect grasp of the language and very little grasp at all of the many subtle expressions and gestures that made up everyday social discourse. She took up residence within a Japanese family, and eventually—because it always seemed to please people when she conformed to their ways, and to make life more difficult when she didn't—she learned to behave like a proper young Japanese woman. She adopted the polite phrases and customs, and over time even modified her body language to make her movements more Japanese and less American. She took up her share of women's chores in the household, learned to cook miso and fish. She adapted so well, in fact, that the recognition of how much she changed came to her as a traumatic flash of insight one day when she was doing the household shopping.

> As I glanced into the shiny metal surface of the butcher's display case, I noticed someone who looked terribly familiar: a typical young housewife, clad in slip-on sandals and the loose, cotton shift called "home wear"

(*homo wea*), a woman walking with a characteristically Japanese bend to the knees and a sliding of the feet. Suddenly I clutched the handle of the stroller to steady myself as a wave of dizziness washed over me, for I realized I had caught a glimpse of nothing less than my own reflection. Fear that perhaps I would never emerge from this world into which I was immersed, inserted itself into my mind and stubbornly refused to leave, until I resolved to move into a new apartment, to distance myself from my Japanese home and my Japanese existence.[7]

The move wasn't entirely successful, as Kondo found only that she then obligingly adjusted herself into slightly different Japanese personas such as tenant and working girl. She decided to return to the United States, became an American anthropologist again, and wrote—from a safe distance—a successful book about the construction of self in Japan.

One dimension of the particularly multiphrenic existences of some women in the present era is that those who pursue nontraditional careers often find that they haven't broken free of the traditional wife-and-mother selves, but rather must retain those while they add new ones to their repertoires. Consider the story (narrated to me by a psychotherapist) of a bright young woman whom we'll call Lupe. Lupe, raised as the daughter of a very traditional Oaxacan family from southern Mexico, emigrated to the U.S., joined the Navy, and was given the opportunity to attend nursing school and be commissioned. She was an officer, but during her naval service she met an enlisted man—of German Protestant descent, from the American Midwest—and they were married. At that time marriages between officers and enlisted men were not permitted, so they had to keep their marriage a secret. They had three children.

Not a spectacularly unusual life; the woman wasn't a person who would stand out in the crowd. But she was in fact living with multiple identities: officer, wife of an enlisted man, mother, dutiful daughter to the parents she sometimes visited in Mexico.

Now, women—especially women who have professional careers, or women who marry outside of their own religions and ethnic groups—often find it necessary to develop a great deal of flexibility. But in Lupe's case there was far more involved than being merely flexible. Her various roles, and the things people expected of her in each of them, had few points of contact. Since her marriage was in violation of Navy rules, she had to deceive her superiors and co-workers. She didn't keep the circumstances of her life in America secret from her parents in Mexico, but she may as well have. Her parents were simple people who had no understanding of how much she had changed psychologically and culturally by being in the U.S., and when she visited them they would assume that she still had all the same values that she had when she was a child. She would try to be the person they wanted her to be, and would feel deeply dishonest about it. At other times she would try to be the person her husband and his relatives wanted her to be and to see the world his way, and would feel unsuccessful—sometimes resentful, sometimes inade-quate—about that effort as well. And meanwhile she was trying to be a suburban wife and mother in a modern American community that was different from not only the village in which she had been raised, but also her husband's hometown. So her struggle, her despair, her pain was in having to keep all these different parts of her life separate—while believing that she was supposed to have them all integrated. And there was really no option, for Lupe, of being an inner-directed person along the lines of the British hunters in the cartoon: She could not behave like a Oaxacan peasant girl at work in uniform, nor like a Navy officer at home with her husband.

Lupe's therapist said, "People feel that they're supposed to be consistent. They feel the demand for consistency from others, and they get subtle—and sometimes not-so-subtle—messages from the various subgroups they belong to that if they aren't the same all the time they are betraying the people who see them in a certain way. The resolution of Lupe's problems began when she saw that as an untoward ethical map, an ideology she didn't have to conform to. She had to say to herself that it was okay for her to be different in Oaxaca from the way she was as a Navy officer. Then it became a management problem, not an identity problem. It was still hard work sometimes, but she began to feel that she was taking better care of the people she was involved with, which was very important to her."

Therapies for the Scattered Self

At the risk of making a very complex profession sound a lot simpler than it really is, let me tell you what is the key to successful therapy with people, male or female, who feel inadequate or even deceitful when they find that life requires them to maintain two or more selves. The key lies in finding a better story.

And there are lots of problems. People all over the world are being torn—and sometimes torn apart—between the belief that they should be integrated selves and the suspicion that they either can't do that or don't really want to any more.

Here the model of mental health becomes so much more than merely an abstract issue for people to read papers about at psychology conferences, because one of the great influences in a person's sense of daily well-being is her confidence in her own normality. If a person is aware of having multiple subpersonalities instead of a single center, or of being a different person in different situations, or of changing dramatically (and frequently) over a lifetime—and thinks that is a crazy or dishonest way to be and that nobody else is that way—she may well be terribly unhappy simply because of those self-evaluations. And often a big part of the psychotherapist's job is merely to revise those evaluations, give the client a better map of what is going on in *other people's* lives. That, too, is a part of our living in history, because right now the times are somewhat out of joint, and there is a wide gap between the prevailing ideas about a self and the actual experiences of most people.

And if consciousness is a descriptive process—that is, if human meaning is constructed in language—then surely the process of experiencing life in satisfactory ways must involve acquiring some knack for telling better, richer, more spacious stories about it. One therapist of this persuasion said:

As practitioners of the art and science of therapy, the work that we do, whichever theoretical models we adopt, involves encouraging people to tell us their stories and helping them deconstruct and then reconstruct those stories in a way that empowers them. In such work it seems to me that we have an inescapable kinship with poets and story writers everywhere, even though, to be sure, we play more the role of editors.[8]

He goes on to say that in a sense, selves are being replaced by stories. Selves are always an abstraction, but the stories we tell ourselves and others, the epics and comedies and tragedies we create to make sense of the moment—these we can feel. And perhaps we can get better at creating them even while recognizing that the world is not going to give us complete poetic license.

One of the stories about our time that is being told by many social critics involves individualism. It is a story of the breakdown of communities and of people being forced to live lost, fragmented, alienated lives. There's enough truth in that account to make it an important part of the public dialogue, but I don't think it's a very good story. In a way people are becoming more individualistic, and in another way scarcely individuals at all. We all are deeply social creatures who respond to—and in many ways conform to—the social contexts in which we find ourselves. But today that context is turning out to be much larger and more spacious (and more confusing) than what is usually described by community. It's the world, and it's where we all live now; it contains many communities, and most of us live in lots of them; we all are selves-in-relation.

"Perhaps," muses F. Scott Fitzgerald's narrator in *The Great Gatsby*, "life is best looked at through a single window after all"—a curious thing for someone to say in a book that is a poetic tribute to a protean hero, self-created out of his own dreams. Neither Fitzgerald nor Gatsby looked at life through a single window, and in the postmodern world, neither does anybody else. We look at life through many windows, and many kinds of windows: the glass windows of buildings; the electronic windows of television sets and computer screens; the conceptual windows of the diverse worldviews that—however strenuously we try to limit ourselves—invade our minds and compel us to see and understand the world in different, often conflicting ways. We learn to tell more complex stories, which may seem terribly difficult for us to do sometimes. But perhaps we have a natural propensity for it—for we have complex brains that seem to possess marvelous, and surprisingly many-sided, storytelling abilities. In somewhat the same way that autobiography served the needs of ego-tripping Renaissance selves like Benvenuto Cellini, narrative today helps people organize their multiphrenic, protean, decentered, relational lives.

Undoubtedly much of the popularity of Mary Catherine Bateson's book *Composing a Life* has to do with the increasing tendency of people to think of life in narrative terms. In the book, Bateson mentions the importance of women's history, as expressed particularly in biographies, autobiographies, and by advocates who take sort of autobiographical views of their own lives—but who think of it more as improvisational art, continually re-creating the plot as things change.

> It is time now to explore the creative potential of interrupted and conflicted lives, where energies are not narrowly focused or permanently pointed toward a single ambition. These are not lives without commitment, but rather lives in which commitments are continually refocused and redefined. We must invest time and passion in specific goals and yet at the same time acknowledge that these are mutable. The circumstances of women's lives now and in the past provide examples for new ways of thinking about the lives of both men and women.[9]

Of course not all women with multiple-self issues to resolve are going to go to a narrative psychotherapist or write their autobiographies. But the kind of thinking that informs the narrative approaches to life—which comes down to taking a more active role in creating the stories that create a self—is seeping through the culture.

Constructing the World, Imagining the Future

According to a group of social scientists associated with the Stone Center at Wellesly College in Massachusetts, many women are evolving toward a more sophisticated understanding of how reality is constructed, and also learning how to play a more active role in the process. Their research places women in five different "epistemological categories"—styles of thinking and being. These are:

> *silence*, a position in which women experience themselves as mindless and voiceless and subject to the whim of external authority;

> *received knowledge*, a perspective from which women conceive of themselves as capable of receiving, even reproducing, knowledge from the all-knowing external authorities but not capable of creating knowledge on their own;

> *subjective knowledge*, a perspective from which truth and knowledge are conceived of as personal, private, and subjectively known or intuited;

> *procedural knowledge*, a position in which women are invested in learning and applying objective procedures for obtaining and communicating knowledge; and

> *constructed knowledge*, a position in which women view all knowledge as contextual, experience themselves as creators of knowledge, and value both subjective and objective strategies for knowing.[10]

Sooner or later, women who have the opportunity to grow, reflect, and learn tend to reach the position of constructed knowledge—which is an evolution beyond the modern self. In the terms of the map we examined in chapter 2, women at the positions of silence and received knowledge are social traditionalists; women at the position of subjective knowledge are neo-Romantics; women at the level of procedural knowledge are scientific rationalists; and women at the position of constructed knowledge are postmoderns—not necessarily postmodern*ists*, not necessarily steeped in any of the sometimes arcane works of postmodern feminist theory—but simply women who have arrived at a way of understanding social reality that carries them beyond the modern world.

The "women's movement" is a global phenomenon now, one of the most powerful political movements of our time—and, for that matter, quite possibly of all time. It is powerful in part because it carries at its core one of the most fundamental and revolutionary discoveries people have ever made: that any society's customs are constructions of reality, that they were invented by specific people at specific times and places for specific reasons, and that they can be reinvented when the need arises. And it is powerful because it affects everyone. It affects all women everywhere, and of course, all men as well.

Fundamental changes are taking place all around the world as women begin to awaken to the revolutionary discovery that *things can be different*, and yet no one who supports such change has any reason to be wildly optimistic. There are backlashes, resistances, dedicated opponents—many of them female—to the feminist cause, and agonizingly slow progress even in the places where the cause appears to have the greatest strength and momentum. Not long ago, a group of leading futurists took a hard look at developments along this front and constructed four scenarios, only one of which showed significant progress toward real global equality for women. Of the other three, one was a story of massive backlash, another a mixed bag of forward steps and backward ones, and a third described a world of separations—not only of smaller ethnic-based (and often traditional and authoritarian) societies from the multicultural nation-states, but also of the sexes as men go about their usual pursuits and women pour their energies into businesses and social organizations created by and for women.

The one bright vision in this rather bleak essay is that of a "golden age of equality" to be achieved early in the twenty-first century as continuing economic and technological progress, coupled with "a profound shift in consciousness," opens up a wide range of new opportunities for women to achieve and develop as fully equal to— although not necessarily the same as—men. One of the things that would make such an outcome possible, according to the authors, would be a worldwide triumph of individual rights over group rights.

Not all women enthuse about the prospect of a global regime of individual rights. That would mean a corresponding diminution in the authority of local communities to enforce their values, beliefs, and rituals. In the disputes over female genital mutilation, for example, you find women on both sides of the argument—some deeply committed to perpetuating the painful rite that they once underwent themselves, others struggling to end it. So it went with foot-binding in China; so too with burning widows on the husbands' funeral pyres in India. Ancient traditions collide forcefully with new stories, changing views of who and what women are.

Border Wars

Feminism isn't any more unified than any other political and intellectual movement—I don't know how it could be or why it should be— and there are plenty of arguments. One of the deepest concerns the matter of establishing the boundary line—if there is one at all— between male and female.

If you read any works of feminist theorists, or for that matter of any postmodern thinker, be on the lookout for the word "essentialist." Any proposition that some quality is inherently, eternally, *essentially* female is likely to be challenged. To the postmodernist, these propositions sound Socratic—abstract realities beyond and more real than our worldly experience. And there are plenty of essentialist ideas around.

They are central to most traditional societies and to religious beliefs in "essentially feminine" qualities ordained by God. They are held by scientists who locate male and female characteristics in the genes. The assumption runs deep through human history that men and women are born different and will inevitably behave differently throughout their lives. Most feminist theorists have rejected this assumption, and many have held out for a more androgynous vision of male and female selves. But old varieties of essentialism persist, and new ones—such as eco-feminism, the proposition that women are inherently closer to nature—come along. Essentialist tendencies even creep insidiously into postmodern feminist theory: Are women *inherently* more relational, or is that the product of social conditioning? Some feminist theorists of a leftward tilt have been dismayed to see the new relational ideas appropriated (and essentialized) by conservatives, such as the lecturer at a Moral Majority conference who told her audience of approving right-wingers, "Women's nature is other-oriented. . . . To the traditional woman, self-centeredness remains as ugly and sinful as ever. The less time women spend thinking about themselves, the happier they are. . . . Women are ordained by their nature to spend time meeting the needs of others."[11]

One popular way to resolve the essentialist issue is to make a distinction between sex and gender. That is, to say, okay, we are born with bodies that are either male or female. That much is given. But *gender*—the roles that people adopt in their lives, and the ways they behave—is socially constructed, and if women are more invested in relationships, it is because the conditions of growing up female have required them to become so.

There's a lot to be said for this theory, but unfortunately the sex lines aren't always all that clear either. They certainly aren't for the growing ranks of "transsexuals" who, with the help of surgery, cosmetics, hormones, and new clothes, move from being male to female, or from female to male. For them, sex as well as gender is a matter of construction and choice. The sex lines aren't clear, either, for people born as hermaphrodites.

Hermaphrodism is being pulled out of the closet these days,

thanks mainly to the efforts of various writers who have reported surprising and disturbing news about not only hermaphrodites, but also what happens to them and our socially constructed concept of a world divided neatly into males and females. Historian Anne Fausto-Sterling reported some years ago that more children than most of us might suspect are born with varieties of chromosomal gender markers and physical apparatus that do not conform to the standard patterns for either sex: a uterus and a penis, or one ovary and one testicle, or a considerable range of other variations that are sometimes called "ambiguous genitalia." She proposed that we should recognize at least five sexes—the usual male and female, and three types of "intersexuals."[12]

According to other writers, the same advances in surgical knowledge that enable some people to change their sex also enable doctors to perform radical surgery on children in order to "correct" such physical deviations and turn them into something resembling ordinary males and females. Critics of such surgery claim that it is barbarous and brutal, hardly better than the genital mutilation of women that is now being widely publicized and condemned—and, in some places, outlawed. The doctors of course resent this argument, and claim that their aim is merely to produce happy and well-adjusted children. But the whole debate suggests that the sexual boundary marking the physical distinction between male and female—while not as wispy and fictitious as the gender boundary—is up for reexamination.

PART 2

Visions
of the
Larger
Person

The data suggest that our mental lives amount to a reconstruction of the independent activities of the many brain systems we all possess. A confederation of mental systems resides within us. Metaphorically, we humans are more of a sociological entity than a single unified psychological entity. We have a social brain.

MICHAEL S. GAZZANIGA[1]

"You," your joys and your sorrows, your memories and your ambitions, your sense of personal identity and free will, are in fact no more than the behavior of a vast assembly of nerve cells and their associated molecules.

FRANCIS CRICK[2]

5

The Multitudinous Brain

Our modern commonsense idea of the self—of that bounded, unique, more or less integrated motivational and cognitive universe—is intimately linked to ideas about our brains and our bodies. The modern self's "organ of thought" is the brain that peers out through your mind's eye at the external world. Its physical persona is the body that you show to the world and that exists separately from your environment—with your skin serving as the living frontier to mark where your self leaves off and your environment begins. In a phrase that has never been improved upon, Alan Watts described the Western self as a "separate ego wrapped in a bag of skin."[3]

But those ideas about your brain and body, like the social and psychological ideas about your identity, are also shifting and dissolving in the postmodern world. The homunculus—the "little man inside your head" that some psychologists used to see as the center of

67

consciousness—seems either to have disappeared or never to have been there to begin with. Contemporary scientists of the brain are happily carving up the Cartesian self into a loose confederation of parts and processes. They are becoming more adept at defining some of these processes in precise chemical terms, and thereby making it possible for other scientists to design chemicals that can alter your mood and character, even your concept of self, in ways that go far beyond what we considered, until quite recently, to be the natural limits. Meanwhile many people—people pretty much like you and me—are changing their ideas about the boundaries of the body, even changing their bodies (and, along the way, their self-images) in new and once-unthinkable manners. All of these ideas and experiences contribute—some in small ways and some in very large ones—to the contemporary identity crisis.

The Freudian Paradox

The modern identity crisis, like the modern self, has been in the making for a long time. Much of the scientific and intellectual history of the past two centuries consists of a series of challenges to the Cartesian "I." These challenges have come from many different directions, and the challengers haven't always been in agreement with one another. We are not talking about one of those neat paradigm shifts here. No field of human inquiry has been more contentious than the study of human cognition. But the various challengers have, in their diverse and sometimes belligerent ways, helped us move toward a new understanding of our own thought processes, and all have contributed something to the founding of a science of the mind that, I suspect, is still in its infancy.

One of the challengers was Sigmund Freud, who reaffirmed the modern concept of the self in some ways, and undermined it in others.

He offered a rather conventional *ideal* of mental health—the inte-grated, purposeful ego, master of its fate and captain of its soul—but drew a new and quite unconventional picture of the human psyche in which that admirable goal appeared devilishly hard, if not impossible, to achieve in practice.

Freudian psychoanalytic theory was built upon a mental trinity of id, ego, and superego. The rowdy and self-indulgent id, Freud wrote, "contains everything that is inherited, that is present at birth, that is fixed in the constitution—above all, therefore, the instincts . . ."[4] The ego emerges at a higher and later level of a person's growth, and serves as the mature, realistic, social actor. "Its constructive function consists in interposing, between the demand made by an instinct and the action that satisfies it, an intellective activity. . . ."[5] So far this idea is not wildly different from older ones about the higher and lower self, instincts and reason; the newer and more characteristically Freudian addition was the superego, the inner agent of civilization, "the suc-cessor and representative of the parents [and educators] who superin-tended the actions of the individual in his first years of life; it perpetuates their functions almost without a change."[6] The superego was pretty much the same as Reisman's internal gyroscope (and of course the model for it), although in Freud's writings it often sounds less like a navigational device and more like an overbearing Hapsburg emperor.

Freud's map of the self—and his various descriptions of how id, ego, and superego wrestle, dance, play hide-and-seek, and occa-sionally cooperate with one another—helped to pave the way for the much more radically decentered view of the self that is now emerging. He made us think of ourselves as populated, mysteriously so, by forces that operate according to logics and motives of their own. The Freud-ian view is almost like the Homeric image of the person driven by gods—except that if you go to a psychoanalyst with the complaint that you are hearing voices, you will be assured that they are not deities broadcasting from Mount Olympus but disguised and mischievous messages coming out of your own personal unconscious mind. Freud's concept of the unconscious was one of the most powerful new

ideas brought into the world in the twentieth century, and one that—
even though it has now faded to the status of everyday jargon—we still
have not fully assimilated. Freud knew how historically important his
contribution was. In an oft-quoted lecture he immodestly described
his work as a blow to human vanity equal to those that had been dealt
already by the discoveries of Copernicus and Darwin. Copernicus had
shown that our Earth is not the center of the universe; Darwin had
revealed us to be descended from the animal kingdom; and Freud
(said Freud) "[sought] to prove to the ego that it is not even master in
its own house, but must content itself with scanty information of what
is going on unconsciously in the mind."[7]

That was the profoundly pessimistic Catch-22 in the Freudian
worldview. Although he prescribed psychoanalytic therapy as an inte-
grative process in which the ego might grow in strength and wisdom,
drawing energy from the unruly id ("Where id was, there shall ego
be"[8]), he was not optimistic about the possibility of a happy outcome,
either for his patients or for humanity as a whole. He once told a
female client that, with luck, an effective psychoanalysis might "succeed in transforming your hysterical misery into common unhappi-
ness,"[9] and in *Civilization and Its Discontents*, the rather gloomy work
written toward the end of his life, he speculated that in the future the
levels of guilt experienced by most people "will perhaps reach heights
that the individual finds hard to tolerate."[10] Freud was one of the first
people to think seriously about the future of the self, and he offered a
bleak scenario.

Localism and Holism

While Freud and the psychoanalysts were forming their picture of the
(at least) tripartite mind, other explorers were (sometimes literally)
dissecting the human brain, searching for new insights into how it

worked, and laying the foundations for contemporary cognitive science and neurology. They found many interesting things, but no single command center.

Some early brain researchers believed there were many centers, and some believed there were none—that the entire brain worked as a nonhierarchical unit. They argued about this through most of the nineteenth century and well into the twentieth. The "localizers" believed the brain was subdivided into specialized regions that control different functions such as speech, movement, and vision, and also different kinds of memories. This was the thesis of the distinguished Austrian anatomist Franz Gall, and also the basis of the quasi science of phrenology, whose practitioners claimed to be able to identify a person's specific talents and characteristics by studying the bumps on his or her head. The leading spokesman for the opposing "holistic" position was the French neurologist M. J. P. Flourens, who believed he had conclusively demonstrated—chiefly through experiments on the brains of birds—that the brain functions as a whole and that it would never be possible to predict any specific defects as the result of damage to a specific part.[11]

Unfortunately for Flourens and for his considerable reputation, his countryman Paul Broca reported in 1861 on the cases of two patients who had lost the ability to speak as a result of injuries to the left cerebral hemisphere. Later case reports and experimental findings appeared to confirm this and to locate further cognitive functions in specific places. However, other case reports and other experimental findings by scientists of the holistic persuasion found evidence to refute the localists. So it went, and so it goes still for a few of the more contentious members of the profession, although today most work in the field is informed by the synthesis view (first put forth in 1949 by Donald Hebb, a Canadian neuropyschologist), in which brain organization is seen to be enormously complex and (at least early in life) flexible, so that both localistic and holistic patterns can be found, depending on how and when you look for them.[12]

Even the most famous of the localizations, the left brain–right brain distinction, is nowhere near as clear or simple as most people believe. Beginning some decades ago, Roger Sperry and his associates at the California Institute of Technology demonstrated that the left hemisphere of the human brain is normally dominant for language and similar conceptual functions, and the right hemisphere is dominant for nonverbal processes such as spatial functions and visual and auditory discrimination—with each hemisphere normally controlling bodily functions on the opposite side. Later Robert Ornstein, a California psychologist, took this idea and ran with it a lot farther than most neuroscientists are prepared to go. In his book *The Psychology of Consciousness* he described the brain as two distinct characters: on the left, "the verbal-logical grammarian [who] can also be the scientist, the logician, the mathematician who is committed to reason and 'correct' proof"; on the other side, "the boatman, ungraceful and untutored in formal terms, [who] represents the artist, the craftsman, the dancer, the dreamer whose output is often unsatisfactory to the purely rational mind."[13] The cover of the paperback edition of Ornstein's book shows an image of the brain as seen from above—its left side superimposed with drawings of hard-eyed scientists and mathematicians, the right with a montage of artists at work and a woman in a sinuous movement that may be ballet or yoga. Largely as a result of Ornstein's popularization, it became a widely accepted truism that the world is divided into rationalistic left-brain people and artistic, intuitive right-brain people. This is not, however, the consensus of cognitive scientists. In fact the leading researcher into left brain–right brain functions, Michael Gazzaniga, has been moved to wonder: "How did some laboratory findings of limited generality get so outrageously misinterpreted?"[14]

Contemporary cognitive science and neuroscience are lively fields with all manner of competing concepts, but I don't know of anybody in the business now who defends a classical Cartesian model of the brain/mind. Descartes is often mentioned in their works, but usually as a combination father figure and standing target. The writer typically begins with a nod to Descartes as the man who in a sense pioneered the systematic study of thought—Howard Gardner calls him "the prototypical philosophical antecedent of cognitive science"[15]—and then proceeds to reject most of his actual ideas, either implicitly or explicitly. Gilbert Ryle's 1949 book *The Concept of Mind* was a powerful and influential attack on Cartesian mind-body dualism—that is, the concept of a material brain and a nonmaterial mind or soul. Materialism prevails in cognitive science now, and recently Daniel Dennett has pointed out that once you have let go of the concept of a nonphysical realm to which thought is relayed, "there is no longer a role for a centralized gateway, or indeed for any functional center to the brain. The pineal gland is not only not the fax machine to the Soul, it is also not the Oval Office of the brain, and neither are any of the other portions of the brain."[16] Francis Crick, the pioneer geneticist who has turned to neuroscience, wrote that the "fallacy of the homunculus"— the little man in the brain—is to be avoided at all costs.[17] Neuroscience remains Cartesian and modern in one respect, however: It still locates our thoughts inside the brain.

But if we are to believe most contemporary investigators of the brain, the little man really isn't there. We don't have a single observer in the center of our heads, and neither do we have a scientist in one side and a ballerina in the other. Instead we have a much more multicentric brain, one in which different functions are distributed in complex ways, but not simply located in a single place.

Modular Brains, Multiple Drafts

This multicentric view is pretty well summed up in two books with somewhat similar titles: Marvin Minsky's *The Society of Mind* and Gazzaniga's *The Social Brain*. The two books express similar ideas, but the authors have arrived at them from quite different directions.

Minsky emerges from the field of artificial intelligence, from the famous laboratory at the Massachusetts Institute of Technology that pioneered what he calls the study "of how machines could do what only minds had done previously." In those pursuits he, like other students of computers and robots, spent much time analyzing the human brain, the model to which we inevitably compare our thinking machines. And he came to the conclusion that the human brain is better understood as a society of "mental agents" than as a unitary actor—mental agents, not necessarily located in a specific place.

Minsky is neither a localist nor a holist, yet he is definitely a pluralist. In his account, the processes of your mind may seem to you to be flowing in a single stream of consciousness somewhat like the famous monologue at the end of James Joyce's *Ulysses*, but they can be much more accurately described as the ever-recombining activities of many different thinking systems. Minsky granted that the idea of a single pipeline of ideas streaming through the mind has certain things going for it—mainly convenience and simplicity—but that it's a convenience we should abandon if we want to gain any understanding of how our minds really work. There are, as he put it, "compelling reasons why it helps to see ourselves as singletons," and added:

> Still, each of us must also learn not only that different people have their own identities, but that the same person can entertain different beliefs, plans, and dispositions at the same time. For finding good ideas about psychology, the single-agent image has become a grave impediment. To comprehend the human mind is surely one of the hardest tasks any mind can face. The legend of the single Self can only divert us from the target of that inquiry.[18]

Gazzaniga's background is in experimental neuroscience. He was a student of Roger Sperry's at Cal Tech and later did pioneering work with epileptic "split brain" subjects in whom the corpus callosum (the neural tract that connects the two hemispheres) had been surgically severed. He uses the term "modules" instead of agents to describe the various brain networks, but he is equally convinced that there are lots of them:

> By modularity I mean that the brain is organized into relatively independent functioning units that work in parallel. The mind is not an indivisible whole, operating in a single way to solve all problems. Rather, there are many specific and identifiably different units of the mind dealing with all the information they are exposed to. The vast and rich information impinging on our brains is broken up into parts, and many systems start at once to work on it. These modular activities frequently operate apart from our conscious verbal selves.[19]

Let's go back and take another look at both of the above statements, because each, in its own way, tells us something about your brain's activities that is even stranger than its being a crowd of agents or modules—and even more threatening to the concept of the unitary self. Gazzaniga spoke of many systems starting at once to work on a new piece of information, and said that many of these activities "operate apart from our conscious verbal selves." Minsky said that "the same person can entertain different beliefs, plans, and dispositions at the same time." It is not simply a matter of different systems of the brain working together to construct our view of the world, but different systems that may be constructing *different views* at the same time—different stories about what is real in that world, and different images of the self who is looking out at it.

So as neuroscience's challenge to the Cartesian "I," we now have what Daniel Dennett calls the "multiple drafts" theory, which says your brain is a noncentralized network of processing units that continually construct and reconstruct the data that comes into it from your sense organs. This idea upsets many of our traditional assumptions about how we think, and offers a particularly self-threatening view of memory. In the "multiple drafts" model, different areas of your brain register different versions of any event. Instead of storing one single official recollection, you may remember things differently—or not at all—at different times and under different conditions. There is no central registry of memory that you can tap to reveal the ultimately accurate recollection of your past, nor is there a single stream of consciousness in the present:

> These distributed content-discriminations yield, over the course of time, something rather like a narrative stream or sequence, which can be thought of as subject to continual editing by many processes distributed around in the brain, and continuing indefinitely into the future. This stream of contents is only rather like a narrative because of its multiplicity; at any point in time there are multiple "drafts" of narrative fragments at various stages of editing in various places of the brain.[20]

Cognitive scientists tend to be skeptical about not only the single stream of consciousness, but also the distinction between conscious and unconscious thought processes as it has been generally accepted—at least by lay people—since the time of Freud. In some ways the scientists extend the boundaries of the unconscious. One psychologist, Carl Lashley, went so far as to assert that "no activity of the mind is ever conscious."[21] What he meant was that although there are thought processes of which you are conscious, you really don't have access to the process itself. If I ask you who Sigmund Freud was, you can answer, but you don't know how you go about retrieving the information. Nor do you know how you go about performing a mathematical calculation or deciding which move to make in a chess game. Nor do I know how I go about finding these words and ideas to shape into a sentence that I will, with any luck, come to regard as a product of conscious thought. All these things pop up rather mysteriously in our conscious minds after a lot of activity under the hood, which we never see. But most cognitive scientists, being scientists, also believe that all unconscious processes are capable of being studied in controlled experiments—and, in that sense, made conscious.

Cognitive scientists are equally skeptical about the idea of the single authoritative memory of an event, stored in your brain the way a book is stored in a library or a file on a floppy disk. Yes, there have been many occasions when, in the course of brain surgery or a laboratory experiment, a stimulus to the brain produced something like a memory of an event, but most cognitive scientists still think memories are stored in many places. Other authorities on the subject—such as Israel Rosenfield of the City University of New York—believe "the fundamental assumption that memories exist in our brains as fixed traces, carefully filed and stored, may be wrong."[22]

The subject of memory often finds its way onto the front pages nowadays, in lurid stories about children recalling sexual abuse—or even, in one case, about a woman who recalled being witness to a murder committed by her own father when she was a child. This theory has something to offer to both camps in the current discussion about "repressed memories" of childhood: It suggests that you can indeed hide memories, and it also suggests that you can create them.

Making Memories

Some years ago I was trying to write an essay about honesty, and I included in it a little anecdote that, I thought, neatly illustrated the contradictions in our culture's values and practices on that subject. I told about overhearing a neighbor as she lectured her daughter who had been caught in a falsehood, saying, "Just remember, Mary Beth, they don't let little girls who tell lies go to kindergarten." Wonderfully ironic, I thought: a lie to teach honesty. It turned out the irony went one floor deeper than I had suspected. My wife read the manuscript and said, "That's a pretty good story about Mary Beth, but you didn't hear her mother say that. I told you about it."

The incident had happened long before, ten years or more. But it had lodged in my mind as a good piece of material, the way all of us (not only writers) recall certain things that people say, little sentences or phrases that somehow strike us as particularly rich or meaningful or useful. And along the way I had forgotten that it was something I had been told; instead I had constructed a new memory with a visual image—one I still retain, by the way—of Mary Beth and her mother on a sunny day in Berkeley, in front of the house where we lived then. (Later I read, somewhat to my relief, that people quite commonly forget the *sources* of things they recall.)

Anyway, I no longer use that little story to make a point about honesty. Now I use it to make a point about memory.

Memory, it turns out, involves acts of creation as well as acts of recollection. The new concepts of it that are emerging and being supported by immense amounts of research disturb some of our deepest assumptions about who we are, what we are, and what is true. Yet even as I sit here reporting (with obvious agreement) about the work of a lot of cognitive scientists who are telling me the mind is multiple and the memories of the past are fallible, I experience myself as an "I"—as surely as Descartes did in his Bavarian bungalow—and I remain confident that my precious collection of memories reflects real things that really happened. Well, maybe not the one about Mary Beth, but I definitely recall my father hooking his leg around a saddle horn and lighting a Lucky. How can a scientific finding be correct when it violates my own conscious experience?

The answer is quite simple, and it has to do with time. At any given instant I experience an "I" and can summon up a horde of memories that support the image of what is sometimes called "the autobiographical self," but the "I" may feel, think, and behave differently at different times. And it is quite clear now that in different situations—if I am, say, responding to a beguiling hypnotist or a hard-nosed cross-examining attorney, or in social surroundings that place some pressure on me—I may remember things differently. I may revise points of fact in my autobiography, forget some things I had once remembered, remember some things I had forgotten. Or—over the course of successful psychotherapy or simply in the process of growing older—I may leave the factual data pretty much intact but greatly change the meanings and interpretations of the events that make up the story of my life. In the same memories I step and I do not step, I am and I am not.

I could be taken for a very large, motile colony of respiring bacteria, operating a complex system of nuclei, microtubules, and neurons for the pleasure and sustenance of their families, and running, at the moment, a typewriter.

LEWIS THOMAS [1]

In essence, we have arrived at a whole other way of thinking about our physical selves—the body not as a fixed-cast that we inherit from our parents and begrudgingly grow old in, but as pliant putty, a work in progress.

CHARLES SIEBERT [2]

6

The Shifting Boundaries of the Body

In everyday life and commonsense thought, our bodies and our selves are more or less the same thing. As our bodies change, as we grow and age, our mental images of who and what we are change also. For most of us, most of the time, the changes are gradual and we aren't intensely aware of them. Once in a while, some of us may find ourselves among the fortunate or unfortunate few who undergo a sudden, dramatic, major physical change such as weight loss, amputation, organ transplantation, plastic surgery—and then, in those moments of profound identity transformation, we come to understand how intimate the body-self congruity really is, how deeply physical are the selves that we experience and present to the world.

Today two important developments are unfolding along this body-self axis: One is that ideas *about* the body are changing, as scientific research forces us to rethink some of our assumptions about what is an integral part of the body and what isn't; the other is that bodies themselves are changing rather more rapidly and readily than they used to, as it becomes easier to transplant organs, remodel faces, and otherwise tinker with the living structures that we inhabit and display to others.

Both of these developments, in various ways, weaken the clarity of the boundary that is fundamental to the common Western sense of self.

Another Worldwide Web

Good old common sense: I suppose we all try to live our daily lives and shape our worldviews on the basis of what we take to be simply, unquestionably *so*. There are all kinds of good reasons for doing that, and personally I propose to keep on trying. Yet I have observed over the course of the past few decades that common sense has a way of moving around, and that what I assume to be unquestionably so at one stage of my life turns out to be questionable, imperfect, or dead wrong in another.

This is certainly true of commonsense ideas about the body, particularly ideas about its boundaries, the separation of the "me" in here from the "not me" out there. When I was a child, the whole thing seemed pretty simple. My skin was the boundary, and I understood that what I needed to do to stay in business was to make sure that boundary remained intact and did its job. If I was wounded, my defenses might be breached by germs carrying any number of dread diseases—lockjaw was one we worried about a lot and had the kind of name that could throw a good scare into a kid. Or I could be invaded by other germs that were floating around in the air or lurking on the surface of things I wanted to eat.

The general arrangement, as I understood it, was that there were a lot of bad things "out there," and that the policy I needed to follow was to prevent them from getting "in here" and making me sick, or crippled (I am talking about the good old pre-polio vaccine days), or even dead. I can't recall that I had any trouble accepting this information and assimilating it into my view of how things worked—although I understand it had a harder sell in nineteenth-century Europe when Pasteur and others were trying to convince rational people that diseases were caused by little living creatures nobody could see.

At a somewhat later stage of my life I accepted without question the news that there were "good germs" as well as "bad germs," and that it was not desirable—as I had once assumed—to be internally germ-free. In fact, as the newer common sense had it, I *needed* to have germs thriving inside me, in considerable numbers, in order to be able to perform a bodily function—the digestion of food—that I had formerly believed I did all by myself. The "not-me" bacteria were, in a sense, indispensable parts of "me." Billions of them, I learned, begin to colonize our bodies the instant we are born, clambering aboard like pirates taking over a ship, and from then on we all sail through life together. We are not so much individuals as walking ecosystems.

More recently I had to absorb another, this time rather more disturbing, revision of my commonsense view of the "me" and "not-me" boundary. I associate this one with Lynn Margulis, the formidable Massachusetts biologist and co-author of the Gaia hypothesis. She claimed that at an early stage in the evolution of life on Earth, the appearance of the eukaryotic or nucleated cell—the basic building block of all higher life forms, including you and me—was achieved through a kind of symbiosis. Bacteria took up residence inside of other bacteria, and what had once been communities—of bacteria or parts of them—became individual cells. This is more of a worldview changer than the "good germs" business. It is one thing to accept the idea that you have a lot of bacteria in the gut busily processing whatever you had for lunch; it is something else to get it that all your cells—body cells, brain cells, and, yes, reproductive cells—are little committees of what had once been separate organisms. It means that we are not only ecosystems, but systems of ecosystems.

This consideration was what led Lewis Thomas to the revision of self-concept that I quoted at the beginning of this chapter. Later on in the same essay, Thomas mused about how this new knowledge threatened his sense of human dignity:

> I did not mind it when I first learned of my descent from lower forms of life. I had in mind an arboreal family of beetle-browed, speechless, hairy sub-men, apelike, and

I've never objected to them as forebears. Indeed, being
Welsh, I feel the better for it, having clearly risen above
them in my time of evolution. It is a source of satisfaction
to be part of the improvement of the species.

But not these things. I had never bargained on descent from single cells without nuclei. I could even make
my peace with that, if it were all, but there is the additional humiliation that I have not, in a real sense, descended at all. I have brought them all along with me, or
perhaps they have brought me.

It is no good standing on dignity in a situation like
this, and better not to try. It is a mystery. There they are,
moving about in my cytoplasm, breathing for my own
flesh, but strangers. They are much less closely related
to me than to each other and to the free-living bacteria
out under the hill. They feel like strangers, but the
thought comes that the same creatures, precisely the
same, are out there in the cells of sea gulls, and whales,
and dune grass, and seaweed, and hermit crabs, and
further inland in the leaves of the beech in my backyard,
and in the family of skunks beneath the back fence, and
even in that fly on the window. Through them, I am
connected; I have close relatives, once removed, all over
the place.[3]

Remember, we are talking about boundaries here. And it appears
that the more you know about what scientists know, the less clear and
sacrosanct the old boundaries become. Your skin isn't the borderline
between you and not-you, and neither, now, is the cell wall. We all are,
physically, much more open systems than we once suspected. And
common sense becomes less commonsensical, and meanwhile other
developments in other fields further complicate the picture.

The New Body Shop

There is, for example, this business about organ transplantation. And I do mean business, because as it becomes possible to move hearts and livers and other body pieces from one human being to another, organs become something they have never been before—namely commodities, and often commodities of almost unlimited value. People buy them and sell them and sometimes steal them. Entire new institutions, sciences, medical practices, codes of law and ethics—not to mention markets—spring into being around the world, all made possible by a once-obscure mold discovered by a Swiss scientist in a sample of Norwegian tundra. That mold is the source of the drug called cyclosporine A, which ushered in the era of organ transplantation by enabling surgeons to violate a boundary created by millions of years of evolution—to suppress the immune system sufficiently so that it will accept an organ from another body.

Organ transplantation involves, first of all, a donor—a person who decides in her lifetime, or for whom the decision is made after her death—to pass the usable parts of her body along to others who need them. It involves a recipient—in many cases a person who will die without such help—who becomes the owner of a new heart, bone, tissue, or whatever. And in between, it involves the growing network of people and organizations who do the work—the hundreds of transplant centers where the operations are performed, the specialized tissue banks and eye banks where organs are stored, the nationwide and increasingly worldwide communications systems that enable organ exchanges to take place, the regulatory agencies that oversee such procedures, and the insurance companies that finance them.

What does it mean when thousands of people—and, in the very likely near future, hundreds of thousands of people—go through their lives with the help of body parts, including major organs, that have been transplanted into them from other people? What does it mean that the bodies of some people become, after their deaths, parts of the bodies of dozens of other people? Is this just a dry scientific statistic, or is it not an indicator of a profound shift in the boundaries between people—and, more important, yet another reason for people to think (and feel) differently about themselves and their selves?

After my book *Evolution Isn't What It Used to Be* was published, interviewers would often ask me how I could say, as I did in the book, that the nature of evolution has changed and that the human being is a fundamentally different kind of creature from what it was a few decades ago. Searching for the sound-bite answer, I would frequently cite organ transplantation. If you saw two schools of fish in the ocean that looked about the same, but were informed that one kind of fish could exchange its organs with others and one could not, wouldn't you agree that they are actually different species, with fundamentally different prospects for survival?

In the previous chapter we noted Gazzaniga's ideas about the "modular brain"—modular in that case meaning made up of distinct parts. But "modular" also means interchangeable. Human brain parts are not yet interchangeable—although scientists are now experimenting with transplants of brain tissue between animals—but human body parts definitely are. And the number of parts appears to be growing steadily as the transplantation system grows. Now when a body is "harvested"—the trade term for the operations performed to retrieve useful parts—the harvest is likely to include heart, kidneys, liver, corneas, mandibles, inner ear, and portions of skin, bone, muscle tissue, cartilage, pericardium, and the brain-cover membrane called dura mater.[4] Some serious observers of this field of medicine believe hand and feet transplants are likely in the future, and I read about one enterprising surgeon who was wondering if the government would support penis transplants.[5]

The individual becomes part of this extended system, dependent upon the tissue bank or the transplant center as surely as a child is dependent on its mother's breast. And people who never see each other engage in an incredibly intimate form of human interaction—the exchange of a heart or other organ from one body to another. These new connections among people mean also, of course, more disappearing boundaries. And still other boundaries can be expected to weaken and move in the not-too-distant future, and new connections will exist between people and other animals—because animal-to-human transplants are definitely on the horizon. And we are already seeing new connections between people and machines, because another option for many patients is a prosthetic device—an artificial arm or leg, a heart valve, an inner ear implant.

Modular Parenthood

Organ transplantation among human beings is one of several developments on the biomedical frontier that challenge traditional concepts of identity. Equally confusing is the ever-expanding field of reproductive technology, which is making childbirth through artificial insemination and various forms of *in vitro* fertilization commonplace, and thus producing a new set of identity problems for the offspring of these multiple parents.

Personal identity for people everywhere has always been intimately involved with biological relationship—particularly with the parent-child connection, but also with other family connections. In many traditional societies, wonderfully elaborate kinship systems define everyone's personal identity and social role, and prescribe rules of behavior for all occasions according to the family connection between individuals. Adoption is the oldest variation on the standard theme—the child becoming in effect a modular human being moved from one set of parents to another—and it is one that most people seem to have accepted. Adoption is an old and widespread practice, but it too is changing now—bringing yet another kind of globalization as prospective parents range about the world in search of adoptable children.

And just a few decades ago, a new kind of reproductive modularity came along—artificial insemination by donor. This way of enabling women to become pregnant came into use in the early years of the twentieth century. At first it was a rare procedure, but as it became more common, it raised legal issues about the status of the child so conceived. In 1921 in a Canadian divorce case, a man charged that his wife, who had conceived a child through artificial insemination by donor, was guilty of adultery. The Canadian courts didn't give a definite ruling on that issue, but a few years later in Illinois, an American court did. The court said that artificial insemination by donor was "contrary to public policy and good morals," that the wife was an adulteress, and the child illegitimate.[6]

Since then other procedures have come along: *in vitro* fertilization, embryo and egg transplantation, surrogate motherhood. Each brings its own new bundle of controversies, its legal and ethical issues. Many of these remain unresolved, but even in the present state of flux and transition they have led to the creation of organizations that would have been unimaginable a century ago—sperm banks and egg banks, for example. Recently, visiting a university community, I picked up a local newspaper and noticed an advertisement requesting sperm and egg donors. Prices were specified—considerably higher for eggs than for sperm. I reflected that in my own undergraduate days, friends, when short of cash, had occasionally sold pints of blood. Inevitably as our various fluids, organs, secretions, and bones become modular, they also become commodities. We can give them and receive them, and we can also buy them and sell them. And we can argue about who owns them and about what status they have in the web of life.

In the summer of 1996, England was embroiled in a controversy about the destruction of more than 3,000 human embryos that had been in cold storage in fertility clinics, awaiting instructions from the couples for whom they had been conceived. Typically, excess embryos are created in the process of an *in vitro* pregnancy; in England the leftovers are frozen and preserved. By law, they were supposed to be destroyed after a five-year period had passed. Many such embryos had been destroyed before, but the buildup resulted because the donor couples had not responded to queries about what to do with them. Many of the couples apparently had moved or changed addresses without informing the clinics and could not be reached. When the news of this mass housecleaning became public, there ensued one of those huge bioethical controversies that periodically arise in this age of genetic wonders. Some officials of the Catholic Church denounced the proposed act as "a prenatal massacre." A group of Italian doctors offered to have all the embryos taken to Italy and put up for adoption. Some people suggested that the clinics, instead of deliberately destroying the embryos, should allow them to "die naturally." Others proposed that they be given a proper funeral.[7] The British Solicitor-General rejected an appeal to intervene—saying he was empowered by law to represent only a "natural person," and the embryos did not qualify as such—and ultimately they were destroyed.[8] But the confusion remained, and remains still.

It was another one of those postmodern boundary wars, people struggling to draw a line, make a clear distinction: self from other, life from nonlife, human from nonhuman, me from you—in this case, person from nonperson. Our worldview was built on the belief that such boundaries exist in nature and that without too much effort, those natural boundaries can be located and enshrined in law and dogma. We become anxious when we draw near places where the boundary is supposed to exist, and find—well, we find nothing particularly definitive. The embryos in this case were minute entities, each consisting of a total of four cells, the whole smaller than the dot on an *i*. Hard to ascribe to such a small thing all the rights and privileges of a human being—all the things that Locke and Voltaire and Jefferson had taught us to view as inalienable parts of the self—but some people were apparently ready to try. The plea that the embryos be allowed to "die naturally" rather than be assassinated by the laboratory technicians struck me as particularly poignant and futile. What is a natural death for a pinpoint cluster of cells? Hard to say. The boundary line between murder and a peaceful sleep was equally hard to define in this case, yet another remnant of a mindset whose time has gone.

Then in 1997 the still-changing human species began to digest another piece of news from the laboratories—the report that Ian Wilmut in Scotland had succeeded in cloning a sheep. The ensuing flurry of public discussion paid little attention to the rather amazing evolutionary implications of what Dr. Wilmut was actually hoping to achieve through his research—animals whose milk would contain medically useful proteins—and fixed on the possibility that it could lead to a cloned human being. What would that mean in terms of identity? As a pair of ethicists at Stanford put the question: "If we had a clone—someone who shared our genes, DNA molecule by DNA molecule, would that new individual be a new self?"9 The general consensus of people who have tried to answer this question has concluded that it would be, as somebody put it, if you cloned Albert Einstein today, you'd probably end up with Steven Spielberg. But yet the possibility of a duplicated human being continues to fascinate the world and to pull away another stone or two from the foundations of familiar ideas about the body and the self, and the boundaries around them.

Protean Surgery

Consider another piece of news along the medical-science front: Plastic surgery is now one of the most rapidly evolving fields of medical practice. The technology is moving beyond the nose-modeling and jowl-tightening that define it for most of us, and at the same time there is an explosive growth in the number of people who resort to it—and in the number of times they are likely to resort to it once they get the habit. In a recent *New York Times* article, a reporter told of a visit to one of the leading centers—the Institute for Aesthetic and Reconstructive Surgery in Nashville—and summarized the main items on its shopping list of available makeovers. These included:

> *Hair replacement surgery.* Through a variety of techniques, among them "scalp reduction, tissue expansion, strip grafts, scalp flaps or clusters of punch grafts (plugs, miniplugs and microplugs)."

> *Brow lift.* To minimize creases in the forehead and hooding over the eyes.

Blepharoplasty. To cut away excess skin and fat around the eyes, eliminating drooping upper eyelids and puffy bags below.

Otoplasty. To reshape ears.

Rhinoplasty. To reduce, increase or reshape the nose.

Collagen and fat injections. To enhance the lips or plump up sunken facial skin.

Liposuction. To remove fat deposits.

Chemical peel. To eliminate wrinkled, blemished, unevenly pigmented or sun-damaged skin.

Dermabrasion. To remove scarring from acne using a high-speed rotary wheel or laser surgery.

Rhytidectomy (face lift). To tighten sagging skin and the under-lying facial muscles over which the skin is then redraped.

Facial implants. To change the basic shape and balance of the face (building up a receding chin, adding prominence to cheek-bones, etc.).

Brachioplasty. To lift and tighten upper-arm skin.

Augmentation mammoplasty (breast enlargement).

Mastopexy (breast lift).

Gynecomastia (male breast reduction).

Abdominoplasty (tummy tuck).[10]

The reporter also documented some other interesting developments in this field—that it is no longer exclusively the province of the rich and famous, the aging and vain. He spoke of "a growing democratization of the desire to redo oneself," as people in the lower income brackets and the younger-age cohorts take their bodies and faces in for minor adjustments of one kind or another—often on a preventative basis, taking advantage of the suppleness of younger skin to have minor sags and wrinkles erased before they become conspicuously noticeable to others.

Not surprisingly, plastic surgery appears to be more popular in the cities than in small rural communities—where people's identities and social situations are less flexible.

I found the news of its growth fascinating, inspiring in some ways and repulsive in others. Certainly it is good news that people who have been born with serious disfigurement, or suffered it as a result of an illness or accident, are not condemned to a lifetime of bearing up under the social and psychological stresses that commonly accompany such misfortunes. I remember how much difference it made to me merely to have a missing front tooth replaced by bridgework, and can well imagine how much plastic surgery could change a person's life. At the same time, contemplation of these wonders reminded me again of the enormous inequity that exists in the world, so that the great majority of people with such disfigurements do not have access to plastic surgery—or, for that matter, to any medical care at all.

But surely whatever we may think about this modern boom in the making-over of human flesh, we are looking at yet another piece of a change in what identity means, for plastic surgery does change identity—sometimes dramatically. In Philadelphia a surgeon was recently convicted of having thoroughly remodeled a big-time drug dealer who was being sought by the police: The doctor had smoothed over prominent gunshot scars on his patient's face, reshaped his nose, sliced nearly 50 pounds of fat from his waist and cheeks, and turned his fingerprints upside down. The criminal was eventually caught anyway, by police who staked out his wife's car and, according to a newspaper report, "arrested a slim, delicate-looking man changing a flat tire who admitted under questioning that he was, in fact, the once-burly drug lord." Offered a shorter prison term instead of life without parole, the drug dealer agreed to testify against the surgeon.[11]

This field of medicine is, whatever we may think of it, yet another piece of the world in which we live. Although it does not affect most of us at all, it affects a growing number of people in small but significant ways, and utterly transforms the lives of a few.

The Futures of the Body

Some years back, Michael Murphy—cofounder of the Esalen Institute, devout sports fan, and lifelong student of the mysterious human body—brought forth a fascinating book entitled *The Future of the Body*. It was an exploration of some of the remarkable things that human bodies appear to be capable of doing—such as self-healing, telepathy, extraordinary feats of strength or perception—and it gave a hint of an evolutionary future in which many such things that were formerly considered to be extraordinary or supernatural will be regarded as within the birthright of all of us.[12] That's one scenario; the various developments we have surveyed in this chapter suggest several others.

Some aspects of the future of the body are totally unpredictable: Who knows what scientist of the Margulis variety may further shatter our commonsense ideas, and how? But it seems inevitable that many of these practices—organ transplantation, technologically assisted reproduction, plastic surgery—will continue to grow and develop. Charles Siebert expects not only that it will develop in its present form, but also will break completely out of that mold: "Some plastic surgery experts suggest that in the near future bodily changes will take place outside the operating room with fat-burning pills, anti-aging growth hormones that promote muscle and bone growth and the application of laboratory-grown skin cells that will, in effect, give people a new coat of actual skin."[13]

Organ transplantation seems to be moving into a new stage now, one with great promise of practical benefits and also with profound philosophical implications. Dr. Thomas Starzl, one of the pioneers of organ transplant surgery and the man who performed the first successful liver transplant, then made liver transplants routine and gained a reputation as a wizard at effective use of immunosuppression drugs, has reportedly decided after three decades at the peak of his profession that he and all the other transplant surgeons have been doing it the wrong way. Now he says, "The mystery was not about [the body's] rejection," but about the intermingling of cells that takes place whenever a transplant is successful; what the successful transplant operation achieves is a sort of identity shift within the body, so that both the host's immune system and the new organ act as if the newcomer is really "self," a recognized member of the host body. This "paradigm shift," as Starzl calls it, is now being put to the test in experiments designed to find new and more effective ways of achieving mutual cell assimilation—known as chimerism—between the donor organ and the recipient.[14] If this research effort succeeds, it will open a new era in transplantation, making transplantations much easier and also increasing the demand for organs, stimulating a global organ-transplant market.

The Wall Street Journal, ever alert to new developments in the world of commerce, reports on the booming international trade in human hair—"an extraordinary supply line, stretching from scalp to scalp halfway across the globe. All around China, India and Indonesia, there are women who sell their hair, collectors who double as barbers, and processors who boil and dye locks by the ton." The Asian women let their hair grow, sell it, and then let it grow and sell it again. "It's a natural product, like corn," one says, and the main consumers of this product are African-American women. Although synthetic hair is normally used in wigs, the women prefer human hair for braiding, gluing, or weaving into their own to achieve dramatic—and more easily changeable—styling effects.[15] There's nothing new about women selling their hair, but this global trade is significant because it serves to remind us that as human body parts become interchangeable, become commodities, the flow is inevitably from the poor to the prosperous, from developing countries to the more developed ones.

I can agree with the free-market economists when we are talking about people voluntarily selling their hair, but the picture grows considerably darker when we consider the economics of organ transplants. Not only is a poor peasant in Bangladesh unlikely to have his life saved by getting a new heart or a new liver, but he may well be tempted—and there are well-documented cases where this has happened—to sell one of his own kidneys to feed his family.

There is much uncertainty, at least in my own mind, about which specific devices or techniques will prove to be technologically practical, economically affordable, and socially acceptable. But I don't have any doubt that a lot of them will leap all these hurdles and become, in the not-at-all-distant future, familiar parts of everyday life, as unremarkable as eyeglasses and hearing aids are now. And every one that does will further weaken the boundary between inside and outside, self and other.

This was who I was to myself. It was who I had always been. I had always hidden myself from my family. It was not that I wasn't the person my friends knew, but I was also someone else, and not just someone else, really someone else, this secret person being the real one.

MICHAEL RYAN[1]

The evidence suggests that we are all born with the potential for multiple personalities and over the course of normal development we more or less succeed in consolidating an integrated sense of self.

FRANK PUTNAM[2]

7
When People
Are Not Themselves

There are undoubtedly limits to how much a person can change over the course of a life, and to how many different selves can inhabit a single mind and body at one time, but we don't know what those limits are. It might be more accurate for us to say we don't *agree* on what they are. As the social consensus about self and identity erodes, we find people challenging, in all kinds of diverse and imaginative ways, conventional ideas about the limits to an individual personality. Pushing the envelope, as the saying goes. We have people pretending to be somebody they aren't, people maintaining two or more identities at the same time, people crossing the lines of sex and gender. Some of these efforts result in spectacular and strange behavior, and sometimes they are hardly noticeable. Sometimes they are quite invisible, because they are kept secret from the world, at least for a while; one of the favorite ways of pushing the envelope is to (switching metaphors) come out of the closet. Most of the envelope-pushing efforts we will consider in this chapter are regarded as deviance. Some, such as multiple personality disorder, are diagnosed as madness. Some look like higher forms of sanity. But all of them are part of the terrain of the human mind, which now seems to have wider horizons than we once suspected.

Among the most fascinating envelope pushers are the impostors who, often with cleverness bordering on genius, manage to construct fictitious identities—serially in some cases, concurrently in others. The newspapers occasionally report on the discovery of some such impostor, and the psychological records are full of case histories. The more remarkable of these are about people who manage to enjoy careers in professions such as law or medicine that require them to learn—or be able to pretend they have learned—highly specialized skills and knowledge. We read in the history books about adventurers like Sir Richard Burton, the famous nineteenth-century English linguist, explorer, and impostor. Burton was one of the few infidels who made the pilgrimage to Mecca. He stained his skin with walnut juice, grew a beard, shaved his head, and represented himself as a physician and holy man from Afghanistan. Showing an uncommon dedication to the art of disguise, he even had himself circumcised, being sure that the operation was performed in the Muslim rather than the Jewish style. Along the way he treated the sick and consoled weary fellow travelers with pious quotations from the Koran.[3]

As we go ever farther into the Information Age, with increasingly sophisticated technologies of identification, the obstacles to such imposture become increasingly formidable. But many people—no one really knows how many—are still managing somehow to get away with it.

Imposture Through the Ages

Imposture has a long history. It appears that as long as there have been identities, names, distinct social roles, there have been people who have dared to play games with them—to pretend to be someone else. Myth and literature abound with stories of disguise: gods disguised as people; people disguised as animals; men disguised as women, and vice versa; pairs of people making prince-and-pauper identity switches.

In modernizing Europe, many people used the transitional nature of their social surroundings—the increasing mobility and urbanization, combined with the lingering reverence for the glamour and power of the old aristocracy—to create new identities for themselves, and in the process to break through the class barriers and live entirely different kinds of lives. Imposture was a significant channel for social mobility. Often the impostors were unmasked—at least the ones we read about in the history books were—but they had some remarkable adventures along the way and achieved an odd sort of prestige that they never would have had if they had remained in their original identities or been born into the ones they created.

There was, for example, the famous Count Alessandro di Cagliostro. Born in Sicily in 1743 as Giuseppe "Beppo" Balsamo, a shopkeeper's son, he showed an early talent for con games and petty crime, and grew up to become one of the many adventurers who scurried about the Continent with assumed—usually aristocratic—identities, in search of suckers. But he made such a mark in his chosen career that the historian Thomas Carlyle called him the "quack of quacks, the most perfect scoundrel that in these latter ages has marked the world's history."[4] With his wife, who apparently went in for a bit of discreet prostitution to supplement his other activities, he became known as a clairvoyant, a maker and seller of elixirs of youth, and, at the height of his career, a leader of a secret spiritual order he called "Egyptian Masonry."

Then there was the Princess Caraboo. Although she didn't rise as high or travel as widely as Cagliostro, she also continued to have a certain fame even after she was exposed as an impostor. Caraboo, a young woman dressed in a rather exotic fashion and speaking no English, appeared out of nowhere one day in 1817, knocked on the door of a cottage in Gloucestershire, and indicated by sign language that she was in need of a night's lodging. She was taken in by a local magistrate and his wife, and lived with them for some time, her origins a complete mystery. Then along came a Portuguese man who had lived in the Far East and who, when invited to the magistrate's house, immediately entered into an animated conversation with the young woman. Through him she communicated that she was a royal princess from an Asian country called Javasu and had been kidnapped by pirates and brought to England, where she escaped and swam ashore.

Eventually her masquerade collapsed: She was revealed to be Mary Baker, a former servant girl, and the Portuguese man turned out to have been an accomplice. But she remained fascinating to the public, and some years later, she put herself on display in London, allowing spectators, at a charge of one shilling per head, to have a look at her in her princess-of-Javasu costume. And in 1995 her story was made into a movie.[5]

Germany also had its share of famous impostors, and there too people seem to have found them rather admirable. One was Wilhelm Voight, an elderly Berlin cobbler and ex-convict, who purchased a Prussian officer's uniform, ordered several groups of soldiers to follow him, and proceeded to take over the city hall in the nearby suburb of Kopenick and walk off with all the cash in its treasury. When he was finally arrested he claimed that he had not really invaded the city hall to get money, but only in hopes of finding there a passport he could use to get the hell out of a country that was so infatuated with men in uniform. This, and the audacity of his act, made him an international hero. A London paper suggested he ought to get a Nobel Prize for exposing the "preposterously extravagant" worship of military uni-forms in Prussia, and even within Prussia a Berlin paper said that if Voight had been acquitted, the crowd waiting outside would have carried him off in triumph. He was convicted, however, and spent four years in prison. But public enthusiasm for him did not diminish: When he came out, a wealthy benefactor gave him a lifelong pension, and dozens of women proposed marriage. Eventually he became a music-hall performer, touring the Continent and America—he finally did get his passport—and always appearing in his captain's uniform.

And then a few decades later, after World War I, the German establishment was embarrassed again, this time by the situation-comedy adventures of a cigar salesman named Harry Domela. An adventurer of rather modest aspirations, Domela was trying only to pass himself off as a baron and do a bit of freeloading in a luxury hotel in the city of Erfurt, when he was mistaken for Prince Wilhelm of Hohenzollern, grandson of the former Kaiser. He had a close resemblance to Wilhelm, whose portrait hung in the hotel, and this led the manager to conclude that he was an impostor—not an itinerant commoner posing as a member of a higher social class, but rather a royal prince posing as a member of a lower one. Domela couldn't quite bring himself to disabuse the manager of his mistake, and soon everyone in Erfurt was calling him "your Highness" and treating him as royalty. Word of his royal presence spread to nearby towns, and for some time he traveled about the region being welcomed at railway stations, attending parties in his honor, accepting the royal box in theaters, making speeches, and being fawned on by the local nobility. The imposture was finally discovered, at which point Domela made a break for the French-occupied Rhineland; he was in the process of enlisting in the Foreign Legion when he was arrested by German police and taken to Cologne to stand trial.

Like the now-legendary Captain of Kopenick—to whom he was inevitably compared as soon as the news of his exploits became public—Domela was completely surprised by the reaction to his imposture. He had no idea that his little caper in the provinces would become big news throughout Europe and America, and he had no idea that it would make him a kind of hero in the eyes of many people. His masquerade was seen as a political gesture, a sort of private revolution. Germany was supposed to be a democracy—these were the Weimar years—and the liberal newspapers praised him for having exposed the reactionary and monarchistic tendencies of the local gentry who had been falling over themselves to get close to the supposed prince. At his trial, nobody really seemed to have much to say against him. The hoaxed hotelkeepers testified that they had made more money from the business he brought in than they had lost by giving him free lodging in their finest suites. The judge sentenced him to seven months—exactly the time he had already served while awaiting trial—and he was a free man. He was also a moderately wealthy one, with a 27,000-mark publisher's advance for his memoirs. He dabbled for a time in show business and at one point went to visit

Cecilie, the mother of the man he had impersonated. The Crown Princess invited him to tea and later pronounced him a charming young man with good manners, but not nearly as handsome as her son Wilhelm.[6]

Adventurers and aristocrats . . . The history books and memoirs of Europe are full of their stories, and cumulatively they tell us a great deal about the social order of that time and place—what it was and what was happening to it. It was the society that had evolved out of feudalism and which still possessed many of the outward structures of the old system—the royalty and aristocracy, the swaggering military men, the Church—but in which old patterns of authority and obligation had broken down, new classes had emerged, and revolutionary political changes had occurred. Ideas of rights and human equality were rampant. Old-guard conservatives and *noveau riche* social climbers still clung to all the trappings of the class system, but others now denounced them as evil, and as the public reaction to the Wilhelm Voight and Harry Domela incidents reveals, a lot of people were beginning to regard them as rather ridiculous.

Every social system is also an identity system. It tells people who and what they are and how they are expected to behave, and when it is working well it does that with great clarity. It may do so also with great cruelty and injustice, but it fills so many psychological needs that the passing of any system is always stressful. Part of the gift of the impostors to the public—and a reason why the public was ready to return the gift with admiration and sometimes hard cash—was that they eased the stress a little, made the collapse of the system seem like fun. No small contribution to social change. And also, of course, they dramatized with their picaresque adventures that identity was not, as people had once unquestioningly assumed, conferred upon a person at birth and unchangeable. In their way, they were early postmodernists, multiphrenic and protean, revolutionaries in spite of themselves.

So far I have been talking about identity-changing in a certain context, that of a society with a relatively rigid class system and relatively few channels for legitimate upward mobility. What is going on in Western societies such as America, where people are obsessed with status but careless about class? Well, obviously we don't have as many phony counts and princesses. But we do have impostors, people who for various reasons keep relentlessly testing the limits of the possible and the permissible. A lot of the impostors seem to be involved in practicing medicine. Sometimes they pretend, for career purposes, to be members of indigenous tribes. Australians were recently scandalized when an award-winning young Aboriginal novelist named Wanda Koolmatrie turned out to be a middle-aged white male taxi driver, and then an Aboriginal painter named Eddie Burrup was revealed to be an elderly white lady named Elizabeth Durack. Both impostors, exercising a much different kind of social mobility from that of Cagliostro and Caraboo, had advanced their artistic careers significantly by switching race, age, and gender.

Hiding—and Revealing—the Secret Self

In a way, we all are impostors: In contemporary civilizations there is nothing unusual about feeling some kind of discontinuity between the private self and the public self. Anybody who has ever really tried to break down that discontinuity knows how difficult it is to erase completely. Years ago I knew a psychologist named Sidney Jourard who wrote a book entitled *The Transparent Self*, the purest statement I have ever come across of the quest for congruence between the self as experienced and the self as presented to the rest of the world. Yet even in that extraordinarily courageous work, he proposed only that we try becoming fully transparent, completely unprivate, with one or a few close and intimate partners.

So we live with the gap and probably figure that's just the way things are. But the gap is not the same for all people. For most of us it's no big deal; for some it is a problem; and for a few—how could we ever know how many?—it is immensely wide, painful, all-consuming. Life—all of life—becomes truly an imposture, except that here the deception is not about name and social rank but about character. The person shown to the world, believed by others to be the "real" person, is the normal and respectable public character. And then there is another person, the secret self, who lives another sort of life entirely.

We have records of this sort of double-living all through history, and Dr. Jekyll and Mr. Hyde is the eternal mythic representation in fiction. Some psychotherapists make a professional specialty of it. Today, with people coming out of all manner of closets, there is a growing body of confessional literature about it. One of the most powerful examples of this genre that I have come across in my research is Michael Ryan's *Secret Life*, a searingly frank memoir of one man's career—hidden from those who knew him as a writer and teacher—as sexual predator. Ryan's career began with his seduction, at the age of five, by a young man who lived next door, and went on for forty years or so through countless sexual adventures with women, men, children, and, I'm afraid, the family dog. It ended—some time after he had been fired in disgrace from his teaching job at Princeton—when he found himself driving to a friend's house in upstate New York for the specific purpose of seducing the friend's fifteen-year-old daughter. It was a moment of supreme clarity, a mixture of total self-loathing with a knowledge that it was time to become another kind of person. He wrote:

> How do you change the person you have always been? How do you change your sexuality, how do you change what turns you on? I had no idea. All I knew was that I was in deep trouble. I couldn't trust my instincts, much less my fantasies. I couldn't trust myself. And I was so tired of being myself, disgruntled and predatory and hungry, creeping around with a secret agenda, trivialized by it, racked by the self-loathing I was beginning to understand I had both blocked and enacted with my sexual behavior. Well, it wasn't being blocked anymore. I felt like a piece of shit with eyes. I felt wrong in the innermost fabric of my being.[7]

The book opens at the end of the story, with Ryan on the way to accept a new job in California—his first permanent teaching job in a decade—and making a resolution, on the way, to completely and radically abandon the behaviors that his secret self had lived for. It would be nice to say that he integrates his two warring selves, but no such happy ending is reported in the book. It is more a matter of one self wrestling the secret self to the mat in the interests of personal survival. But there is a certain dignity even in Ryan's outburst of self-loathing, an implicit statement that the truth and wholeness of human existence are more spacious than any self, either the public one or the private one. Living two lives is one way of pushing the identity envelope; going public with the secret self is another one, another kind of personal revolution.

Among the secret-lifers are all the homosexuals or bisexuals who live behind the façade of a "normal" heterosexual identity and maintain another existence after hours. These are the people we are most likely to think of when we hear about "coming out of the closet" and "outing"—the people by and for whom those terms were invented.

It's an interesting sign of our times that the terms *were* invented and have taken up residence in everybody's vocabulary. Usually they refer to revelations of previously suppressed homosexuality, but now are also likely to be applied to any concealed behavior, trait, or opinion. I have heard people referred to (or referring to themselves) as closet liberals, closet racists, closet almost anything, with the double meaning of something concealed but not successfully concealed, or of something once concealed but now revealed.

In earlier times you didn't hear much about people coming out of closets voluntarily, or even of people being involuntarily "outed" with this mischievous, consciousness-raising intent that now commonly accompanies such acts. What you heard about were the scandals, sometimes huge ones, that rocked entire societies and shattered lives: the Oscar Wilde scandal, which forced the British Empire to look with uncharacteristic frankness at "the love that dare not speak its name"; the Redl Affair in Hapsburg, Vienna, when the bourgeois Austrians— kindred spirits of the Victorian English—learned that the distinguished Colonel Alfred Redl, deputy director of the army's intelligence division, was a spy in the pay of the Russian Tsar and had been using his secret income to finance a wild, secret homosexual life.[8]

Coming out of the closet has now become not only a familiar term but in some circles a socially recognized life transition, entitled to be formalized with a rite of passage. I have heard of coming-out-of-the-closet parties with religious ceremonies invented for the occasion. There are self-help books and support groups specifically designed to help the coming-out person take on a new identity, and in the process to feel a little more like a "normal" human being and a little less like a protean pioneer. All these signify a profound shift in social values, and one that is still far from complete.

I don't mean to imply that the act of coming out has been rendered painless. I have known people, and worked with people in therapy, for whom it was the most difficult and wrenching process of their lives. And recently I was reminded of another side of it, the effect on family or friends—and especially spouses and children—of the out-comer. I had given a talk on the general subject of this book to a church group, and afterward a woman who had been in the audience sent me a copy of a book she had written, which was a collection of case studies of homosexuals and bisexuals, male and female, as they struggled through accepting and revealing their secret lives.

The book told of some aspects of coming out that most of us never think about: The confused, sometimes repressed anger of children whose homosexual or bisexual parents reveal their true orientations. The feelings of sexual rejection often experienced by spouses who have to endure their own pain and confusion alone while their partners gaily celebrate their new lives in the company of homosexual friends and sympathetic support groups. The legal battles for custody of children. The enormous difficulty some people have in discovering (or deciding) what their sexual preferences really are. The occasional discovery by a couple that *both* of them have secret homosexual lives. And, perhaps most touching of all, the long unhappy marriages that couples sometimes endure when a secretly homosexual partner does *not* come out.[9]

There is much agony in such stories, and much of it being felt out there in the world right now by people who are struggling with such issues in their own lives. Yet the overall picture that I see is one of slow and difficult progress, a huge social learning process as more people learn to accept those secret selves and to give them public lives and identities.

From Mars to Venus, and Vice Versa

Sex and gender are very high on the list of categories by which we define who and what we are. Even as other identifiers fade in importance, being male or female still feels, for most of us, central to our inner sense of self and our presentation of self to the world. Because sex and gender do matter, we are fascinated by anything that claims to have the last word on what it means to be male or female: by feminist psychology that searches for ways of being that are essentially female, by chest-thumping movements to get men back to their primal manhood, by pop psychologies with new deep truths about the difference between the two—men are from Mars, women are from Venus, and all that.

Because sex and gender do matter, advertisers spend uncountable millions offering us products, everything from mascara to Marlboros, that they claim will help us be more totally, fashionably, attractively, irresistibly, unmistakably, female or male.

And because they do matter, people who are striving to define their identities—hoping to locate and live out their true selves—often fix on sex and gender as the problem, the thing that most needs to be *changed*. So words like "transgender" and "transsexual" find their ways into our vocabulary, and many people embark on strenuous, often costly quests for selfhood. This is old terrain in a way—as old as the myths of gender-changing deities and the sly impersonation games of Shakespearean comedies—but for most people who actually have to deal with such quests, it feels like unexplored territory. The transgenders and transsexuals are true pioneers, and like all explorers, they lose their way sometimes. Not surprisingly, many of the people who experiment with sex and gender—who cross-dress in secret or present themselves in public in the role of another sex or who go through any of the complex surgical and medical procedures (hormone treatments, etc.) that are now available for people who want to take a permanent transfer from one sexual identity to another—feel the need for some help from psychotherapists along the way. There was a time when such psychotherapy was overwhelmingly on the medical model, that is, diagnosis of the "problem" and "treatment" to get the patient to overcome such crazy urges and become a normal human being. Quite possibly that is still what happens in most cases, but there are now a number of therapists who lend a more sympathetic ear and try to help the client live whatever lifestyle he or she chooses, and do it with satisfaction and dignity.

Recently, at a psychology conference, I sat in on a presentation by two such therapists—Niela Miller and Maureen O'Hara—and found it an eye-opening and mind-expanding experience. I thought I already knew a thing or two about the subject. From my years of working in group therapy, I knew that cross-dressing males weren't necessarily— or even ordinarily—homosexual. I had worked with a woman who complained that her fireman husband liked to put on her dresses when he came home from his heroic efforts in burning buildings, and with young men looking for ways to manage their cross-dressing urges within the nonprivacy of army barracks and college dormitories. I had just finished writing a book that dealt with all kinds of happenings on the medical frontier, including transsexual surgery. I had spent most of my life around San Francisco, which is an education in itself. But I was still carrying around a number of assumptions which, I learned that day, were fairly primitive.

I had assumed, for one thing, that most people who decide to change sex are single, relatively young, and still trying to establish their gender identities. But Miller talked about married people with families and about the enormously sensitive counseling that may be called for when a man with several children and a reasonably successful marriage decides to become a woman. It means he has to tell his wife, of course, and also tell his children, and tell people with whom the family interacts as a family.

I had assumed, too, that whatever the practices or the direction of change, everybody made a choice to be one sex or the other, at least most of the time. But then I heard about the case of the person who spends six months of the year as a male and six months as a female—one gender on the west coast, one gender on the east.

What we are looking at here is not just a curious kind of deviance or a new growth industry for psychotherapists, but an enormous chunk of the human condition that has always been with us in some form or another and is now surfacing in response to a whole range of converging events: the breakdown of old sexual taboos, the feminist challenge to traditional sex and gender roles, the medical advances that enable men or women to change sex.

Some societies are now beginning to accept homosexuality, but transsexual and transgender changes are hard for "ordinary" people to get used to. A homosexual is at least a recognizable type, even if a "deviant" one. Cross-dressing, especially by heterosexual males, really doesn't occupy any familiar social niche, and it's something most of us can't quite take seriously. For most heterosexual men, cross-dressing is in the "secret life" category, and often remains there even when they share their secret with lovers or wives. According to Miller, sometimes a man will want to reveal his cross-dressing to other family members, and this often causes problems. One kind of problem results from the wife's reluctance to let others in on what she still regards as a somewhat embarrassing secret. Another kind of problem results when the wife angrily decides to go ahead and tell them herself.

The Twenty-two Faces of Eve

Of all the deviations from the approved one-self, one-sex, one-identity path, perhaps the most bizarre is multiple personality disorder (MPD). Even psychiatrists get upset about it.

In 1988 the annual meeting of the American Psychiatric Association featured a debate that was as much an insight into the current identity crisis as the psychological debate about the self that we noted in chapter 3. The theme of this one was "Resolved: That Multiple Personality Is a True Disease Entity." Through the debate, the association attempted to grapple with a really astonishing phenomenon: the veritable population explosion of people with this form of madness. It was then only eight years since MPD—a disease whose "essential feature is the existence within the individual of two or more distinct personalities, each of which is dominant at a particular time"—had been recognized officially by the Association as a legitimate diagnosis. Things were moving so quickly, though, that in 1982 an article in a psychiatric journal called attention to the "multiple personality epidemic."[10] Never before had a form of madness gone in such a short time from virtual nonexistence to great prominence in both the psychiatric world and the popular imagination. Canadian philosopher Ian Hacking, a bemused observer of this strange piece of human history, reported that "ten years earlier, in 1972, multiple personality had seemed to be a mere curiosity. . . . You could list every multiple personality recorded in the history of Western medicine, even if experts disagreed on how many of those cases were genuine." At the outside, there had been perhaps something more than one hundred cases since 1791, when the first clear description of such a condition was given by a German physician. But then by 1992, "there were hundreds of multiples in treatment in every sizable town in North America. Even by 1986 it was thought that six thousand patients had been diagnosed. After that, one stopped counting and spoke about an exponential increase in the rate of diagnosis since 1980. Clinics, wards, units, and entire private hospitals dedicated to the illness were being established all over the continent. Maybe one person in twenty suffered from a dissociative disorder."[11]

It was no wonder the psychiatrists were exercised about whether MPD was a true mental illness that had simply not been discovered until quite recently—or whether (as some of them thought) it was a sort of hoax, part mass delusion and part hucksterism, created out of a collusion among suggestible mental patients, empire-building therapists, and sensation-seeking newspaper reporters and TV talk show hosts. There was cause for concern either way: If it was a legitimate illness only now being discovered, then countless people in the past must have suffered from it with no understanding of what was happening to them, and no competent help; if the whole business was spurious, it hardly spoke well for the mental health of the mental-health profession—or for the ethics and competence of those members of it who were building careers as experts on multiple personality.

The subject first came to my attention, as it did for many other people, in the 1950s. At about the same time people were reading and talking about *The Lonely Crowd* and its affirmation of the inner-directed man, they were also reading and talking about a book entitled *The Three Faces of Eve*, which told the remarkable (and apparently true) story of a woman who had three separate personalities. Or they saw the movie, in which Joanne Woodward brilliantly portrayed the three: Eve White, the dowdy and neurotic housewife; Eve Black, the hot hussy who hung out in the bars and picked up servicemen; and Jane, the smart, sane, straightforward woman who emerged later. This was a powerful story, although what it offered was in some ways a rather bland, Eisenhower-era version: The causative event seemed to be one single traumatic occasion when Eve, as a child, was forced to kiss the corpse of her dead grandmother. And the therapy proceeded to a thoroughly upbeat ending in which both of the inadequate personalities obligingly disappeared, leaving sane Jane to take over, get a handsome new husband, and live happily ever after.

Some forty years later, when I was in the early stages of thinking about this book, I had occasion to meet the original "Eve," Chris Sizemore, and to hear her talk about her experiences and show samples of her artwork—paintings done in entirely different styles by her different personalities. By this time MPD had become not only an important and controversial item in the psychiatry world, but also a small literary movement. Numerous accounts of other multiples had been published, and other movies had been made. And another kind of population explosion, no less astonishing than the rise in the number of diagnoses of this disease, had taken place: an increase in the number of personalities per patient. The human skull was getting to be a mighty crowded place. Some years after the book and movie successes of *The Three Faces of Eve*, Mrs. Sizemore had published her own story, in which she said that she had not merely three personalities, but somewhere around twenty-two. In another account, *When Rabbit Howls*, a patient described more than ninety personalities. Identity inflation.

And yet another development had taken place. It had become generally understood that the cause of multiple personality disorder was generally child abuse, and that most MPD patients were women. This meant that MPD was becoming controversial and politicized in new ways; it was a feminist issue, and also part of the dispute about the recovery (or creation) of repressed memories of childhood sexual abuse. And it is of interest to people concerned about gender and sexual orientation, because multiples frequently push those envelopes: A woman may have one alter who is an active lesbian, another who is a heterosexual male.

But is MPD *real*, in the modern, objectivist sense of the word? The issue that the psychiatrists debated in 1988 is still a controversy in the mental-health professions. And outside of those ranks there are plenty of people who just don't quite buy the lurid accounts of people who have absolutely distinct personalities that take over their bodies at different times, that are physically different in some ways—that is, they may have different blood-pressure levels, like different foods, or require different eyeglass prescriptions.

MPD is real in at least two ways, and possibly real in a couple more.

It is, first of all, a real mental illness that is suffered by real people—and suffered in other ways by their families, friends, and associates. At the present time it appears that the average number of alters is around sixteen.

It is also—and this is the least controversial point of all, but one whose importance we haven't yet fully grasped—a real part of contemporary culture. Millions of people have now read one of the books, read an article in a newspaper or magazine, seen one of the movies, seen multiples discussing their symptoms on a TV talk show. The multiple has become familiar to us all, part of our common image of the human mind. It is the trademark psychosis of our time, a madness appropriate to the era of multiphrenia and multiple drafts of memory.

It may well be—because it is now a part of our culture—a kind of map that is available to people experiencing severe psychological breakdown. Some skeptics suspect that suggestible patients may be consciously or unconsciously plagiarizing Mrs. Sizemore, developing MPD because it seems like a rather attractive way to handle their problems. This is normally taken to be evidence of the phoniness of MPD, but it also may suggest complex, and in some ways perhaps healthy, choices being made by people who cannot allow themselves the power to make such choices consciously. A woman may find, for example, that one strategy for dealing with the pain of confinement to the role of submissive female is to develop a strong, perhaps male, alter ego. A man may find that creating a homosexual alter is his way out of an unbearable everyday "normality." Hacking thinks this may, in some cases, open up new possibilities for therapy:

> Initially multiples in therapy are ill; they do not choose roles self-consciously. But suppose they acquire suffi-cient maturity to see that they have options open to them, and aim not so much at integration as at finding the kind of person they want to be. Then a formerly pathological gender could become the chosen way to be a person. This must be treated as a sophisticated idea. We should not think that the patient discovers some "true" underlying self but that she had broken through to the freedom to choose, create and construct her own identity. Rather than being a pawn in a deterministic game, she has become an autonomous person.[12]

I suspect that MPD is real in precisely the way that patients and clinicians say it is, and that it is also a constructed reality peculiar to the present time. Similar experiences probably were understood as trance or possession states in other times and places, or simply not understood at all and therefore noticed as little as people could possibly manage. Stanley Krippner, after reviewing various inter-cultural studies of MPD and similar phenomena, wrote, "I would interpret the findings to suggest that there may be a physiological predisposition to dissociation in general and to MPD specifically which, if activated by trauma in a society where there is an awareness of MPD, spawns alters."[13]

Yet it's an amazing manifestation of the human mind. Regardless of whether you choose to approach it as a psychiatric diagnostician, as a true believer in trance and possession, or as a skeptic who thinks the whole business is a therapeutic con job, you have to grant that there is something impressive about human beings who can manifest so many different characters of widely varying ages, personalities, sexes. It says something about the complexity of the brain that is now being studied by the cognitive scientists. It is a bit awe-inspiring to contemplate some of the case histories, and equally awe-inspiring to turn around and look within oneself and consider the possibility that, as Frank Putnam, one of the leading authorities on MPD, said, the potential exists in us all.

The Envelope Pushes Back

The limits that people encounter when they begin to explore different styles of self and identity are not always passive, benign, and yielding. Societies, being systems of identity, can become coercive and punitive when confronted with people who, in one way or another, just don't fit the recognizable identity categories. This reaction is most evident when people change sex and gender, but the same kind of pressure is also likely to be present when we push the envelope in less spectacular ways.

I have been putting words like "abnormal" and "deviant" in quotes, because those categorizations are under fire now, the boundary between abnormal and normal as questionable now as all the other boundaries that once defined social reality.

Clearly it is becoming easier in some ways for people to acknowledge that they have many sides to themselves, and to go through major changes of identity. The culture is developing multiphrenic and protean myths, rituals, and values. Yet there are many kinds of resistance, not only the social and cultural ones, but also others that have more to do with technological change and the needs of public and private organizations. Even as we become more protean in some ways, the bureaucratic systems evolve and improve, keeping records of our identities so effectively that we never really abandon old official selves completely. Inventions such as DNA testing make it easier for the record-keepers to nail down, process, categorize, and enforce our identities in all the ways the keepers of such systems deeply love to do. The modern identity crisis could be described accurately as the identity wars, a million little skirmishes between people trying to change, and an enormous range of forces—cultural values, categories of mental health and normality, expectations of others, bureaucratic inertia—that resists those changes.

*Some years ago I myself made some obvserva-
tions on . . . nitrous oxide intoxication, and
reported them in print. One conclusion was
forced upon my mind at that time, and my
impression of its truth has ever since
remained unshaken. It is that our normal
waking consciousness, rational consciousness as we call it, is but one special type of
consciousness, whilst all about it, parted by
the filmiest of screens, there lie potential
forms of consciousness entirely different. . . .
No account of the universe in its totality
can be final which leaves these other forms
of consciousness quite disregarded.*

WILLIAM JAMES[1]

*Fifty years from now we may have drugs
that can alter personality profiles. Things
are moving very fast.*

JEROME KAGAN[2]

8

The Chemical Connection

Most of us, most of the time, manage to organize our consciousness around whatever "I" we happen to be at the moment, and to persuade ourselves that that's more or less the way we are all the time. Some people, in moments of psychological trauma or in the radical confrontation with other realities we call "culture shock," may become much more strongly aware of a complete break with what they had thought they were. More people nowadays are having experiences of profound change in their personal consciousness and sense of self, because a considerable number of other people all over the world are in the process of making and selling chemicals designed precisely to cause such experiences. That is also a part, and a big one, of the identity crisis.

Drugs "Я" Us

We live in a time of moving and disappearing boundaries: psychological boundaries, physical boundaries, conceptual boundaries. For me, and for a lot of other people in the Western world, something funny happened somewhere in the 1960s to the boundary that separated the respectable people from the dopers.

Before that time, we on my side of the boundary enjoyed our coffee and cigarettes and booze, and regarded people on the other side of the boundary—the unfortunates who "took dope"—with disapproval, fear, and perhaps pity, because we knew that all those narcotics were addictive, leading to lives of violence and despair. Even if we had not personally seen *Reefer Madness*, we understood that dope fiends did terrible things.

Then things got strange. Along came the Beatles and the hippies, Timothy Leary and Alan Watts. People were singing songs about the joys of marijuana, writing books about the marvels of LSD. Some of the books—following the lead of Aldous Huxley's groundbreaking *Doors of Perception*—were saying that drugs could bring profound religious experiences, even spiritual enlightenment. Friends began breaking out the joints at parties, and a lot of us tried them, and most of us—unlike President Clinton—inhaled. The LSD trip became something that many people had experienced and wanted to tell you about. Some of my friends were involved in the studies that were being conducted by the National Institutes of Health—yes, official government acid trips—and others were doing their own explorations in the private sector. Personally I never ventured very far into psychedelia, and of course many people did not venture at all. But it really didn't matter, because the walls had come tumbling down around all of us. And they have stayed down. We no longer have that tidy division between the drugged and the drugless. Instead we find ourselves in a complex and tangled world, a world awash with chemicals—some of them probably addictive, some of them not, some of them helpful to us under certain circumstances (although we're not altogether sure what those circumstances are), and some of them harmful to us under certain circumstances (although we're not too sure what those are either). Some of the drugs are legal, and some of them not, but enough of them are legal that it's possible for any law-abiding citizen to be under some kind of chemical influence most of the time if he needs it and can afford it.

Although there is an immense amount unknown about drugs—why and how they do what they do—it is certain that many of them have the ability to alter the quality of human life. We can see that in the experiences of addicts, in the changed behavior of mental patients, in the enormous literature about people's adventures with psychedelics such as mescaline, psilocybin, and LSD. Concerning LSD—which became a literary movement unto itself in the '60s—we can read of humans turning into animals, inanimate objects coming to life, people magically appearing and disappearing, personal encounters with Christ, enormous waves of joy or despair, moments of profound religious insight, visions of great beauty, excursions into higher sanity, and/or descents into fearful madness. It appears that with a little chemical help, those agents and modules in the brain can get mighty frisky. And this adds a whole new dimension to the discussion about multicentric and protean selves—all the psychological issues—because drugs can enable people to discover quite different personalities within themselves and to change dramatically over rather short periods of time. There's ample evidence of chemically assisted multiphrenia and personality transformations that old Proteus would have envied.

Drugs, in short, can be changers both of the self and of fundamental ideas *about* self. We would have reason to recognize the truth of this and to take it seriously even if the old boundary were still in place. But it isn't. We now have down-and-out street addicts, rich and famous addicts, people using drugs for what they call recreational and spiritual purposes, and increasing numbers of people who identify with no drug subculture but are doing their daily doses of one or more prescribed medications. Psychopharmacology is a recognized field of medical practice and research, an enormous worldwide industry, and an intimate part of the personal lives of millions of people. Prescription drugs are being used for everything from mild anxiety to schizophrenia and manic-depression. They have transformed mental hospitals, where dispensing "meds" to patients has become the central administrative activity. They are in the process of transforming the mental-health professions, changing diagnoses of mental illnesses as doctors discover which disorders respond to which medications. And they are inexorably moving the public toward regarding more and more emotional ailments and problems as biologically caused and therefore chemically treatable.

One of the most popular and controversial drugs to come along in recent years, Prozac, has been particularly influential in this respect. Prozac, more than any other item in the modern pharmacologist's bag of miracles, raises fundamental questions about the self and about how the growing use of chemicals in psychotherapy may affect the future of the self.

Although fairly new on the scene—it hit the market in December 1987—Prozac was soon being used by millions of patients. In 1990 it made the cover of *Newsweek*, which reported its sales in 1989 had reached $350 million—more than was being spent on *all* antidepressants just two years earlier. It appeared to be not only the most safe and effective antidepressant, but also an all-purpose wonder drug: Doctors were prescribing it for a whole range of ailments including anxiety, addictions, bulimia, and obsessive-compulsive disorder.[3] The biggest excitement of all, however, was not about its usefulness as a treatment for ailments, but about the possibility that it simply improved the quality of life—turned its users into new people. A psychiatrist, Peter Kramer, who wrote a monthly column for a trade paper, *Psychiatric Times*, began reporting about his experiences with patients who, on Prozac, had obtained not just a relief from symptoms but, in effect, entirely different personalities and new levels of understanding about themselves. They had become, as he put it, "better than well."[4]

The burst of publicity and controversy about Prozac was in some ways similar to the big excitement about LSD in the 1960s. The promise of chemical transformation of the self is capable of arousing tremendous interest and high hopes—and equally strong social disapproval. Dr. Kramer found that out during his Warholian fifteen minutes of fame, and during the backlash that soon began. There had been reports and rumors of unpleasant side effects, and these attained a level comparable to the initial flood of uncritical enthusiasm. Prozac was accused of having led people to suicidal thoughts and even to committing suicide. Some lawyers used it as a defense in murder trials, saying, in effect, that Prozac had pulled the trigger. And other lawyers of course got busy suing the manufacturer, Eli Lilly & Company. Most of the suits involved patients who claimed to have been somehow harmed by the drug. One suit was brought by the survivors of a mass shooting in Kentucky, where a man had gone berserk in a Louisville printing plant, allegedly under the influence of Prozac. In a way the most rabid enemies of Prozac were saying the same thing as the most rabid fans—that it turned its users into different people.

As of this writing that furor has subsided somewhat. Prozac is certainly a commercial success. More than 22 million people have used it worldwide, and current yearly sales are more than $2 billion. But it remains controversial, and it should—because the controversy is about not only the relative benefits and downsides of a drug, but also the chemical reconstruction of the self.

The Future of Drugs: Four Questions and One Answer

The controversy around Prozac raises urgent questions about the role of drugs in personal life and in human societies. Actually, I suppose I should say it re-raises them, since all these questions have been circulating for some time—at least since the psychedelic revolution of the 1960s. Here I'll mention four of the big ones—the cosmetic question, the real-self question, the real-humanity question, and the Columbus question—and close with a speculation about the future.

1. THE COSMETIC QUESTION. It was Kramer, in his columns about Prozac, who coined the term "cosmetic psychopharmacology" for drugs prescribed not to treat an illness but to tinker with the emotions and behavior in ways that seem desirable to doctors and their patients. Since all manner of nonchemical self-improvement and self-actualization therapies are already among us—techniques designed not to make the sick well but the well weller—he asked reasonably, why not drugs for the same purposes?

Some people might prefer pharmacologic to psychologic self-actualization. Psychic steroids for mental gymnastics, medicinal attacks on the humors, antiwallflower compound—these might be hard to resist. Since you only live once, why not do it as a blonde? Why not as a peppy blonde? Now that questions of personality and social stance have entered the arena of medication, we as a society will have to decide how comfortable we are with using chemicals to modify personality in useful, attractive ways.[5]

Some people find this kind of proposition repugnant, reject it totally on moral grounds—a form of response that another scientist has called "pharmacological Calvinism."[6] Others of us, including myself, have no objection on that basis, but worry about cosmetic pharmacology for what we like to think are less puritanical reasons: the inevitable misuses, bummers, bad side effects, slides into addiction. The matter of inequity: If such drugs turn out to be a good thing, will all people have equal access to them? (You know the answer.) The style problem: Will people turn to cosmetic drugs in response to social pressures or fads, striving to become more vivacious, languid, poetic, assertive, or spiritual according to whatever happens to be popular at the moment among certain groups? (You know the answer to that one, too.) All of these concerns are with us now, and they will be with us in the future, and they are virtually identical to the concerns that arise around that other booming field of self-transformation, cosmetic surgery.

2. THE REAL-SELF QUESTION. Kramer wrote about the case of a woman—called Tess, in his narrative—for whom he prescribed Prozac not long after its approval by the U.S. Food and Drug Administration. The aim was to relieve her depression, which it did quite effectively. The surprising thing was that it did a great deal more. Tess began to report feeling more relaxed and energetic, more gregarious and socially competent, less emotionally fragile, more effective in her work.

She was, in short, a new woman.

After about eighteen months, Kramer took her off the medication. She soon began to report that she was backsliding into all the destructive feelings and behaviors that had brought her into therapy in the first place. And in reporting this to her doctor, she made a remarkable statement: "I'm not myself," she said.[7] Kramer put her back on the medication but was left wondering about what it *meant*. "How," he asked, "were we to reconcile what Prozac did for Tess with our notion of the continuous, autobiographical human self?"[8]

How indeed? And to sharpen the concern, he had a similar experience with another patient, here called Julia, whose difficulties were more in the obsessive-compulsive direction. Her behavior had been causing repeated upsets with her husband and children, and virtually unbearable stresses in her work as a nurse. Under Prozac, everything changed: Work and family tensions eased, compulsive drives subsided, and she even began to consider giving in to her children's pleas to get a family dog. After about five or six months, Kramer lowered the dose:

> We lowered the dose of medicine, and two weeks later Julia called to say the bottom had fallen out: "I'm a witch again." She felt lousy—pessimistic, angry, demanding. She was up half the night cleaning. And there was no way she could consider getting a dog. "It's not just my imagination," she insisted, and then she used the very words Tess had used: "I don't feel myself."[9]

What is particularly fascinating here is that in both cases the women believed their "real selves" to be what they had experienced during the short period of treatment and not the way they had been for the rest of their lives. Which, then, is the real self? And who decides? If the patient decides, who is the self that makes the decision? Each of these is, in its way, a profound philosophical question. None yields an easy answer, and perhaps there is no final answer to any of them. And they all are closely related to the question coming up next.

3. THE REAL-HUMANITY QUESTION. One of the issues that troubles many—even those who are prepared to grant that Prozac's benefits far outweigh the various minor side effects that are sometimes reported—is whether something is not lost, something precious and essentially human, when people so effortlessly iron out the wrinkles in their personalities.

Some critics, for example, have worried that the use of drugs such as Prozac might lessen people's "affect tolerance"—their ability to put up with their own unpleasant feelings—and stunt the emotional growth that would come from simply learning to accept the rocky realities of life. Others, approaching the subject from the viewpoint of evolutionary biology, have argued that all our unpleasant feelings evolved for good reasons—anxiety as a warning against danger, for example—and that it might be best to allow those feelings to carry out their ancient survival functions without interference. Yet others have pointed to the vast historical literature on men and women who have lived lives of immense suffering—suffering that might easily be dispelled today by a pill or two—but out of which they brought forth great artistic, intellectual, and spiritual gifts to the world as a whole. Would the world be better off if Dostoevsky had taken Prozac or if Nietzsche had been on lithium?

These concerns, I believe, go far deeper than the worries about medically or socially undesirable consequences—side effects, dependence on doctors, growth opportunities for illegal suppliers, obscene profits to drug companies. They are saying, in effect, that we have even more to fear if the chemicals work precisely as they are supposed to. Because if they do, then people will irrevocably embrace them and their presumably even more effective successors, and something essentially human—something connected to the tragic grandeur of how we cope with our miseries—will have been lost forever.

Walker Percy constructed a whole novel, *The Thanatos Syndrome*, around such concerns. In his book a group of arrogant mental-health professionals introduce into a town's water supply a chemical called Heavy Sodium, which smoothes out everybody's neuroses without their knowledge of what is happening. But the book's hero and narrator is troubled by this, and after observing the behavior of a couple of his patients, he muses:

> In each there has occurred a sloughing away of the old terrors, worries, rages, a shedding of guilt like last year's snakeskin, and in its place is a mild fond vacancy, a species of unfocused animal good spirits. Then are they, my patients, not better rather than worse? They are not hurting, they are not worrying the same old bone, but there is something missing, not merely the old terrors but a sense in each of her—her what? Her self?[10]

The author had to load up his story quite a bit in order to inject some drama into this rather subtle existential argument. Heavy Sodium, we discover eventually, does have undesirable side effects when taken in sufficient quantities: It turns people into subhuman child-abusing sex maniacs. But still we are given to understand the central moral message, which is that chemicals—other than, perhaps, the occasional shot of Early Times favored by the book's protagonist—should not be used to modify the human condition.

The question here is, What is the human condition? Or the optimal human condition? Are we nobler and more truly *homo sapiens* when living with our familiar neuroses and sufferings, or might we evolve, in a sense, beyond them? Kramer's response to the Prozac critics, although certainly not putting all their concerns to rest, hit that central issue. Referring to the easing of his own early concerns about Prozac, he said, "Our worst fear . . . was that medication would rob us of what is uniquely human: anxiety, guilt, shame, grief, self-consciousness. Instead, medication may have convinced us that those affects are not uniquely human, although how we use or respond to them surely is."[11]

Those affects are not uniquely human. I repeat the doctor's statement, set it out for your special attention, because what we are dealing with here is a controversy about the nature of human life, and about the future. It is a philosophical issue right up there with the great topics that were wrestled with by heavies from Socrates to Descartes. But it will not be settled by philosophical discourse. It will not be settled at all in our lifetimes, and during the unsettled period—which may well have no end—a lot of people will cast their votes according to their own convictions, by dropping a pill or by choosing not to. There are no easy answers to this question, either, although you may be sure it will be before us in the years ahead.

4. THE COLUMBUS QUESTION. This is the hardest question to ask, the easiest to trivialize, and yet, I suspect, the one that will turn out to be the most important: To what extent can drugs enable us to explore consciousness beyond the self, the outer reaches of human reality, the realms beyond the filmy screen that William James discovered in his own mind? This was the question that Aldous Huxley raised in *The Doors of Perception*, and for a while, in the psychedelic decades that followed, it was not at all hard for many people to see the advocates of LSD and the astronauts off there on the moon as simply different kinds of pioneers in a great human adventure. Humphry Osmond, who had given the world the word "psychedelic," was one of those who believed the human race was receiving, in its growing medicine cabinet of mind-altering drugs, a gift of inconceivably great importance, an opportunity to pull itself up by its own bootstraps to a new level of evolution. He wrote:

> I believe that the psychedelics provide a chance, perhaps only a slender one, for homo faber, the cunning, ruthless, foolhardy, pleasure-greedy toolmaker, to merge into that other creature whose presence we have so rashly presumed, homo sapiens, the wise, the understanding, the compassionate, in whose fourfold vision art, politics, science and religion are one. Surely we must seize that chance. . . .[12]

Well, it doesn't seem to have worked out that way. Not yet, at least. The reasons the psychedelic enterprise went off track are of course many and varied, but one reason is that the drugs were widely misused, often by young people and often with disastrous results that stampeded many parents and authorities into panicked overreaction. Sex, drugs, and rock 'n' roll seemed to be but different faces of the same threatening beast, whose ugly characteristics also included political radicalism and a general up-yours attitude toward all things respectable and square in mainstream Western culture. Timothy Leary, who no doubt did a great deal to popularize the psychedelics, probably did more than any single person to unpopularize them. Opinions hardened, new laws went on the books, research funds dried up, and the media—which for a while had treated LSD with something akin to reverence—went their fickle way to other fads.

Yet of course LSD hasn't gone away, and neither have the other chemicals, such as mescaline, which had been taken up by the psychedelic explorers. Undoubtedly a lot of people are still using them and still making the same kinds of amazed discoveries of what one of the pioneers called "the beyond within."[13] But the whole enterprise is no longer before the public in the way it once was. We still have drugs as global crime problem and drugs as therapy, even drugs as emotional cosmetic, but not much is heard these days about drugs as aide to inner exploration, drugs as key to religious experience, drugs as—in the most buoyantly hopeful descriptions—tool for the further evolution of the human species.

And that is a grievous loss, because the best of the psychedelic explorers were engaging the real-self question at a much deeper level than anything we find today in the psychiatric context. The patients on Prozac are making decisions about what kind of personality to have, what face to present to the world, and those are anything but trivial issues—but they are nowhere near as close to the foundations of human reality as the experiences commonly reported by LSD subjects. For example, Walter Pahnke of Johns Hopkins, whom I remember as a frequent speaker at psychology conferences in the 1960s, identified experiences of "undifferentiated unity" as a common feature of the states of mind achieved by subjects in controlled double-blind laboratory experiments. In these states, subjects reported a fading

away of the empirical ego or sense of individuality, while consciousness remained:

> In the most complete experience, this consciousness is a
> pure awareness beyond empirical content, with no ex-
> ternal or internal distinctions. In spite of the . . . dissolu-
> tion of the usual personal identity or self, the awareness
> of oneness or unity is still experienced and remembered.
> One is not unconscious but is rather very much aware of
> an undifferentiated unity.[14]

A curious business, a consciousness that is aware of itself and at
the same time aware of not having a self. No wonder the subjects also
identified feelings of "ineffability," a sense that the experience was
"beyond words," as well as a certain "paradoxicality."[15] Yet such
experiences were quite commonly reported, and the literature is still
available—most of it gathering dust in the libraries now. For whatever
reason, despite all the current explorations of self and issues about self,
that particular area of science is no longer quite within the realm of
intellectual respectability. Yet if there is any truth at all in what researchers such as Pahnke discovered, it is a subject far more important
than most of what is currently being pursued in the laboratories; it may
be, in fact, one of the most important things in the world.

THE ANSWER. Where do we go from here, in relation to all the
behaviors, issues, discoveries, mysteries, crimes, tragedies, and delights that are loosely gathered together under the heading "the drug
problem"? The answer, I believe, is that we will go as we have been
going—in all directions. I have sometimes cited as my favorite futurist
the former Kansas City relief pitcher Dan Quisenberry, a man given to
Satchel Paige-like musings on profound subjects, who once said to a
sportswriter, "The future is just like the present, only longer."

I think he had something there. What we have at the present time
is an enormous range of chemical substances—all the way from milk
chocolate to crack cocaine, from ginseng tea to LSD—that have some

effect on how we feel or think. We have many drugs, and many categories of drug use: addictive, nonaddictive, good for you, bad for you, recreational, spiritual, therapeutic, cosmetic. We also have an enormous body of what might loosely be called information about the effects of these chemicals and the best ways to use them, which includes everything from ancient cultural traditions (such as Native American peyote rituals) through household wisdom (take a couple aspirins for a headache), and street drug-culture lore to research-based scientific data and treatment protocols. We also have a wide range of opinions about how this information should be dealt with by people and societies—all the way from huge, federally financed wars on drugs and "Just Say No" education campaigns to libertarian and neo-Hippie calls to decriminalize or legalize the use of all or some drugs. We also have a wide range of opinions about just what constitutes a "drug," and about which drugs are helpful and which harmful. This is what we have, and in the future this is what we'll have more of. More drugs are on the way. So is more information about them. Society may not be comfortable with the idea of drugs as tools for spiritual exploration, but it is obviously willing to accept drugs as tools for psychotherapeutic and even cosmetic purposes. Current research in genetics and neuroscience guarantees that there will soon be much more information about what roles the genes (and the chemicals the genes make) play in our emotional lives—and that will lead to the development and use of still more psychoactive chemicals. Consider a science writer's semiserious vision of the near future:

> It's winter 2030. Work is going badly, your love life is in tatters. Feeling irritable and melancholic, you reach for your computer and call up Normopsych, an on-line drug service specializing in personality restructuring. After downloading your life history and personality profile data and completing virtual reality tests of rejection sensitivity and mood, you sit back in your chair. A few seconds later the screen fills with a rotating, three-dimensional image of the brain. A handful of neuro-

transmitter pathways are flashing ominously. The diagnosis reads: "Seratonin levels 15 percent below par in limbic system. Boost with 100 milligrams per day of MoodStim and AntiGrief."[16]

The writer hastened to add that the scenario is just a bit fanciful, but that such glimpses of the road ahead can't simply be dismissed as wildly improbable. If anything, they may be on the conservative side. As he pointed out, "For a minority of psychiatrists, the era of the personality pill has already arrived." All this has many implications, but for this discussion there is only one that needs to be clearly read: Human consciousness—definitely including the sense of self—is mediated not only by genes and childhood experiences and social environment, but also by the chemicals that we take into our bodies.

At the present time we are moving into a global civilization that is sometimes described as postmodern, sometimes as an information society. Both are accurate and useful definitions, but we should probably add, to be realistic, that we live in a global drug culture and drug economy. The manufacture and distribution of drugs are industries of astonishing proportions. I can read in today's newspaper report on the cocaine trade that "after 20 years and eradication programs totaling hundreds of millions of dollars, cocaine can be bought on every continent, in virtually every major city."[17] I imagine this is more or less true for all the other major narcotics as well, and for most of the minor ones. The world is awash in chemicals.

This is true now, and will be in the future. The future of the self will be determined in part, perhaps in very large part, by the drugs that are available and by how we use them.

PART 3

Toward a
Post-Identity
Society

*How an [Internet Relay Chat] user "looks"
to another user is entirely dependent upon
information supplied by that person. It
becomes possible to play with identity.
The boundaries delineated by cultural con-
structs of beauty, ugliness, fashionableness
or unfashionableness, can be by-passed on
IRC. It is possible to appear to be, quite
literally, whoever you wish.*

ELIZABETH M. REID [1]

*When people find out that Uncle Jim is
online cruising for teenagers, or that
HotGirl4U is actually a boy, those
identities vanish, and the people behind
them reemerge under different names.*

ROBERT ROSSNEY [2]

*Tools are to a great degree the way we
understand our identity. As our tools
evolve, our concept of who we are evolves,
and as our concept of who we are changes,
how we behave with each other changes.*

VICTOR GREY [3]

9
The Self's Adventures in Cyberspace

The essence of life in a post-identity society isn't that people have no identities at all—we can scarcely imagine such a world. Rather, it's that people have more identities than they know what to do with, that identities change or cease to mean what they once did.

Although the business of constructing and maintaining a personal identity is mysterious in many ways, it's fairly obvious that plain old geography is a powerful piece of it. If you live your life within a single village or a single patch of forest or mountain and in the company of people you've known through a lifetime, you are not likely to spend much time agonizing about who you are. It is when you start moving into other spaces and other societies—or when strangers invade your territory, or when some message from a foreign culture (say, a television broadcast) invades your psychological territory—that things start to get interesting.

Today, things are getting mighty interesting, and mighty fast. People are moving around the world in unprecedented numbers, and so are symbols and information of all kinds. I read an article recently about advances in global telephone communication, which proclaimed "the death of distance." That's overstating it a bit; distance isn't dead, but it certainly matters less as a limit on the social environments we inhabit than it did only a short while ago.

It matters least of all to people whose professional and social lives are lived, in some degree, through the media of computers and the connections among them. Cyberspace. It's a significant sign of our times that we have had to coin a new word, snatched from the pages of a hip science-fiction novel, to describe a new dimension of human interaction, a place that really isn't a place at all in the geographic meaning of the word.

Yet a place where a lot of people seem to want to hang out.

Other Voices, Other Rooms

The advice columns in the newspapers are great windows on the world through which you can catch some interesting and useful glimpses of what is going on in people's lives. In recent years I have noticed quite a number of letters from people complaining about a relative or a friend who has become addicted to the computer. And not just to the computer, but to one or more of the various electronic social settings where they converse, play games, gossip, flirt, and argue with people they have never seen face-to-face. Usually in these cases the addict in question is a nerdy young man, but not always: I particularly recall one fretful note concerning Grandma, who sat in her room all day drinking Cokes and tapping on the keyboard, and who clearly preferred the company of those shadowy figures in cyberspace to her flesh-and-blood relatives. In most cases the worried letter-writers assume that any such preference, any such immersion in "unreal" relationships, must be pathological.

Is it? I suspect most people would say that it is not entirely healthy to spend a major part of one's life online if one has the option of being with flesh-and-blood folks. But I have come to know many others who find life in cyberspace vibrant, rewarding, and expansive, and who insist that it adds to, rather than detracts from, their existence in the old-fashioned four dimensions.

I'm inclined to take them at their word, but that really isn't quite the issue we want to explore here. The subject before us is the self and the various events in our time that change our ideas about it and experiences of it—and it appears that cyberspace is a whole new playground for self-construction and self-transformation, a dimension of life in which people are allowed to be almost infinitely multiphrenic and protean, a matrix for new relationships.

Because so many people are now living some part of their lives in cyberspace, discovering (and creating) new rules and rituals and social orders, the study of such electronic goings-on has become an important growth industry for academics. It's a stroke of luck for them, in a way: Just as modernization appears about to sweep away all the distance, difference, and mystery from exotic lands and primitive civilizations, technological change opens up a fresh terrain with a civilization in the making, and intellectual opportunities galore to create what some call a "postorganic anthropology."[4]

A Surfeit of Society

Cyberspace contains a virtually infinite multitude of communities. Membership in multiple communities is, as we've already noted, a natural inducement to self-diversification. And since the world of computer-mediated communication (CMC) contains so many different communities of so many different kinds, most users find it a shame to participate in only one. A single individual may be significantly involved in, say, a self-help group for overeaters, a religious-study group, a professional or scientific group focused on solving tasks and exchanging information, a multiuser domain (MUD) for playing a fantasy game, and a political-issues group for arguing about current events, and of course may also spend some time unhooked from the machine and participating in various other such activities in the domain that old computer hands refer to breezily as "IRL"—in real life.

It's not even necessary to restrict your socializing to just one electronic community at a time. With good equipment and sufficient technological skill, you can connect to two or three or more at once. Sociologist Sherry Turkle, whose *Life on the Screen* is one of the best studies of the social dynamics of the computer world, said that "people are frequently connected to several MUDs at a time." She described an eighteen-year-old MIT freshman, sitting before a net-worked machine at 2 A.M. and looking at a screen with four boxed-off areas. "On this MUD," he said, "I'm relaxing, shooting the breeze. On this other MUD I'm in a flame war. On this last one I'm into heavy sexual things. I'm traveling between the MUDs and a physics home-work assignment due at 10 tomorrow morning."[5]

Obviously this isn't looking at life through a single window, it's multiphrenia running wild. This might not mean much if all those involvements were fleeting and superficial, with no serious personal involvement, no more sense of relationship than you might get, say, from browsing through magazines at a newsstand. But people *do* get personally involved, and do live important parts of their lives in those contexts. I know a number of people—perfectly adequate folks who possess all the usual social skills and have no trouble functioning in real life—who insist that their electronic socializing is real life, too, in its own way, and a rich addition to their existence. Howard Rheingold, for example, is a smart and amiable guy with whom you might sit around and talk in a bar—as I have done, in fact—but who also relishes the conviviality of cyberspace and has written a book, *The Virtual Community*, about its delights. He said:

> [M]y world today is a different world, with different friends and different concerns, from the world I experi-enced in premodem days. The places I visit in my mind, and the people I communicate with from one moment to the next, are entirely different from the content of my thoughts or the state of my circle of friends before I

started dabbling in virtual communities. One minute I'm involved in the minutiae of local matters such as planning next week's bridge game, and the next minute I'm part of a debate raging in seven countries. Not only do I inhabit my virtual communities; to the degree that I carry around their conversations in my head and begin to mix it up with them in real life, my virtual communities also inhabit my life. I've been colonized; my sense of family at the most fundamental level has been virtualized.[6]

Being Somebody Electronically

Being a member of different online communities of course offers you the opportunity to be different—not only to behave differently from the way you do ordinarily, but even to take on an entirely new identity.

Each region of cyberspace has its own rules about identity, and hence, different opportunities for playing around with it. In the relatively prosaic realm of e-mail, and on the WELL (Whole Earth 'Lectronic Link), where I do most of my geeking, your real name is right out there on your messages, for all the world to see. You may, of course, have ongoing relationships based on the exchange of messages with people you never meet in the flesh, but that in itself is nothing new. You can do that on the telephone. People were doing it hundreds of years ago via the medium that is now known as snail mail. However, in Microsoft World I can go into a chat group, where I am identified only by the member ID I use as my address on that service. This happens in my case to be WALTANDER, which is hardly what you would call a foolproof disguise, but I could as easily have registered with the service as Whoozis or Cagliostro. Other online services make it even easier by allowing their users to have a number of "screen names," which they can change at any time. In the MUDs, you are known only by the nickname you invent for that particular domain, and you may participate in many of them with many different identities. This is also possible in the fast-moving Internet Relay Chat (IRC) conferences, where all the action is live—where people read your comments as you write them, and respond in real time.

The MUDs and chat groups are the places where the identity-creating becomes most free and imaginative. Turkle cited another college student (male) whose online life is played out mainly by four characters: a seductive woman; a macho "Marlboro man" cowboy type; a rabbit named Carrot who has a passive, innocuous personality; and another furry animal who participates (with other furry animals) in a MUD that apparently has a heavy orientation toward erotic play. "I split my mind," he declared proudly. "And I just turn on one part of my mind and then another when I go from window to window."[7]

Great practice, I should think, for being multiphrenic in real life. The MUDs and the electronic role-playing serve the same function as a flight simulator, giving young people—thousands and thousands of them, out there at this very moment, improvising and creating themselves in cyberspace—invaluable training for lives that will be lived in multiple and ever-changing contexts. And Turkle and other students of life in cyberspace insist on the importance of *simultaneous* multiplicity: "The self is no longer simply playing different roles in different settings at different times, something that a person experiences when, for example, she wakes up as a lover, makes breakfast as a mother, and drives to work as a lawyer. The life practice of windows is that of a decentered self that exists in many worlds, and plays many roles at the same time."[8]

For many people the cyberspace experiences can be significant learning opportunities, tools for psychological growth. One leading investigator called MUDs "identity workshops."[9] People express parts of themselves that they repress in real life, or gain useful social insight by discovering how people respond to them when they take on different genders, ages, personalities, social roles. Gender switching is probably the most common form of identity experimentation online— Rheingold estimated that "the population of online gender-switchers numbers in the hundreds of thousands."[10] The numbers are impossible to nail down precisely—everything is fluid in cyberspace, and few records are kept—but there is no doubt that this is the most common form of electronic imposture. It's particularly common for men to appear as women, and people have wildly different opinions about the reason for this. There are the usual Freudian explanations: the repressed feminine revealing itself electronically; and there are also more prosaic ones: the number of men wandering around in cyberspace vastly exceeds the number of women, and the women—I should say the online characters who identify themselves as women—tend to get a lot more attention. Sometimes the gender-switching games become unbelievably complex—women pretending to be men pretending to be women, for example. All this may seem bizarre and futuristic, but one cyber-scholar pointed out that it's a bit old-fashioned in a way. After all, the male and female arrangement of the world still prevails:

> On the nets, where *warranting*, or grounding, a persona in a physical body, is meaningless, men routinely use female personae whenever they choose, and vice versa. This wholesale appropriation of the other has spawned new modes of interaction. Ethics, trust and risk continue, but in different ways. Gendered modes of communication themselves have remained relatively stable, but who uses which of the two socially recognized modes has become more plastic. A woman who has appropriated a male conversational style may be simply assumed to be male at that place and time, so that her/his on-line persona takes on a kind of quasi life of its own, separate from the person's embodied life in the "real" world.[11]

Such experimentation with self, such free wandering across all the usual categories of identity, can be great fun, and it can also be a kind of therapy. In the case studies of online lives, you often come across accounts of people who expand and mature in those playful spaces, take on new responsibilities. Sherry Turkle, for example, told of a young man named Matthew who, unlucky in love and repelled in his efforts to be helpful to people, developed a new personality in a MUD—just one MUD, incidentally—in which he became a leading citizen:

> On the MUD, Matthew carved out a special role: He recruited new members and became their advisor and helper. He was playing a familiar part, but now he had found a world in which helping won him admiration. Ashamed of his father in real life, he used the MUD to play the man he wished his father would be. Rejected by Alicia in real life, his chivalrous MUD persona has won considerable social success.[12]

While reading such accounts I sometimes am reminded of the great 1960 Roberto Rossellini film *General Della Rovere*, an identity parable in which a small-time con man is forced to impersonate a famous Italian general, then takes on the role so completely that he develops integrity and courage he had never exhibited in real life, and dies a hero.

The Dark Side of Cyberspace

Yet clearly all is not merely sweetness and light in this new electronic world. Some people do become unhealthily obsessed with their online lives—even the most enthusiastic defender of digital social life will concede. Players in MUDs and chat groups do sometimes get hurt, frustrated, scorned, defeated, or used, and with no guarantee of any psychological growth as a result. And then there are the stories we all have heard—and some of which I know to be true—of people who establish wonderful relationships online, determine to carry them forth into real life, and are terribly disappointed when they meet their online lovers face-to-face. Cyberspace has its sexual predators, psychological predators, desperate neurotics, deceivers, destroyers—in short, everything that plain old nonelectronic life has. Because it is truly a different medium, a different space with new and as yet somewhat shifting and uncertain rules, it offers new opportunities not only for personal growth, but also for the acting-out of personal craziness. It is kind of a psychological Wild West, with the masks a good deal more effective than the old desperado's bandanna.

There is a story—undoubtedly true, although somewhat confused in a few details as a result of much telling—that has become a part of the lore of cyberspace. It concerns a male psychiatrist named Alex who (like many men) experimented with presenting himself as a woman online. He found that many people, particularly women, were able to relate to this fictitious persona with surprising emotional depth and honesty, and he began to embellish it. Her name was Joan; she was seriously handicapped as a result of an auto accident caused by a drunken driver; she had suffered brain damage that impaired her ability to walk and talk; and she was also badly disfigured, so that she, conveniently, was reluctant to have face-to-face meetings with any of the women to whom she was becoming an important mentor and friend, and who admired her tremendously for her ability to cope with such enormous misfortune.

So Joan was not physically accessible, but she was very much present online, listening to people's stories and offering them advice and support. And she had a rich, interesting personality, with characteristics—warmth, humor, earthiness—that her creator had never been able to express in his own life. In some versions of this story she introduced some women to lesbian "netsex"—simulated sexual activity online. In others she referred them to her creator, Alex, who had affairs with them in real life. Some women became increasingly persistent to meet Joan, and Alex then developed a classic case of impostor's cold feet. A few decades earlier, Harry Domela had tried to enlist in the French Foreign Legion when it looked like the game was about up; Alex decided to kill off Joan. A new character, Joan's husband, came online and announced that she was in the hospital and seriously ill. Her online clients, lovers, and admirers were distraught, and wanted the name of the hospital to which they could send cards and flowers. Alex, making his fatal mistake, gave the name of the hospital where he worked as a psychiatrist. Somebody called the hospital, and "the case of the electronic lover," as it is known in the history of cyberspace, came to its (for Alex) embarrassing and (for Joan's friends) emotionally traumatic end.[13] A woman who was one of the friends, and who wrote an article about the deception for *Ms.* magazine, said:

> Even those who barely knew Joan felt implicated—and somehow betrayed—by Alex's deception. Many of us online like to believe that we're a utopian community of the future, and Alex's experiment proved to us all that technology is no shield against deceit. We lost our innocence, if not our faith.
>
> To some of Alex's victims—including a woman who had an affair with the real-life Alex, after being introduced to him by Joan—the experiment was a "mind rape," pure and simple.[14]

When Worlds Collide

Life in cyberspace may supplement and enrich life IRL, but it may also complicate it in serious ways. We've noted, for example, that there is a lot of sex play online, known variously as netsex, tiny sex, or teledildonics—a surprising amount for a medium that offers no semblance of physical contact. Maybe, as some psychologists have said, the brain is the real sex organ for human beings. These conversations range from lightweight flirtations and friendly discussions of sexual and emotional issues to explicit simulations of sexual activity. Much of the heavy stuff occurs between people who have agreed to meet in private chat rooms, so our knowledge of what takes place there is no more accurate than our knowledge of what takes place in other people's bedrooms. Some of this leads to IRL friendships, to real affairs in real bedrooms, and in many cases to marriages. And some of it leads to serious problems with preexisting marriages and other nonelectronic relationships.

Adulterous affairs are apparently rampant in cyberspace. Married people dissatisfied with their spouses find enormous opportunity—and irresistible temptation—to flirt. That's clearly and explicitly what a lot of chat groups are about. If you come to an online chat room headed "Married and Flirting" or "Married Affairs" or "Lonely Wife" or "Hot Hubby," you are not going to be too surprised at what you find when you enter it. All too easily, the electronic flirtations develop into serious affairs. The online magazine *Self-Help and Psychology* conducted an Internet poll on this subject and found dozens of computer users who said they had conducted online extramarital relationships. These may, of course, be superficial adventures with no real-life contact, and I have heard of instances in which a husband or wife knowingly tolerates them as harmless diversions. But they may also scuttle a marriage, in at least two different ways: when the spouse does *not* tolerate them and then finds out about what's going on, and when the adventuring husband or wife decides the online partner is preferable to the IRL one. I read a San Diego newspaper report on this subject, which told of a young wife who was seriously considering dumping her husband in favor of a man she had never met in the flesh:

> "He's charming, witty and funny," Jenny, 28, said of the man she now spends sizzling hours with, electronically, into the later hours every evening. "My husband is a good man, but he doesn't know the nurturing aspects of a relationship. This man does; he provides sheer attention."[15]

The whole institution of marriage is already threatened in many ways, and this looks like more trouble. True, marriages do result from online relationships. Sometimes people get married online, with corresponding IRL marriages, and sometimes people get married online and never meet. But the opportunities for multiplicity and change that open up with cyberspace make me wonder about the future of stable, monogamous relationships of the traditional kind. Marriages, after all, depend on a certain continuity of identity. Psychotherapists often find that when one partner changes in some fundamental or dramatic way and the other does not, the unchanged partner feels deeply threatened and destabilized, and the marriage may well collapse if this crisis can't somehow be managed.

Online Identity Crises: Privacy and Piracy

The movie *The Net* was an Information Age thriller that dramatized the plight of a woman who lived most of her life in cyberspace rather than in direct face-to-face contact with other people, and whose identity was hijacked by a sinister organization of super-nerds. They took all her documentation, her bank accounts, even her house, and she had nobody who knew her except a mother who was in an advanced stage of Alzheimer's. The filmmakers may have overstated their case somewhat, but clearly all of us are now "known" and "identified" by digitized information, which is becoming at least as important as being known or identified by personal contacts among other people, as in more traditional societies. Thus the new society being created by computer communication presents a quite different set of problems, equally disturbing and equally relevant to the present identity crisis.

Privacy, we noted in chapter 1, is one of the distinguishing features of modern life, one of the forces that, historically, helped to construct the modern self. And in the information era it seems increasingly threatened. Cyberspace is not only the world's largest singles bar; it is also the world's largest filing cabinet. All kinds of information about you and me is floating around out there. According to science writer James Gleick, all of the following exists about you in government and corporate computers, even if you are only a moderate participant in the new electronic economy:

- Your health history; your credit history; your marital history; your educational history; your employment history.

- The times and telephone numbers of every call you make and receive.

- The magazines you subscribe to and the books you borrow from the library.

- Your travel history; you can no longer travel by air without presenting photographic identification; in a world of electronic fare cards tracking frequent-traveler data, computers could list even your bus and subway rides.

- The trail of your cash withdrawals.

- All your purchases by credit card or check. In a not-so-distant future, when electronic cash becomes the rule, even the purchases you still make by bills and coins could be logged.

- What you eat. No sooner had supermarket scanners gone on line—to speed checkout efficiency—than data began to be tracked for marketing purposes. Large chains now invite customers to link personal identifying information with the records of what they buy, in exchange for discount cards or other promotions.

- Your electronic mail and your telephone messages. If you use a computer at work, your employer has the legal right to look over your shoulder while you type. More and more companies are quietly spot-checking workers' e-mail and even voice mail. In theory—though rarely in practice—even an online service or private Internet service provider could monitor you. . . .

- Where you go, what you see on the World Wide Web. Ordinarily Net exploring is an anonymous activity, but many information services ask users to identify themselves and even to provide telephone numbers and other personal information. Once a user does that, his or her activity can be traced in surprising detail. Do you like country music? Were you thinking about taking a vacation in New Zealand? Were you perusing the erotic-books section of the online bookstore? Someone—some computer, anyway, probably already knows.[16]

Although the various businesspeople who hope to turn cyberspace into the world's largest department store assure us that all the data about us is being protected, we hear or read horror stories about people whose identities are borrowed and used:

> It could happen to you. Suddenly, banks, stores and collection agencies are demanding that you pay for things you never bought.
>
> And it's not as simple as someone stealing your credit card. Someone has actually stolen your identity, making it almost impossible to prove to creditors that it wasn't you who made the fraudulent purchases.
>
> It's called ID fraud and it's happening to more and more people, wreaking havoc with their lives for years, while remaining a low-priority crime for law enforcement agencies.[17]

As a result there has been much pressure for improved protection —better software, tougher laws, more aggressive enforcement—and I am sure that this will prove reasonably effective. The potential profits from online merchandising and finance are enormous—enormous enough to guarantee that governments and businesses will do all they can to make the public feel secure in the new electronic economy. But this doesn't mean there will be no sacrifice of privacy. On that score, I am inclined to agree with sociologist Amitai Etzioni:

> The chance of restoring old-fashioned privacy is about as likely as vanquishing nuclear weapons. The genie is

out of the bottle. We must either return to the Stone Age (pay cash, use carrier pigeons and forget insurance) or learn to live with shrunken privacy. . . . We are properly distressed when we are denied credit or learn that the wrong person has been arrested because of mistakes in data banks. But this is not the effect of a violation of privacy, but rather the consequence of data poorly collected and sloppily maintained. We need quicker and easier ways to correct dossiers rather than to try to ban largely beneficial new information technologies because they need fine-tuning.[18]

Etzioni, looking at the privacy issue through the window of his communitarian philosophy, believes that giving up some measure of privacy is "exactly what the common good requires." He points out that computerized data performs such socially useful functions as keeping records on incompetent and negligent physicians, defective airplanes, sexual offenders, deadbeat fathers.

Somewhat ironically that aspect of our new electronic civilization does provide a certain stability of personal identity. However much we may go happily morphing and mutating through MUDs and chat rooms, or even changing our real-life personalities and physical appearances, certain information about us—such as our credit records—usually lives on tenaciously in the data banks. Yet I don't think anybody believes that information represents the true self. It's just data, loosely attached to our lives, another facet of our multidimensional identities.

Infinite Connections: The Future of a Wildcard

Professional futurists, the people who make a living constructing plausible scenarios of what may lie ahead, have a term— "wildcards"—for the events that nobody can predict, the developments that come seemingly out of nowhere and radically alter the course of history. Wildcards may be disastrous or wonderful or some combination of the two, but they are always unpredictable. The only thing you can predict with any certainty is that some wildcards will be dealt. You can do no more than speculate about what they will be or what they will do.

The emergence of the personal computer was such a wildcard, and it may well turn out to have been one of the biggest and wildest of all time. The technology itself was not the surprise—many people expected it to evolve more or less as it has. The surprises were who began to use PCs and how they used them. Computers assume roles in society and in the lives of people completely unrelated to the scientific, commercial, and military realms where such technology has been used in the past. Nobody thought computers would create a new kind of human connection, a new social space, a whole new way for people to experiment with their personal identities.

Well, now we know. What we don't know is where it goes from here.

I realize that in most of this chapter my tone has resembled that of an anthropologist or traveler describing another country— someplace that he has seen and knows fairly well; a place whose language he speaks well enough to get around but that he still regards as somewhat exotic, not quite home. Which is just about where I stand in relation to cyberspace. I spend a fair amount of time there— I log on daily for my e-mail and use the Web more and more for research; I have participated in many different conferences, geeked around some in chat groups and MUDs to see what they look like, even taught online courses. But it's still not quite home. Not the way it is for Howard Rheingold. Not the way it was for my late friend Tom Mandel, a famous citizen of cyberspace who was one of the first people to die online—talking about how it felt to be going under with inoperable lung cancer, being berated in various conferences for never having given up his cigarettes, and, finally, being mourned by many people he had never met IRL. Not the way it is for my son, who, as soon as we acquired our first family computer, plunged gladly and fearlessly into it the way he had—at a much earlier stage in life—jumped off the diving board before he knew how to swim.

I, being thus in it but not entirely *of* it, consider with some skepticism the wild and hubristic claims of its various cheerleaders—such as most of the people who write for *Wired*—and wonder if we are, as they confidently believe, looking at the emergence of a new civilization.

And I finally conclude, still without accepting all of their pronouncements about what it will look like or how it will work, that yes—yes, by God, we are. And that means the computer revolution is happening to us all, and not just to those who are actively participating now in the various subcultures, networks, and industries that are built upon the new technology.

The Gutenberg revolution happened to the world, not just to those who were literate or able to acquire books when it began. And although there are still people who can't read or write and don't have access to books, that revolution is now ancient history. It has been stepped on and walked over by revolutions hurrying along behind it—the revolutions of telegraph, telephone, wireless radio, television. Each of these has changed the rules of societies and politics and personal life in various ways. None of them is finished, in the sense of having reached everybody.

Yet new wires are being rolled out, new satellites being launched into space, and inevitably the tendrils of communication will reach into more places, touch more lives. Those options of community and identity that are now available to a fraction of the world's people will become—with all their joys and all their problems—available to most, and perhaps to all.

And the technology will not only spread, but also evolve—become easier to use and more powerful, offer new opportunities for expression and creativity. The first generation of chat groups and MUDS were limited to keyboard communication, and that is still—as of this writing—the main medium in cyberspace. You write things, and you read on your screen what other people have written. But already there are numerous new services that provide for much more visual interaction. In Worlds Chat, for example, you enter what appears on the screen to be a three-dimensional space, and you choose an "avatar"—an image of some sort—to represent you, as well as a nickname. ("Avatar" is the standard cyberspace jargon for such a visual persona. The word means, in Sanskrit, a manifestation of the Divine.) Some of the ready-to-wear avatars that you can choose for yourself in these spaces are fairly ordinary-looking human beings of various ages, genders, and races. Others are more imaginative: angels and devils, monsters, fish, birds and wild beasts of all description, flowers, creatures from outer space. In some of these you can make your avatar change its facial expression (if it has a face) or gesture. Some allow you to design your own avatar. A new one, OnLine Traveler, requires you to have a microphone on your computer, and with that, you can talk to other people. Some people are enthusiastic about one called Worlds Away, which has some far-out avatars and also some strange interactions—one of the most common of which is hustlers who try to con you into removing the head from your avatar and giving it to them.

What we are seeing here is one piece of the evolution of technology, and it is impossible to say how far it will go. Some speculate that it may go as far as to create an entirely complete yet different alternate reality, a "Metaverse"—in the term of a science-fiction writer—so satisfying and rich in its complexity as to rival the real one.[19] Others predict that much more realistic interactive networks, complete with sound and visual communication, may soon become commonplace online and widely used. A writer in *Wired*, bucking this trend of thought, holds out for the joys of unreality:

> The online world is full of things that are just like real life—but not quite real. Email is not mail. A conference online is not the same thing as a conference in real life. Virtual communities share many attributes with real-world communities, but they differ in many ways.
>
> The same will be true of metaworlds. If you try to evaluate them in terms of how well or how poorly they

mirror the real world, then you're asking the wrong questions. We shouldn't be expecting metaworlds to supplant the real world or fix it. They won't. What they will do, though, is give people something they are ceaselessly searching for: new ways to connect with each other.[20]

And, I would add, new ways to experiment with self.

Among ethical philosophers, there is nothing approaching agreement on where we might turn for basic moral values—except, perhaps, nowhere.

ROBERT WRIGHT[1]

Transforming our epistemologies, liberating ourselves from that in which we were embedded, making what was subject into object so that we can "have it" rather than "be had" by it—this is the most powerful way I know to conceptualize the growth of the mind.

ROBERT KEGAN[2]

10

Post-Identity Ethics

In the spring of 1996, those of us who live in the San Francisco Bay area read in the local newspapers about a man who was about to be executed for murder. The man's name was Daniel Williams, and he had, according to the reports, grown up more or less the way many other men who reach Death Row had grown up: born in extreme poverty to migrant farm workers; a victim of fetal alcohol syndrome at birth; mercilessly beaten by his stepfather through childhood; in and out of different schools, as many as twelve in one year; progressing into adolescence in a stupor of drugs and alcohol; soon in and out of federal and state prisons for a variety of offenses including rape, car theft, assault, and kidnapping; subject to blackouts, double vision, and other symptoms of manic depression. When he was thirty-one he went on a furious one-day crime binge in which he killed three people—including a woman whom he shot while he was in the act of raping her—and was duly arrested, convicted, and sentenced to die.

Seventeen years of legal delays ensued, until the appeals ran out and it appeared that the time for Williams's execution had finally arrived. But by then he had changed. He was on medication that controlled his manic symptoms and had become a quiet, gentle person, known to everybody as Danny, whose main pastime was reading Irish and English history books. A woman, one of his defense attorneys, who had spent much time with him, said, "When he's on his medication, he is respectful, thoughtful, caring—he is like the grandfather everyone wants."[3]

A different man, in short. He was haunted by remorse and claimed to have been "out of his mind" when he committed the murders. Ten relatives of his victims believed that he had fundamentally changed, and asked that his sentence be reduced to life. But according to the law he was the same man who had committed the crimes, and some people—including the son of one of his victims—insisted that he should die, whether his present behavior had changed or not. And after a final appeal to the U.S. Supreme Court was refused by Justice Sandra Day O'Connor, Danny Williams was executed by lethal injection. Case closed.

But of course the case isn't closed. It is still with us, standing as one of the many paradoxes of self. We have a legal order and a culture that are riddled with contradictions—insanity defenses that in some cases will excuse almost any behavior for a person judged to be "not himself" at the time of the act, yet penal systems and social values that amount to little more than institutionalized vengeance. And vengeance requires resistance to any belief in fundamental personal change.

The attempt to save Williams from the executioner is yet another example of pushing the identity envelope—by making the claim that a person can become so different that he is not legally accountable for the criminal acts of the person he used to be—and yet another example of the envelope pushing back. It illustrates another kind of conflict about the limits to change. We have, in this instance, people arguing that a middle-aged prisoner living quietly with his medications and his regrets is not the same person as the raging young manic-depressive who slaughtered three people one day in the San Joaquin Valley.

In many ways, identity issues are ethical issues. And under the enormous pressure now from so many people moving beyond the modern age's assumptions about the self, we are forced to rethink many ethical questions—not just to rethink them once, either, but to keep rethinking them. Cases refuse to remain closed, issues refuse to remain settled to the satisfaction of all concerned, and we find ourselves in a never-ending engagement with ethical principles. Furthermore, ethical issues are not just abstract matters to be debated at leisure—and in the most incomprehensible language—in the philosophy departments. The issues are on the streets and in our homes. We live by them and sometimes die by them. Go ask somebody who is considering an abortion or waiting for a heart transplant.

Ethics, Time, Place

The most important thing we need to understand about ethics and morality, the great lesson that is being widely learned now—and deeply feared and fiercely resisted—is that all ethical and moral systems are created by people, and by people as they are at a certain time and in a certain place. This discovery is difficult for all of us, made more difficult by the inseparability of morals and self. What you think is right is inseparable from who you think you are. Whenever the foundations of morality shift, so do the foundations of identity; we give up a part of what we were, or believed we were, or pretended to be. The philosopher Alasdair MacIntyre reminded us that the words we use—"ethics" and "morality"—derive from the Greek *ethikos* and the Latin *moralis*, both of which, he said, "mean 'pertaining to character' where a man's character is nothing other than his set dispositions to behave systematically in one way rather than another, to lead one particular kind of life."[4]

Some see the present era as the new Dark Age, the utter collapse of all foundations of moral behavior—not only religion and social tradition, but even the rationality that some philosophers had once believed would be the shining path to lead all people everywhere toward a common, reasoned understanding of right and wrong. This perception of collapse is a favorite theme of reactionaries and Romantics, for whom the prescribed remedy usually begins with the magic words "Back to . . ." Back to religion, back to patriotism, back to community, back to the philosophy books. In *After Virtue*, MacIntyre gave a sophisticated but nevertheless bleak account of how that collapse took place and of what we are left with in the aftermath. The prevailing morality now, he said, is what the philosophers call emotivism: "Emotivism is the doctrine that all evaluative judgments and more specifically all moral judgments are *nothing but* expressions of preference, expressions of attitude or feeling, insofar as they are moral or evaluative in character."[5] What this means, to put the matter in somewhat more blunt terms, is that we all do what we damn well feel like doing. We may feel like being ethical, generous, religious, abstinent, chaste, or even old-fashioned, but the feeling is still the determining factor. And since feelings change whenever the person changes, nobody really operates from any permanently rational or coherent moral code. "Everything may be criticized from whatever standpoint the self has adopted, including the self's choice of a standpoint to adopt."[6] The emotivist self "is a self with no given continuities, save those of the body which is its bearer and of the memory which to the best of its ability gathers in its past."[7]

MacIntyre is anything but cheerful about this situation. His own preferred way out of it is also in the "back to" category—in this case, back to the sort of moral thought described in Aristotle's *Nicomachean Ethics*, a rational quest for principles of "virtue" that might be agreed upon by all people, at least by all people in a community or at a certain stage of history.

One thing you can't fail to notice about the present age, regardless of whether you personally happen to find it dark or bright, is that there is a hell of a lot of talk about morality. Issues of rightness and wrongness are copiously discussed and debated. Ethics is a growth industry, and professional ethicists are hard at work on codes of business ethics, medical ethics, legal ethics, scientific-research ethics, cyberspace ethics. Biotechnology, a subject in which I have been involved over the years, is a particularly rich field for ethical discourse. As this sort of ethical activity goes on, I see no evidence of any shortage, either, of moralizing and preaching. We hear secular preachers everywhere, exhorting us to be nonracist, nonsexist, less individualistic, environmentally responsible, fiscally responsible, kind to animals. And meanwhile the more traditional types of preachers are still hard at work over the airwaves, in the churches, and sometimes on the street corners, waving the Bible and telling us to obey the Ten Commandments and get right with God. In comparison to our present situation, the old-timers in Salem had it easy: At least they got hit over the heads with only one belief system. With morality, as with community and identity, the problem is not too little, but too much.

Community profusion and morality confusion are actually two sides of the same situation, different aspects of a single problem to which we all have to keep improvising daily solutions as we live our postmodern lives. We move in and out of different communities, every community has its own values and beliefs, and sometimes one community's morality is different from—even diametrically opposed to—another's. And each time we move in and out of them, we change. Periodically we may make a resolution to be more consistent, but it's not easy. Most of us simply do not live full-time within a single moral structure that gives us a set of instructions on how to be, or even a good clear set of guidelines on how to figure it out for ourselves. Nor do we, as individuals, have ironclad "characters" with solid personal ethical codes that apply wherever we go. We just don't have, most of us, what you could call a clear moral identity any more than we have an enduring psychological one.

Ethics and Culture Wars

To make the matter yet more perplexing, there is a war going on. Lots of them, in fact: culture wars.

Whenever we struggle with the moral dilemmas that all of us encounter at some time or another in our daily lives—whether or not to follow the teachings of a religion, what to do with our sexual urges, how to treat somebody we don't like—we are probably becoming foot soldiers in the culture wars. Those wars, those conflicts over how literally to take the codes of morality handed down from the past, are going on all over the world. And nobody gets to be entirely neutral.

Sociologist James Davison Hunter defines the contemporary culture wars as conflicts between two different impulses: the impulse toward orthodoxy, and the impulse toward progressivism. Those impulses surface within all belief systems—organized religions, political ideologies, the traditional cultures of tribes and nations—and have caused a tremendous amount of conflict within some religious denominations. Hunter calls orthodoxy *"the commitment on the part of adherents to an external, definable, and transcendent authority,"* and progressivism *"the tendency to resymbolize historic faiths according to the prevailing assumptions of contemporary life."*[8]

The culture wars are everywhere, but they take different forms. In the Christian churches the orthodox are likely to be proclaiming the infallibility of the Bible or the Pope, while the progressives are trying to ordain women and gays and make up new rituals. In the Muslim world the orthodox are happily stoning adulterers to death and exhorting women to cover up the parts of their bodies that might incite a man to uncontrollable lust—which turns out to be just about all parts—while the progressives are trying to live a more global and tolerant variety of Islam. In the Communist world the orthodox are struggling to hold on to the eternal verities of Marx and Lenin, while the progressives are opening stock markets. In the American schools, the orthodox are teaching children basic traditional principles of right and wrong in hopes of turning them into inner-directed solid citizens with clear moral identities, while the progressives are teaching skills of "moral reasoning" that will, they believe, equip them to function as civilized human beings in a relativistic, pluralistic world.

Most of us aren't moral philosophers and don't want to be, and we try valiantly to be a little bit orthodox here and a little bit progressive there, a little bit spiritual in one place and a little bit scientific someplace else. You can do that. It will get you into trouble with the warriors of orthodoxy, but you can get some moral support from progressive theologians such as Martin Marty, who has written of the need to commute between religious and secular ways of thought depending on the situation: "I am a Christian," he declared, "but I think in secular rational ways all the time. If I am ill, I don't want Mormon brain surgery, I don't want Baptist blood transfusions and I don't want Lutheran proctology. I just want the job done. This mode of rationality isn't fortified too much by a heavy philosophy, but is likely to stay with us for many dimensions of life simply because it works too well."9

Something else that is likely to stay with us—not because it has such obvious practicality but simply because a lot of people seem to find it satisfying—is the practice of making choices about which parts of a religion or tradition to accept and which parts to reject. If you examine the birth rates of some heavily Catholic countries such as Italy, you are likely to get the impression that a lot of people are no longer following the Church's teachings about birth control. If you talk to an American Catholic you may find that she loves God and loves the Church but doesn't believe in the Immaculate Conception or Original Sin. Huston Smith, another of our leading theologians, says that most Christians have now come to regard the Ten Commandments as the Ten Suggestions. This kind of picking and choosing—which gets some people accused of being "Cafeteria Catholics"—doesn't necessarily come from being self-consciously progressive. It may not lead to any deliberate attempts to remodel the Church, but it does reflect a way of relating to official codes of morality that is far more radically postmodern than most of the people who are doing it consider themselves to be. It's also extremely widespread, and deeply disturbing to those of a more orthodox persuasion who view such mix-and-match morality as worse than no morality at all—only feel-good morality, rudderless emotivism.

Orthodoxy, at least in its grumpier and more militant forms, becomes what we usually call fundamentalism these days. Martin Marty says that fundamentalism is basically a postmodern movement. There have always been conservatives, true believers, and just plain intolerant people, nothing new about that. But the movements that have erupted within most Christian denominations, and in places where people once preached their Hinduism or Islam less furiously, have a different character now, and a new enemy: They are opposed not merely to deviation from the old teachings, but to globalization, to postmodern pluralism and relativism, to the mass media and the popular consumer culture. Political scientist Ben Barber aptly caught the essence of this global phenomenon in the title of his book *Jihad vs. McWorld*.

Identities and Moralities

If you do happen to be born into a strictly fundamentalist culture, or choose to join one, you get ready-made answers to two of life's most perplexing questions: Who am I? and What should I do? A strong traditional belief system is usually a system of roles defining the different parts that people play in the social order, and also a system of morality with a solid set of instructions about what's right and what's wrong. That is the appeal of such systems, the siren song of all religions and cults. Join up, and you have the answer to who and what you are—and with that identity you get, at no extra charge, a set of values and beliefs, a worldview, a moral code.

So I read in the paper of a young fighter in the armies of the Taliban, the fiercely fundamentalist students of Islam who are battling in the endless wars of Afghanistan. "I am a soldier of Allah," he told the reporter. No identity crisis there. No question about right or wrong, either. Only the Sharia, the Muslim codes that prescribe behavior, dress, sexual conduct, punishment for wrongdoers.

And I think of various acquaintances who, in the 1970s, became disciples of Bhagwan Shree Rashneesh, the Indian holy man whose particular brand of New Age spirituality was winning converts by the hundreds until it became apparent that the Bhagwan had more Rolls-Royces than good sense, and his movement went into a tailspin. If you formally joined his movement, became a *sannyasin*, you were given a new name and vowed to dress always in the clothing—first orange, later a shade of crimson—that proclaimed your faith to everyone who saw you. Your identity was thus welded to the guru and his teachings, and that was a *primary* identity that claimed dominance over all your other labels, including the name you had been given at birth. Good psychology, there, an antidote to multiphrenia. For a while it effectively kept the faithful from wavering. But eventually they wavered anyway when the ship began to go down, and today I rarely meet young Americans with names like Krishna Prem.

Most people in the West do not succeed in achieving anything like the secure identity and moral certainty of the young Taliban soldier. Some do reasonably well without either. They improvise, borrow from here and there, shop around, adjust to the situations in which they find themselves. But others don't, and it's hard to know where to turn when the going gets tough, how to learn the skills of navigating in a world that has as many different moral codes as styles of cooking. That is the real moral challenge of our time. Society is not going to find an overarching moral code, spiritual or secular, that will work uniformly for everybody. Not all individuals are going to find clear moral identities. What we have to do, whether we do it singly or collectively, is find ways that people can learn how to be responsible in this kind of world.

Morality and Mental Health

Psychotherapy is one of the ways. And by psychotherapy I mean not just the high-priced shrinks in Manhattan and Beverly Hills. There are many, many different ways that people seek and find help in dealing with their lives—sessions with counselors of all kinds, marriage encounter weekends, self-help groups, addiction programs, dialogues with priests and pastors, work with personal coaches and management psychologists. And in all these variations of psychotherapy, a big part of the work involves what are essentially ethical and moral issues. Many psychotherapists would as soon keep this truth in the closet, because much of the leadership in that profession is marching in lockstep toward a more mechanistic, medical model of mental illness and mental health. You won't get much insight into dealing with your moral dilemmas from the *Diagnostic and Statistical Manual*, the Bible and cookbook of the American psychotherapy establishment.

If you want to get the feel for that moral-search side of therapy, you have to consult the works of some of the old humanistic psychologists like Rollo May—*Love and Will* is definitely not a book of symptoms and prescriptions—or the renegade psychiatrist Thomas Szasz, who says mental illness is a myth and psychotherapy is merely applied philosophy. Or you can get it, as I have, in informal conversations with psychotherapists who are willing to talk about the difference between what they learned in grad school and what they actually deal with in their practices.

What they often encounter in their clients—the force that impels many people into psychotherapy, makes them willing to spend their money and time on it—is a powerful moral energy. And in saying this I am not merely offering praise or a simple declaration of human goodness. It's far more complex than that, because a lot of that moral energy is toxic. People mobilize it in creating endless melodramas of guilt and vengeance in which their family and friends get to play the villains. It is a Force that definitely has its dark side. But nevertheless it's there—a desire to do right, to find dependable moral guidelines, to feel like a decent person.

Consider again the case of Lupe, the Oaxacan daughter/Navy officer/nurse/wife/mother, and her travails. Her problems did not have to do with psychosis or neurosis. Nor did the solution to them lie in taking a pill—not even Prozac—or recovering memories of childhood trauma. They were ethical problems and identity problems. Dealing with them required not just finding the rules in some book, because no such book has been written, but struggling through to new under-standings of right and wrong and finding better ways to take care of the people she loved. Her therapist said, "What she had to do was move up a level of mental development, see that she's the one who has to make that decision, say whether her behavior is ethical or not. I don't mean in a vacuum, in a solipsistic way, like if it feels good to me I'm going to do it, but in a way that understands her place in a complex situation and takes responsibility for it. Her conversations with me were really conversations about that." The therapy was a matter of engaging the client to develop as a moral animal.

On Hope and Complexity

Human beings *are* moral animals, and moral in specific ways. We are *socially* moral because no matter how individualistic we may be, all morality is defined in some social context. And we are *symbolically* moral, because moral understanding is done with language. In saying that we are moral animals I don't mean that we are naturally disposed to be trustworthy, loyal, helpful, kind, or any of the other virtues on the Boy Scout list. We obviously have strong abilities in the opposite direction on all of the above counts. I mean that we moralize. We operate by principles of right and wrong, and those principles are part of our continuing effort to make sense of the world, to organize the raw material of experience—the "blooming, buzzing confusion" that William James famously described—into some kind of coherence. "Organisms organize, and human organisms organize *meaning*" is the way the pioneering psychologist William Perry put it.[10] And he meant that *all* human beings organize meaning. The organizing drive, and the moral energy that is an essential part of it, is shared by all members of the species. It may lead in a virtually infinite number of different directions. An individual may solve those organizational problems by becoming a Taliban warrior, an urban sophisticate, a loyal gang member, an orthodox Jew, a liberal Protestant, an environmentalist, a murderous sociopath, or a crusader for global peace. But the drive for meaning is universal. It is the source of all our problems, and our only hope.

That organizing process always involves feeling—the "emotivist" charge is correct as far as it goes. It goes on in several versions at once, as the cognitive scientists now tell us. It goes on continually, through all our waking moments and a good part of the time we're asleep as well. It is endlessly producing new versions of reality as we become slightly different people in slightly different situations and surroundings.

Because this organizing process involves such complexity, and because it can be hard work, people have historically made it easier by participating in the lie of self. They pretend to be less complex than they are, less changeable, less multidimensional.

We love anything that reduces the burden of complexity. We love labels of race, gender, and nationality; movies of good guys bashing bad guys; songs of undying love; stories in which people are propelled through life by a single motive. We all would like to be the Count of Monte Cristo for a while, with nothing to do but pursue righteous revenge. Identities are one fiction that serves this complexity-reducing purpose, formal codes of morality another. And I don't say it's time to simply give them up, because our consciousness and our civilization are built on them. But it is definitely time to push the envelope, to look at wider visions of our own humanity.

Ethics in Evolution

We have available now, to help us get through what might appear to be an unimaginably complex and confusing world of conflicting moral claims, richer maps of the meaning-making human mind—psychological maps that take account of how our styles of thinking about right and wrong change during our lifetimes. These are usually called developmental or evolutionary models, and they have to do with growing up.

The godfather of all such mapmakers was the great French psychologist Jean Piaget, who studied children's cognitive development. He described in some detail the child's continual restructuring of her relationship to the environment—how she perceives the world, how she understands it, how she organizes her sense of self.

Then along came Lawrence Kohlberg, who described another kind of growing up—the movement from one stage of moral development to another. At the lowest "preconventional levels," according to

Kohlberg, the child has begun to develop some idea of the cultural rules and labels of good and bad, right and wrong. These aren't understood as abstract principles, but as general guidelines for getting along. There are powerful folks out there in the world, and you are likely to get punished if you do what they say is bad and get rewarded if you do what they say is good.

The child matures toward the levels of what he called "conventional morality," which involve desire for approval from others, conformity to social roles, respect for authority, and maintaining the social order for its own sake. The person who has reached one of these stages of development has internalized the cultural rules and labels, made them a part of his view of how the world is ordered. He still may be responsive to reward and punishment, but it is now the social, symbolic feedback that counts.

At the highest levels of moral development, according to Kohlberg, are the stages at which "there is a clear effort to define moral values and principles that have validity and application apart from the authority of the groups or peoples holding these principles and apart from the individual's own identification with these groups."[11] One of these stages is the "social contract orientation," a relativistic worldview in which the person sees that there are a lot of possible standards and rules and that the best ones are those agreed to by people through constitutional and democratic procedures. (This, he says, is the official morality of American governance.) And finally there comes a "universal ethical principle orientation," an advanced stage of moral wisdom in which the person recognizes—or chooses—abstract principles of justice and respect for others which he regards as logical, universal, and consistent.

Kohlberg's moral-development theory was much praised in his time because it was conscientious, groundbreaking work that afforded a powerful—and essentially hopeful—vision of the human being as a moral animal. But he took a lot of criticism, too, and the strongest criticisms came from feminists. Any reference to Kohlberg's work now is likely to be paired with a reference to Carol Gilligan, who charged that much of it had a hidden sexual bias, a kind of Lone

Ranger mystique that might be relevant to the moral development of men—or to their ideals of it—but didn't speak for women. Women, she claimed, speak of such things with a different voice; they understand moral obligation, and hence moral development, in terms of relatedness rather than in male terms of individuation and separation.[12]

There's plenty of room for argument about the specifics of moral development, but it remains our deepest and most useful understanding of how human beings really deal with moral issues and how we might get through the present crisis in cultural evolution without becoming either fundamentalists or sociopaths.

One of the best systems of this sort is the one constructed by Robert Kegan of Harvard. It's particularly useful to us here because Kegan is explicit about the connection between a person's morality and sense of self. His system has five levels of development, and the key process involved in moving from one level to another—the process that is central to our lives as we mature, and central to the human race's struggle upward from barbarism—is a conversion of subjective to objective modes of experiencing the self. This may not be immediately clear (I said only that Kegan's theory was the best, not the easiest to understand), and a bit of explanation is in order. Kegan said:

> Subject refers to those elements of our knowing or organizing that we are identified with, tied to, fused with, or embedded in. We *have* object; we *are* subject. We cannot be responsible for, in control of, or reflect upon that which is subject. Subject is immediate; object is mediate. Subject is ultimate or absolute; object is relative.[13]

So what we do as we mature is to keep turning around and *seeing* thoughts, ideas, and feelings that had previously been invisible because we took them to be inviolable realities. Then once we have seen them we can begin to consider them; evaluate them; wonder where they came from; compare them to other thoughts, ideas, and feelings that we might choose to have in their place. Or we can simply continue to entertain them, but with a different awareness of their role in our personal consciousness. In any case, we are reorganizing the self and our understanding of the world in a major way.

Kegan calls his system constructivist and developmental. Constructivism refers to the various schools of thought that deal with the creation of social reality by people or systems; developmentalism to "the idea that people or organic systems evolve through qualitatively different eras of increasing complexity according to regular principles of stability and change."[14]

The first two levels in Kegan's system have to do with childhood and adolescence. The next three—where things get interesting—have to do with different levels of development in adults. They describe the moral growth of any individual, you or me, and also represent different stages of historical cultural evolution. He calls them traditionalist, modern, and postmodern.

At the third (traditionalist) level, people seek a clear, external guide to morality: "An infallible guide outside ourselves, in which we comfortably invest authority and to which authority we pledge loyalty, fidelity, and faith—this is the essence of psychological dependence. It is the essence of the premodern Traditional state of mind, and it is the essence of third order consciousness."[15]

When we move beyond that consciousness—if we do at all—we do it by reorganizing our worldviews and redescribing our lives in ways that may not be at all apparent to others. We begin to recognize that there may be some element of *choice* involved in matters that we once accepted without question. This certainly involves some serious thinking, but it doesn't imply that the person at a higher level is more intelligent: "What we mean by maturity in people's thinking is not a matter of how smart they are, it is a matter of the order of consciousness in which they exercise their smartness or their lack of it."[16] We do some thinking, we reconstruct our worlds, and we do it with the help of words. We tell new stories:

The idea that leaving the third order of consciousness is akin to leaving the family religion does not mean that the move to modernity of necessity requires us to leave the family or the religion. What it requires is that we construct a new relationship to the family or the religion. Like all such metaphors sent in to aid the remaking of mind, the new spaces it can create are not necessarily separations between people but distinctions within a person, differentiations within a relationship or a faith. The prospect of leaving the family religion can foster a host of such distinctions: the distinction between . . . "finding my own way of practicing what is still a form of the family religion" and "leaving the faith altogether"; between "leaving behind some of what my parents believed" and "leaving behind my previous sense of connection to them." The creation of such distinctions builds a trembling bridge from the third to the fourth order of consciousness.[17]

As people edge their way into the fourth (modern) level of growth, they become more inclined to exercise personal choice and responsibility. They are increasingly aware of the existence of other societies with different sets of roles and boundaries. It is a more complex worldview, and has produced more complex devices—ideologies, legal systems, conflict-resolution mechanisms—for explaining and managing the differences among people. The dream of getting everybody to reason together and arrive at universal principles of morality, sometimes referred to as the Enlightenment Project, is a product of fourth-order mentality. So are the two highest levels of moral development in Kohlberg's system. Kohlberg never really got to a postmodern view; Kegan does.

Kegan describes a fifth level of adult development, in which people recognize the "fictive, constructed" nature of all values and beliefs, all codes of ethics and morality.[18] At this level of cognition and maturity, which he calls postmodern, people form an entirely different way of thinking about conflict. They become more likely to accept it as an ever-present opportunity for growth and change rather than as a deviation from some "normal" situation in which it is a problem to be solved. They become more likely to examine their own attachment to their own positions. They may see a protracted conflict as "a reminder of our tendency to pretend to completeness when we are in fact incomplete. We may have this conflict because we need it to recover our true complexity."[19]

A political system based on fourth-order (modern) thinking will recognize different cultures as "whole and distinct," and search for principles of self-determination and peaceful coexistence—that's how we got the present global political system. An individual operating at that level will recognize other people as whole and distinct, respect their rights, and demand that his own rights be respected as well. At its best it represents a high order of moral thought and civilized behavior. But it does not solve all problems, in part because it cannot see beyond the modern view of the self, and human development does not rest there.

Kegan's research with married couples gives a good example of how fourth-order thinking may lead couples to different ways of understanding their relationships. In a third-order (traditionalist) marriage, the couple is a unit with a shared identity. In fourth-order (modern) marriages, people let go of that kind of closeness and learn (or think they ought to learn) to view each other as whole and distinct selves. But couples may also let go of that belief as well. Kegan described one such case:

> For the Bakers, the good working of the self and its recognition by the other begins with a refusal to see oneself or the other as a single system or form. The relationship is a context for a sharing and an interacting in which both are helped to experience their "multiple-ness," in which the *many* forms or systems that *each self is* are helped to emerge. While the Ables (a couple operating at the fourth order) begin with the premise of

their own completeness and see conflict as an inevitable byproduct of the interaction of two psychologically whole selves, the Bakers begin with the premise of their own tendency to pretend to completeness [while actually being incomplete] and see conflict as the inevitable, but controvertible, byproduct of the pretension to completeness.[20]

What he means by "incompleteness" is that any idea we have of another person (or of ourselves), any role, any persona, any personality, is only a limited and temporary construction of all that the person is.

The reader will probably get the impression, from my brief summary of Kegan's ideas, that he thinks the world is in the process of making a transition from modern to postmodern. Not so. He sees most people and societies barely struggling into modernity, searching for "full participation in the modernist world of personal and collective empowerment, dignifying one's own and one's people's voices and having a hand on the levers and dials of one's own destiny."[21] I think he's quite right, and that much of the political turmoil we see in the world at the turn of the century has to do with the aspirations of people to be whole and distinct individuals with rights. They aspire to live in modern, self-determining, whole, and distinct societies something like what Europeans and Americans had—or thought they had—some decades ago. But most peoples who are pursuing that goal are going to find that they are trying to catch a train that has already left the station, and perforce be required to inhabit social orders much more pluralistic and changeable, and not always comfortably distinct from the world beyond their borders. These are the situations that push us to rethink and rethink as we struggle—and we are all engaged in it—either to fight our way back into tradition or to fight ahead into much more complex understandings.

Kegan's book, the one I have been quoting from here, is entitled *In Over Our Heads: The Mental Demands of Modern Life*, and he means it. Most people, he believes, are simply not ready for the "admirable but currently out of reach" worldview of postmodernism.[22] That may be quite correct, but the great changes of the past—the discovery of the New World, the Industrial Revolution, the revelations of Darwin and Freud and Einstein—didn't wait until everybody was ready for them, and I don't think this one will either.

Staying Afloat in the Meme Pool

The human species is moving beyond one stage in its evolution—a historical period in which most people live in traditional societies and some live in modern ones—and has not yet reached the next. We're not even altogether clear on what it will be when we get there.

Since we are talking evolution, let me borrow an image from biology to talk about the more hopeful side of the present situation. Steve Jones, a noted British geneticist, believes that global migration and the resultant intermarriage among people from different regions may be a very healthy development. "Wherever we look," he said, "one thing is clear: there has been a drop in inbreeding in human populations in the recent evolutionary past. An increase in mating outside the group is one of the most dramatic changes in recent evolutionary history. Its effects may outweigh anything that medical genetics is likely to be able to do,"[23] which, ironically, is just the opposite of what was feared during the heyday of "eugenics"—when the priests of genetic improvement thought the natural vigor of their peoples was going to be sapped by mixture with the inferior genes of foreigners—and is still feared by many defenders of national and ethnic purity today.

Borrowing metaphors from biological evolution to talk about cultural evolution is a dangerous business (see social Darwinism), but it's useful as long as we keep in mind that a metaphor is just a descriptive tool. Comparing what's happening to human genes with what's happening to human cultures is not all that far-fetched, however, because it's all part of the same process—globalization. As the world becomes truly one world, there is much mixing of genes, and also mixing of memes. (Memes, for anyone who may have escaped exposure to that trendy term, are cultural symbols and ideas.) God knows we have had plenty of cultural inbreeding; the contemporary world, for all its cacophony of conflicting moralities, is an incredibly rich field of opportunity.

I wouldn't go so far as to say that this mixing leads inevitably to health and moral progress. But I would go so far as to say that it can if we get clear on what is happening now and have the courage to go fully into it and through it. Many codes of ethics are handed down to us, but the wisdom to know how to live with all of them is not. We have to figure that out, learn more about how people develop, and create the situations that facilitate their moral growth. We need principles that will provide better help and guidance for a woman who is trying to live in three or four cultures at once, perhaps some better understanding of what to do with a manic-depressive mass murderer who is also a sad, kindly man reading history books. In neither case are the traditional answers satisfactory, nor are we ever likely to be completely satisfied with the modernist belief that at some point a new whole and distinct individual—a completed modern woman, a rehabilitated criminal— stands before our vision.

Is there any hope for such progress, or am I being incurably idealistic in even suggesting that the human species as a whole can evolve into higher levels of understanding and behavior? Certainly, as you consider a few of the things that are going on in the world, the stuff that you find while reading the day's news, you can hardly be optimistic.

Out there in the world are some six billion human brains, each one spinning out its multiple dramas, organizing and reorganizing its world, telling its ever-changing stories of self and other, right and wrong. I have no hope that all those minds are going to become engaged in thinking things through together, as prescribed by some of the great philosophers of moral reasoning. Neither do I have any hope that they are going to be united under a single religious teaching, as is still dreamed of by some of the priests and mullahs. If there is hope, it rests in the ability of those busy brains to discover new ways of seeing the world—and then newer ways still. Some part of that will involve understanding how fictitious and changeable are all those public truths, how limited are all the stories we tell ourselves and others about who and what we are. I don't think it is really a matter of optimism, or even of hope: We are being pushed into the unknown by the force of our own consciousness, and will not let ourselves rest until we see how much of our world is of our own making and stop being afraid of our own complexity.

This new social character—ambiguously enterprising, abandoning a vacuous authenticity for a particular artificiality . . . and operating on a model of the individual traditionally gendered as female—hardly fits the picture of the hardy, self-reliant individual of pre-organization-man days or of the inviolable, creative authentic self that arose in reaction to [the organization man].

PAUL LEINBERGER AND BRUCE TUCKER[1]

Firms now prosper less by making commodities than by endowing tradable products, whether material objects or human performances, with the heightened capacity to appeal—in short, by making icons. And consumers in turn make their way in this world through heightened iconographic receptivity.

ERNEST STERNBERG[2]

11

The New Economics
of Identity

It's impossible to think about identity without, sooner or later, thinking about money. We all are economic beings, however reluctantly some of us may embrace that fact, and we literally buy and sell our selves. As consumers we purchase things not only because of their blunt usefulness, but also because they help us craft our self-images. As workers we can't help being reminded that we are, in a sense, commodities. And we all have grown up with an understanding that your occupation is a huge part—if not all—of your personal identity.

But both buying and selling are undergoing great changes now as we proceed headlong into a global, high-technology, information-driven economy. Consumption is being transformed by the appearance of new ways of buying and new things to buy, and by the emergence of any number of international cultures and lifestyles that are defined by things people possess and use—everything from T-shirts and sneakers to luxury cars and designer suits. Work is being transformed, too, as we all are drawn into a huge and ever-changing supermarket of skills and knowledge in which it becomes increasingly

175

difficult to rely on using your occupation as a permanent, universally recognizable badge of self.

Identity and Work

As long as there have been occupations—and the division of labor is an ancient and near-universal human practice—work has been a shaper of personal identity. We have a legacy of work-based names—Baker, Mason, Knight, Carpenter, Smith, and all their equivalents in other languages—to remind us of times when what you did was who you were. The Industrial Revolution, a major force in the creation of the modern self, brought forth new occupational roles: the Working Man, the Working Girl, the Captain of Industry, the Organization Man, the Company Wife. People's sense of self and ways of working changed and changed again, but beneath the surface of those transformations the deeper assumption held: the belief that a person was defined by his or her occupation. It was, in some ways, made even stronger by modernizing forces—the physical and social mobility, the rise of egalitarian and pluralistic values—that tended to weaken old identity definers such as class, religion, and ethnicity. But even that powerful source of personal identity is now being shaken by the transition into a postindustrial information economy. Work is changing so dramatically that even though it continues to occupy a central place in the lives most of us lead, it no longer plays quite the same role in our construction of self.

One facet of this change is a decoupling of work and jobs. Until quite recently the two were more or less synonymous. If you had a job, you worked; if you didn't, you didn't. And in the modern era having a job usually meant being employed by an *organization* in a clearly defined and stable occupational role, with duties, hours, rates of pay, and promotion all more or less standardized.

But the job, in that meaning of the word, is a social invention, and a fairly recent one. As management consultant William Bridges pointed out, "Before 1800—and long afterward in many cases—job always referred to some particular task or undertaking, never to a role or a position in an organization."[3] You might *do* a job, but you didn't *have* one. You might have a recognized craft or occupation, but it was not framed by the structure of a large public or private bureaucracy. The change—Bridges calls it "the first job shift"—came with industrialization and urbanization.

That job shift was, for many people, a traumatic adjustment to fit the routines of the factories and offices. But nevertheless the job—the kind that you had or hoped to get—became a central fixture of life in industrial countries. It was an invention that served many purposes: For managers and efficiency experts, job assignments were the key to assembly-line manufacturing; for union organizers, jobs protected the rights of workers; for political reformers, standardized civil-service positions were the very essence of good government. Jobs provided an identity to immigrants and recently urbanized farm workers. They provided a sense of security for individuals, and an organizing principle for society.

Jobs functioned in so many ways until so recently that it is amazing how many organizations are now opting for other ways to define and manage work. The second job shift is well under way. You can see it in the industrial countries of the North with the renewed interest in telecommuting and job-sharing, the increasing use of temporary and part-time workers and contracted-out services, the changing relationships between workers and management, the growing popularity of self-employment and small businesses. Indeed, "de-jobbing" is proceeding at such a pace that many economists, management experts, and futurists are now talking freely about the end of the job. Bridges predicts that the job as we now know it will disappear entirely and be replaced by new kinds of flexible work assignments in post-job organizations. It will be remembered, then, only as a quaint artifact of the Industrial Age.

Work has to change, because the organizations that employ workers are changing. And organizations have to change to survive in the new global economy. In the advanced industrial countries, businesses are rushing to remodel themselves into what some experts call "agile companies." "Agility," as defined by Steven L. Goldman of Lehigh University, means "the ability of a company to thrive in a competitive environment of continuous and unanticipated market change—to respond quickly to rapidly changing, fragmenting global markets that are served by computer-networked competitors with routine access to a worldwide production system, markets that are driven by demand for high quality, high performance, low cost, customer-configured products and services."

One kind of agile company is the "virtual corporation," the loosely linked network of organizations and people with a minimum amount of the hierarchy, bureaucracy, and permanent structure that distinguished the classical corporations of a few decades back. This corporate model has become a hot topic in the management literature, and some companies have been quite successful in making it work. A prime example is Verifone, currently the world's leading producer of electronic credit-card validation systems. Although the company grosses nearly a half-billion a year, it doesn't have anything resembling the showplace headquarters that a traditional company would consider absolutely necessary to its effective functioning and corporate image. It has something—some leased offices in a suburb of San Francisco, where about 180 of its 2,800 employees work—that its managers refuse to call "headquarters." Instead they call it "SFO," which is the designation of the nearest airport. All its other offices, scattered around the world, are known by airport initials. Its various activities are carried out in thirty or so different offices and plants. Its executives come and go from continent to continent, communicating with one another by e-mail and voice mail. Most of them do their work without that other badge of executive rank, the private secretary. Sometimes as many as twenty-one different offices dial into a teleconference at the same time, and the decisions made that way become immediate global policy.[4]

Obviously this is a radically different kind of organization, a different way of working—and a different kind of employment, since agility and virtual organization hardly lend themselves to having a stable, bureaucratized workforce. One management consultant believes that such corporations "will maintain a 'contingent workforce,' but white collar employees will become more like construction workers, taking work by the job and often working at home."[5] Goldman said, "It is easy to project a growing body of people who will never have a stable job, and certainly not a middle-income job, in a society adapted to the characteristics of agile production."[6]

The nature of work is also changing for the people who *do* have jobs. Management guru Peter Drucker has talked and written at great length about the emergence of the "knowledge worker," whose occupation involves not merely performing routine tasks but also applying theoretical or analytical skills. Such workers are replacing the industrial laborer as the dominant part of the workforce, and their productive activities are always organized and structured differently from those of their assembly-line predecessors. They have different relationships, and both managers and workers develop a different sense of self within these contexts. Many companies now refer to both managers and workers by trendy new terms like "associates."

The kind of de-jobbing that results from such corporate metamorphosis is getting a lot of attention from the economists and the management theorists, but that is far from the whole story. At all levels of society, all over the world, people are improvising livelihoods that do not fit either the industrial-era model or the agriculture-and-crafts-based economy that preceded it. Immigrants to developed countries, often unable to find steady jobs, nevertheless find places in the new landscape by being mobile, flexible, resourceful, and imaginative. They moonlight, work part-time, share jobs, start small businesses. Their lives are often precarious and hard, but what they do and how they do it are instructive to those of us who believe you either have a job or you're out of luck. And yet another kind of job shift has been taking place in much of post-Communist Eastern Europe, where people are surviving not because the old command system is still in place—or because the shiny new Western-style one has taken hold—but out of sheer ingenuity. Forced to adapt, people become hustlers, traders, independent manufacturers, freelance deal makers. Even in much of the developing world, the best hope for the future may lie in creating innovative new kinds of non-job employment. For example, the International Commission on Peace and Food (in its 1994 report) pointed to the urgent need to create employment for hundreds of millions of poor people, and at the same time dismissed the notion that most of these people could be employed by new jobs in the corporate sector or by government-sponsored activities. Instead it argued strongly in favor of a different approach, giving central importance to self-employment and entre-preneurship, with emphasis on agriculture, agro-industry, and small firms in the informal sector.[7]

It's impossible to see all the implications of this vast transforma-tion of work or to evaluate it in any final way as simply good or bad, but clearly the current job shift is as rough a transition as the last one, causing great hardships for many workers and their families. And it is forcing policy makers, political activists, and labor leaders to do some agonizing reappraisals of their values and positions. For example, the increase in the number of part-time workers—which the International Labor Organization (ILO) estimates has soared to 60 million in industrialized countries—is generating new concerns about workers' rights. A few years ago in Geneva, delegates to the ILO's seventy-fifth-anniversary conference adopted a new convention calling for part-time workers to get the right to organize, occupational safety and health standards, and social security. The same document recognized the growing importance of part-time work and called for employment policies to take it into account as an important way of creating new job opportunities.[8] I don't see much sign that governments have rushed to implement these recommendations, but the recommendations them-selves are a significant indicator of change. Historically the labor movement has tended to cherish the traditional permanent, full-time job as the only acceptable form of work, and to be highly suspicious of the variations. But the variations—all the ones I have mentioned here, and probably others we haven't heard of yet—look like the future of work.

Also changing are expectations of occupational stability. Young people are being told that instead of learning the skills of a lifetime trade or profession, they should learn how to survive in a fluid, fast-moving economy, in which they may have to change occupations several times in the course of their working lives.

The New Individualists

This new economy is bringing forth a new kind of social character, quite different from that of the "organization men" who punched the time clocks a few decades ago.

That term "organization man" is itself an important piece of history. It's associated with William Whyte's 1956 book, *The Organization Man*, which drew a detailed and unforgettable picture of the sort of social character that had evolved in response to the needs and values of industrial economies at mid-century. Whyte's book fits nicely on the shelf next to *The Lonely Crowd* as a document about how people of that not-too-distant past lived and worked, and also about how social scientists of the period understood them. Whyte, a young editor at *Fortune* magazine, based his study on extensive research with American employees, and out of his efforts emerged a vivid image of a type of person—prudent, risk-averse, and security-conscious—who thrived within the framework of large paternalistic organizations. It was a type of person, by the way, that was found in not only the corporations. Whyte wrote:

> The corporation man is the most conspicuous exam-
> ple, but he is only one, for the collectivization so visible
> in the corporation has affected almost every field of
> work. Blood brother to the business trainee off to join
> Du Pont is the seminary student who will end up in the
> church hierarchy, the doctor headed for the corporate
> clinic, the physics Ph.D. in a government laboratory,
> the intellectual on the foundation-sponsored team proj-
> ect, the engineering graduate in the huge drafting

room at Lockheed, the young apprentice in a Wall Street law factory.[9]

Whyte, like the authors of *The Lonely Crowd*, was alarmed by what he saw as the loss of the old individualism and, more specifically, by the loss of the kind of moral force it had exerted in the marketplace and the workplace. He believed that the hardy "Protestant ethic" of the nineteenth century had been replaced by a conformist "social ethic" and that the old *self-reliance* was giving way to an *organizational reliance*, based on the assumption that the way to get ahead was to become a smoothly moving cog in the corporate machinery.

More recently a pair of social scientists, Paul Leinberger and Bruce Tucker, went back to some of the same people who had been interviewed by Whyte, and interviewed them again—and also studied their children and grandchildren. And they reported that the organization man is on the way out as a major player in the workplace. He's not yet an extinct species—there are still some huge organizational structures where such people find stable niches and feel right at home—but he's definitely on the endangered list. They say that things have been moving quickly since mid-century and that the busy decades of the recent past have produced *two* different post-organization-man value systems, one following the other: first a passionate infatuation with the character ideal of the "true self," and then a virtual abandonment of it.

The first step produced a new burst of individualism, but not the kind that had been prevalent in the previous century. For the offspring of the organization men, they said:

> Individualism became synonymous with individuality, and with the cultivation of the private self. In effect, they took individualism, which had previously had a political and social component, and redefined it in psychological terms. . . . As the organization offspring came of age in the sixties and seventies, they were exhorted to find themselves or create themselves. They undertook the

task with fervor, as self-expression, self-fulfillment, self-assertion, self-actualization, self-understanding, self-acceptance, and any number of other *self* compounds found their way into everyday language and life. Eventually, all these experiences solidified into what can only be called the self ethic, which has ruled the lives of their parents. Many people mistakenly regarded this development as narcissism, egoism, or pure selfishness. But the self ethic, like the social ethic it displaced, was based on a genuine moral imperative—the *duty* to express the authentic self.[10]

This commitment to self-expression, they found, took the form of a yearning for the life of the artist as an occupational ideal. All kinds of people in all kinds of occupations—whether or not they were actually involved in any artistic activity either professionally or recreationally—turned out in the course of interviews to have artistic aspirations or fantasies. "They want to be musicians, filmmakers, screenwriters, actors, poets, novelists, dancers, or visual artists or to work in related fields."[11] These desires expressed their conceptions of who and what they were, a way of affirming true, authentic inner selves different from their organizational roles and the social conventions to which they might outwardly conform. People aspired to be not only artists, but social critics and political activists, because a movement or a cause was an effective way to "find yourself" while contributing to the greater good. And as those of us who are old enough remember from the 1960s and 1970s—the decades in which that ethic was riding high—this development produced great criticism of corporations and of modern civilization generally. Yet for all its vigor and moral fervor, the era of the self ethic is, according to Leinberger and Tucker, drawing to a close. They offer several reasons for the short happy life of the authentic self, of which I'll cite three:

· Alternative and more inclusive conceptions of the self, especially those introduced into organizations by the influx of women, now challenge almost daily the more traditionally male conception of unfettered self-sufficiency.

· The rise of a genuinely competitive global marketplace linked by instantaneous communications has accelerated the diffusive processes of modernity, further destabilizing the self.

· The centuries-old philosophical bedrock on which all our conceptions of individualism have rested, including the highly psychologised individualism embodied in the authentic self, is being swept away.[12]

In place of the authentic self, they say, is arising a new social character with yet another kind of individualism. They call this newcomer the "artificial person," but hastened to add that

the designation *artificial person* does not mean these people are becoming phony or insincere. Rather, it refers to a changing conception of what constitutes an individual and indeed *makes* someone individual. In the recent past, the organization offspring believed that individuality consists of a pristine, transcendent, authentic self residing below or beyond all the particular accidents of history, culture, language and society and all the other "artificial" systems of collective life. But for all the reasons we have cited and many more besides, that proposition and the way of life it has entailed have become untenable. More and more the organization offspring are coming to see that the attributes they previously dismissed as merely artificial are what make people individuals—artificial, to be sure, but nonetheless persons, characterized by their particular mix of these ever-shifting combinations of social artificiality of every variety. Starting from this fundamental, and often unconscious, shift of perspective, they are evolving an individualism that is "artificial" but particular, as opposed to one that is authentic but empty.[13]

What this describes—although in different language—is a transition from the neo-Romantic kind of modernism to postmodernism. The organization men (and women) of mid-century had been chiefly social traditionalists, their senses of personal identity inseparable from their social roles. The opposing, countercultural reality language that blossomed quickly among their offspring, borrowing heavily from the old Romanticism, resurrected the ideal of the inner "true self." Its view of the world carried a strong conviction that the public self of any person who worked in an organization had to be a false, dehumanized façade. But, as the authors reported (and they seem to have discovered it to their surprise in the course of their research), that ideal has been fading, even among some of the organization offspring—the baby boomers who had once espoused it. They learn to live in a world that can be described in many different ways, in which all social reality is artificial—not false, just artificial, built up out of creative variations on all kinds of hand-me-downs from older cultures. As they do they become more like Richard Rorty's postmodern "ironists," who are "never quite able to take themselves seriously because [they are] always aware that the terms in which they describe themselves are subject to change, always aware of the contingency and fragility of their final vocabularies, and thus of their selves."[14]

Whatever Became of Loyalty?

A *Wall Street Journal* columnist contemplated the present postmodern scene and saw a dismal downward slide of one of the great virtues: loyalty. He reported on a conspicuous lack of long-term allegiance in the field of politics—with people showing less loyalty to institutions and communities, and communities showing less loyalty to citizens—and, even more dramatically, in the workplace, with employers and employees showing less loyalty to each other:

> Denise Mitchell is a senior official of the AFL-CIO, and she has sat in on several focus-group discussions with union members in recent months to get a better sense of their concerns. "What I heard again and again was that there is no loyalty," Ms. Mitchell says.
>
> In short, employees are less and less likely to feel that the companies they work for will show allegiance to them. And who's to blame them? Corporate downsizings, merger mania and white-collar job losses have guaranteed that almost everybody suspects they can't count on any employer for long. Workers still tend to stick with their jobs as long as before, recent statistics show, but Ms. Mitchell says their sense of any "social compact" is fading.[15]

According to the Leinberger and Tucker thesis, this isn't just a few workers with a bad attitude, or a reaction to what employers are doing. It is a manifestation of a deep shift in how people think about themselves. It doesn't necessarily mean, as conservatives of the organization-man era almost invariably assume, that such workers are less productive on the job. They may well be highly productive, responsible to their work obligations, and happy with what they are doing. They just don't assume that in the future they will still be doing the same thing for the same employer, or that what they are doing defines who they are. Nor are they likely to feel the deep pangs of the idealists who are convinced that there is an unbridgeable gulf between an inner "authentic self" and their present occupations. They aren't the inner-directed rugged individualists on the old model. They aren't the conformity-driven organizational units described by Whyte. But neither are they the authenticity-bound self-discoverers of the counterculture and Charles Reich's once-famous Consciousness III. In practice, "they change jobs and even careers with startling frequency, choose where they want to live and only then look for work, desert orthodox career paths in favor of fashioning their own situations, and prize personal freedom over job security."[16]

Like many other aspects of the postmodern identity crisis, this shift can easily be lamented as a collapse of morality. Such laments inevitably give way to calls for renewal, which in practice inevitably turn out to be some form of regression: back to the organization man; back (it now looks better than nothing) to the heady days of the baby-booming quest for the inner self; back to community. But it doesn't have to be lamented; it can also be accepted as a challenge, as Tucker and Leinberger suggested:

> The artificial person is, for better or worse, the kind of dominant social character we are likely to get. The real challenge of the coming decades will not lie in trying to whip such people back into shape, but in understanding them; not in trying to protect organizations from them, but in accommodating organizations to them; not in bemoaning the loss of authentic community, but in see-ing how narratives of care may be humanely elaborated in a mobile and fragmented society that is likely to become more so.[17]

What's Your Mix?

Some years ago I accepted an appointment as a visiting lecturer at the School of Public Policy at Berkeley. This experience was bemusing for me in many ways. It was, for one thing, the first time I had taught at Berkeley. I had labored on other occasions as a part-time academic field hand at various universities, but had never been on the faculty at the place where I once had been an undergraduate. Another thing that gave the experience a quixotic sense of history for me was that the school is located in a building I had known as a fraternity house, and it always seemed interesting to me that our meetings were held in the same room that once had reverberated to the rowdy songs of fifties fraternity boys. (This wasn't the only postmodern fraternity house in the neighborhood: One just up the hill had turned into a Tibetan Buddhist institute, where I sometimes went to meditation classes.) And yet another contribution to the mild sense of unreality that always hovered about me there was the fact that the School of Public Policy tended to reflect the neoconservative politics of its founder, Aaron Wildavsky, and I wasn't much of a conservative, either neo- or paleo-.

Anyway, there we all were, and the faculty were a civilized bunch. The regulars would make it a point to introduce themselves to the visitors, and I recall one such polite conversation with a woman who asked, "And where *are* you?" I knew what she meant, of course: *At what university are you a regular faculty member?* But since I had never been a full-time faculty member at any university, did not expect or aspire to be, I didn't know quite how to answer. "I'm right here," I answered lamely. It was one of those times—and I have known many of them during a life spent mainly outside the boundaries of the usual job descriptions—when I had the feeling that the maps didn't have a place for me and the ways I earned a living.

More recently I have discovered that in the intellectual world as well as in the world of business, there are any number of kindred spirits who also wander, occupationally multiphrenic, beyond and across the boundaries of work and of the traditional academic disciplines. They are variously employed as teachers, writers, lecturers, consultants. Some of them have adopted fancy new job titles—like "independent scholar"—to describe what they do. Mary Catherine Bateson proposes that instead of asking somebody "What do you do?" we should now ask "What's your mix?" I like that one, although I haven't yet actually tried it on anybody; I suspect they would think I was offering them a drink.

I know that all of the people thus occupied do not really prefer such footloose working lives and would happily settle down in some campus with tenure, benefits, and a few grad students to do the chores. But the traditional colleges and universities are also being shaken—some believe threatened with extinction—by the various technological, economic, and social changes that are racing through the world, and it becomes harder and harder to be an academic organization man even if the lifestyle appeals to you.

The Nonmaterialistic Consumers

As employment changes, so does consumption. Consumption is now absolutely inseparable from identity. With the breakdown of other definers of status and group membership, we have had no breakdown at all of the human preoccupation with status itself and the need for belonging. In place of rigid social classes and unchanging social roles, we now have lifestyles that are made and maintained through purchasing habits. So our purchases are creations of *meaning*. We have an economy in which consumption is inextricably intertwined with symbolism, an economy that has gone far beyond simple materialism.

This game is new in some ways, old in others. There's nothing really new about a symbolic dimension to the things people own and use and rely on as indicators of whether they are wealthy or poor. In every economic system—definitely including those of the most primitive traditional societies—people value possessions for reasons that go beyond their simple instrumental usefulness. The other reasons have to do with aesthetics here, religion there, status somewhere else. You can find endlessly varied accounts in the anthropology books and the history books of the human tendency to place great value on all kinds of things for symbolic reasons. You can find accounts, too, of changes in style, when things once valued lose their charm or new things take on great value for reasons that now seem utterly incomprehensible. Read Charles Mackay's classic *Extraordinary Popular Delusions and the Madness of Crowds*, in which he tells of the great tulip craze that gripped Holland in the early seventeenth century, when the mania for the new plant became so intense that people were paying huge fortunes for a few grubby bulbs of particularly desirable varieties.[18] You could take that for an aberration, but on last night's TV news I saw one feature about Japanese youths paying hundreds of dollars for used American sneakers—yes, smelly old secondhand shoes—and another of people battling each other in a store for the current Christmas season's tulip toy, the Tickle Me Elmo doll.

Naturally people who are looking to make some money—and that designation takes in quite a few of us—try to see if they can't make those things happen rather than just waiting for the winds of human folly to blow in their direction. Makay mentioned that tulip pushers in London and Paris tried hard—but with only modest success—to reproduce the Dutch phenomenon in their own countries. That was more than three centuries ago, and since then people have grown more skillful at sales promotion. The symbolic manipulation of desire has become a huge industry in its own right. Advertising isn't new, either, but it now plays a different and more important role in our lives. It's interesting to browse back through the ads that appeared in publications and posters in the infancy of that art, when people were just beginning to discover that there might be a bit more to selling a product than just making it and letting people know it was available. Advertising began as an outgrowth of the Industrial Revolution, changed enormously throughout the modern era, and in the postmodern era saturates all cultural experience.

One of the things you can't help noticing in the advertising of the nineteenth century was its class consciousness. The ads for clothing, jewelry, and many other items teased the consumer with the invitation to be an impostor in a safe and harmless way. Perhaps you couldn't become a member of a higher class, but you could *seem.* Middle-class people could imitate the upper classes. Lower-class people, if they had a little extra cash, might imitate the middle classes. People of color imitated whites, and children imitated grown-ups. And everybody imitated royalty. At any given time there was basically one "right" style—and it was handed down from above.

Cut to California in the 1970s. At SRI International, researchers in the Values and Lifestyles (VALS) program helped advertisers understand the consumer preferences of the times, so they could fashion and target their messages more effectively. Note the appearance of the word "lifestyles," and the nonappearance of the word "class." The VALS program was (and is) consumer research: serious thinking about what makes people buy things, aimed for advertising and marketing executives. And like much other work of that sort, it had evolved well beyond the idea of selling people things so they could imitate their betters. It assumed that people lived different lifestyles, and furthermore that these changed over time. The VALS typology—which has a distinct 1970s feel to it—mapped two different paths of development, with two different fundamental types of consumers. They called one the other-directed group, and the other the inner-directed group. The other-directed group contained such types as the Belongers ("traditional, nostalgic, and patriotic"), the Emulators ("youthful, ambitious, macho, status-conscious, and competitive"), and Achievers ("self-assured, materialistic builders of the American dream"). Along the inner-directed path were the I-Am-Me consumers ("exhibitionist, narcissistic, impulsive, dramatic, experimental, active, and inventive"), the Experientials ("person-centered, artistic, and intensely interested in inner growth"), and the Socially Conscious ("highly educated and prosperous . . . many people in this mission-oriented group support causes such as conservation and consumerism").[19]

All this sort of work—and there's plenty of other research of the VALS variety—is based on the recognition that our buying activities involve much more than simply getting things we need and then using them, and is also more than the "conspicuous consumption" described decades ago by Thorstein Veblen. It is a way that people construct their identities and present themselves to the world. And this kind of work is based also on the recognition that there is no longer a single hierarchy of style. We don't have one consumer culture; we have an economy made up of consumer subcultures. Within this huge and varied bazaar freely wander people of all ages, educational levels, ethnic groups, and degrees of wealth, purchasing things that appeal to their senses of who they are or want to become, things that give them status in whatever society of style they want to be identified with.

Jim Collins, one of my favorite commentators on postmodern society, equates popular culture with postmodernism. Both, he said, "reflect and produce the same cultural perspective—that 'culture' no longer can be conceived as a Grand Hotel, as a totalizable system that somehow orchestrates all cultural production and reception according to one master system."[20] He argued against promiscuous use of terms such as "mass culture" and "dominant styles." What he means is that there isn't as much up and down in culture, style, and in consumption habits as there once was. This certainly doesn't mean equality or leveling, nothing like it. There is tremendous diversity, great inequality, obsessive status-seeking, and constant change. Consumption is multiphrenic, protean, decentered, relational.

In this postmodern consumer economy you don't really know the value of something except with reference to a particular lifestyle or subculture. A pair of blue jeans with holes in the knees may be a throwaway item to a person living one lifestyle, a precious piece of clothing to someone living another. We now have what Ernest Sternberg of SUNY Buffalo calls an "economy of icons," in which all goods and services are made, sold, bought, and used as icons. An icon isn't just an image; it is a thing—a physical object such as a car, an intangible such as an insurance policy, or even a person—that has been endowed with symbolic meaning to the extent that we can't ever separate the symbol from the thing itself. And the value of an icon is in the eye of the beholder.

In the old days, manufacturers used to make things and then try to sell them. The symbolic dimension was always there, but it was rooted in class and tradition. Then to stimulate sales they began to advertise, to pay more attention to packaging and to marketing devices such as displays in stores and windows. Symbolism invaded the factories, stores, and marketplaces, conquered them completely and occupied the territory. Now the advertising, packaging, and marketing are not afterthoughts but forethoughts—integral parts of the design of products, the creation of new services.

Consumption serves as an identity definer for everybody who consciously plays the game and also, in different ways, for those who don't. If you are one of those who chooses to live more simply, you have discovered yet another way to define who and what you are. You can even buy books and subscribe to magazines that tell you how to do it. You can—such is the pervasiveness of consumption in our lives—find stores that will sell you clothes, garden tools, and other items that subtly proclaim your personal dedication to a life-style closer to nature. I happen to live near a branch of one such, Smith & Hawken, and find it instructive to wander through the store and consider such items for the gardener as goatskin gloves, rubber boots from Scotland, and seventy-dollar indigo-dyed cotton shirts. More icons.

Beyond the Consumer Society (Don't Hold Your Breath)

One Sunday, accompanied by an old friend and colleague, I was driving home from a conference in Monterey. We stopped in Santa Cruz for lunch, located a likely place, and I parked the car a few blocks away. As we were strolling toward the restaurant we stopped to look in some store windows, and I recall his comment as we stared at one particularly rich display of elegant items of silver and crystal: "How are we going to get beyond this consumer society?" I should mention that we had been talking, at the conference and on the drive home, about the future of global civilization. He had weighed in among those who think the world is being strangled—ecologically, culturally, and spiritually—by consumerism. And as you undoubtedly know, he's not alone in that view.

How are we going to get beyond this consumer society? Well, we aren't. Maybe someday—anything is possible—but not in any immediate future. Because at the same time thousands of intellectuals in the West fret about the consumer society on their way to lunch, billions of people in the rest of the world are rushing to get in on the act. I can think of—and hope for—ways that consumption may become less wasteful and inequitable, but can't imagine its ceasing to be an enormous force in shaping global civilization. If our future does indeed reduce to the simple proposition that we either abandon consumerism or destroy the planet, then we are in what is technically known as deep shit.

The world's ecological problems—which are enormous and frightening—may be solved, but it will not be done by shutting down the immense power of consumption. Nobody has a hand on that lever. There's no such lever.

We are beginning to recognize consumerism as a political force in a way it has never been before. Consider the world's largest subculture: teenagers. Teens are notoriously conformist and style-conscious, and the globalization of communications media makes it possible for them to conform globally, style globally. This means, among other things, big, big profits. A *Fortune* writer reported:

> In a world divided by trade wars and tribalism, teen-agers, of all people, are the new unifying force. From the steamy playgrounds of Los Angeles to the stately boulevards of Singapore, kids show amazing similarities in taste, language, and attitude. African Americans and Asians, Latinos and Europeans are zipping up their Levi's, dancing to the Red Hot Chili Peppers, and punching the keyboards of their Macintosh PC's. Propelled by mighty couriers like MTV, trends spread with sorcerous speed. Kids hear drumbeats a continent away, absorb the rhythm, and add their own licks. For the Coca-Colas and the Nikes, no marketing challenge is more basic than capturing that beat. There are billions to be earned.[21]

We might wish that the evolution of global consciousness would take place in some more elegant fashion and not come rushing in on a wave of Cokes and Big Macs. But whether or not we like the way it is happening, the first truly global generation has come into existence, its members knowing one another and identifying with one another. We have no idea what will come of this, but clearly consumption and pop culture are among the forces that are redrawing the global map of political consciousness.

What ethnic identity politics had in common with fin-de-siecle *ethnic nationalism was the insistence that one's group identity consisted in some existential, supposedly primordial, unchangeable and therefore permanent personal characteristic shared with other members of the group, and with no one else. . . . The tragedy of this exclusionary identity politics, whether or not it set out to establish independent states, was that it could not possibly work. It could only pretend to.* ERIC HOBSBAWM[1]

The American achievement is not the multicultural society, it is the multicultural individual. . . . Identity is the promise of singleness, but this is a false promise. Many things are possible in America, but the singleness of identity is not one of them.

LEON WIESELTIER[2]

Americans have no identity, but they do have wonderful teeth.

JEAN BAUDRILLARD[3]

12

The Global Politics
of Not Being Had

A famous politician—Jesse Unruh, speaker of the
California Assembly and all-around big-time power broker—once
memorably said that money is the mother's milk of politics.

And this is undoubtedly true if you're talking about the cost of a
political campaign. It's true if you're talking about the power wielded
in democracies by fundraising lobbies and fat-cat contributors. It's the
truth, but not the whole truth. Because if money is the mother's milk of
politics, identity is its lifeblood and the personal self is its heart.

When young men march out to die on battlefields, as they have by
the millions since time immemorial and are still doing today, they are
rarely doing it for money—there are lots of easier ways to make a
living. They are doing it because they have accepted their country's
noble lies about who and what they are, and who their enemies are.
When a Hitler or a Mussolini rallies his followers, it is with flattery of
their greatness as citizens of a great nation. When a flag or a national
anthem touches our feelings, it is because we identify with it, accept it
as a symbol of what we are. When a million black men march on
Washington, it is to affirm and celebrate their black—and male—

identities. When women struggle for rights, it is because they know that sex is, in the eyes of the great majority of human beings, a powerful definer of who and what a person is, and what she should be doing in life.

Identity is the heart of politics, and yet identity itself is changing. As people become multiphrenic and protean, decentered and relational, they are less inclined to cling to those group identifications as the final and permanent essence of their selves. And a new kind of political controversy stirs to life, not just another controversy between different groups with conflicting claims or aspirations—black against white, tribe against nation, women against the patriarchy—but a controversy about self. Wieseltier's quotation at the opening of this chapter is from an article entitled "Against Identity." I cannot imagine seeing an article in a national magazine with such a title a few decades ago. Nobody would even have known what it meant: How could you be against identity? Now we know: You can be against identity if having an identity means having to cram your complex, mysterious, and shifting human existence into the confines of a given designation—like one of the overnight guests of that famous innkeeper Procrustes. You can be against identity when you discover that any label comes at a price—often a high one. You can be against identity when you begin to suspect that *none* of the labels currently in use really stands for any "primordial, unchangeable and therefore permanent personal characteristic," in Hobsbawm's words. You can be against identity when you choose to have more than one of them, and begin to agree with Wieseltier that "there is a greater truth in the plural. There is also a greater likelihood of decency."[4] You can be against identity when you decide to have identities but not be had by them.

The signs of this newer kind of politics are all around us, but we haven't quite grasped it yet with sufficient clarity to see which way it is headed or to speculate on how far it may go. So much political thought and action has been blinkered by premodern and modern concepts of identity—chiefly tribal and regional ones in the first case; racial, nationalistic, and ideological ones in the second—that it is hard to think in other terms. Both premodern and modern kinds of politics are still here, making their claims upon people and upon institutions of governance, yet both kinds are also being weakened by the multiple stresses of transition into a postmodern world. As identities change, so does the whole global political system that was linked to those identities. The new secular order expresses different ideas about identity, and also about citizenship and rights. It moves—amid confusion and conflict, with many steps in the opposite direction—toward a world in which governments and people are open systems.

Going Forward, Looking Back

The change is most evident—and also most disturbing and least understood—in the places where premodern cultures still survive, where people still organize their personal and social lives around traditional customs, values, roles, religions, and worldviews. In tribes and villages, people are taking sides—"traditionalists" against "modernists"—about globalization. Both sides are aided and abetted by outsiders, some of whom are agents of modernization, and some of whom are "cultural preservationists" dedicated to keeping things as they were. The word "indigenous" is increasingly heard in such political dialogues and, like so many other terms of political rhetoric, tends to be used with more fervor than precision. As the Australian political scientist Alastair Roderick Ewins noted:

> "[I]ndigenousness" is linked with the concept of identity. To identify oneself as indigenous to a particular place is to distinguish oneself from other residents who are not. But . . . the term is highly relative; its meaning depends on the particular circumstances of any one place. For example, a Fijian descended from Tongans who settled in Lau in the eighteenth century is considered indigenous, while an American descended from Europeans who settled in Virginia in the seventeenth century is not.[5]

Ewins interviewed many people on the Pacific islands of Fiji and Tonga, and found that the distinction between traditionalists and modernists was as murky as the definition of indigenous. The traditionalists understood the world differently from their premodern ancestors, who were not aware of the existence of multiple realities. Their thinking was more like that of inner-directed moderns—nineteenth-century British, for example—who knew there were many civilizations in the world but insisted the others were inferior and factually inaccurate. The more cosmopolitan modernists were actually "modernists-going-on-postmodernists" learning to think and live in eclectic and relativistic ways. But to complicate the matter still further, some of the traditionalists seemed to be distinctly postmodern, such as the university-educated woman, one of the strongest supporters of the old Tongan monarchy, who said:

> Just because I've gone to university, I'm therefore expected [by Westerners] to be different. I can only be Western or backward Tongan; I'm not allowed to be both. I don't think Western society will ever grow out of that kind of misconception. . . .
>
> A lot of us are bi-cultural. . . . We have some *palangi* (European) concepts, we have some Tongan concepts. Some of us are honest to say we are both. . . .[6]

Most people in traditional societies know that "going back" is not really an option, but few understand that "cultural preservation" is not an option either—that cultures are living things, created by people in response to the conditions around them, and that efforts to preserve cultures always, inevitably, involve further acts of creation. Yet that more complex kind of understanding is on the rise. In many parts of the world, not just modernity but postmodernity—in the form of multiple identities and reluctant recognition of the social construction of reality—is spreading more quickly than most observers suspect.

Upstairs, Downstairs

It's not always as easy for Westerners to notice the changes that are going on within their own social orders, but there is much evidence that all of the labels we have used in the modern world, such as those of class, race, and nationality, are losing their potency as a result of the impacts of globalization and, as the French call it, informatization. And of all the identity systems that served to order society and politics during the modern era, class is the one in the most advanced stages of decay.

There was a time when class was "real." People knew, then, that God was the divine sociologist who had created a world with multiple strata of humanity, descending from the obscenely high to the unspeakably low, and that the identity of any person was a matter of where he or she stood—and was stood upon—in that hierarchy. Just like we now explain human characteristics in terms of genes and environments, people of the not-so-distant past (not to mention a fair number of holdovers into the here-and-now present) confidently explained characteristics—the strength and wisdom of kings, the sensitive grace of lords and ladies, the stolid ignorance of peasants—in terms of class. Class defined who and what you were, and your civic duty was, as the British put it, to "keep your station" in life. Charles Dickens wrote a mocking hymn to that worldview:

> *O let us love our occupations,*
> *Bless the squire and his relations,*
> *Live upon our daily rations,*
> *And always know our proper stations.*[7]

Now we know that class is a socially constructed reality, and we see the idea of "proper stations" as a noble lie (i.e., a lie of the nobles) designed to keep subjugated people content with their misery. This understanding erodes not only the conservative political ideologies that aspire to preserve the class system, but also revolutionary ones aspiring to unite one class against another. Fewer people seem to be willing to dedicate their lives to the Marxist vision of class as the basic structure of all politics, the engine that drives the laws of history.

I wouldn't say that class has faded away entirely: My British friends still identify one another by class as quickly and surely as if people had "Upper," "Middle," or "Working" tattooed on their foreheads. In India the pernicious caste system keeps its hold on party politics. But there aren't many places left in the world where hereditary rank and political power are synonymous.

In the United States we manage to be obsessed with lifestyle and status while rather careless about class. Americans don't have a clear idea of the difference between class and status; they're inclined to assume that if you are rich, famous, and/or powerful you have more or less become an *ex oficio* member of the upper classes—a mistake an Englishman would never make.

Status has replaced class in much of the world, particularly among youth and in popular culture. And it is yet another kind of diversification along lifestyle lines, another collapse of the Grand Hotel, because there is not one single hierarchy of status but many of them. You can be world-famous to all the members of one subculture (or age cohort) and totally insignificant to everyone else. A friend of mine, a man about my age, recently remarked to me that he is amazed at how many famous people there are that he's never heard of. I knew what he meant.

Class as we know it was a modern invention, an attempt to give the hierarchies of feudal society a primordial status and carry them forth into a postfeudal social order. Status, although ancient, comes into its own in the postmodern era. Like consumption, it is multiphrenic, protean, decentered, relational. It is an open system. Status comes and goes, and few people have any illusions that it is an eternal or even terribly meaningful arrangement. Andy Warhol's silly statement about everybody getting to be famous for fifteen minutes is so widely quoted because it makes about as much sense as the way things actually work. Nobody thinks that status represents any deep inner characteristic of the person who has it; nobody thinks all people with status should stick together, conform, be loyal to one another. In the 1930s it meant something when grumpy conservatives called President Franklin D. Roosevelt—the aristocrat-turned-champion of the downtrodden—a traitor to his class. I have never heard of anybody being called a traitor to his status.

The great enemy of class is mobility. Social mobility is the worst kind, because a class system must be a *closed* system, with entry into its upper levels slow, rare, and difficult; too much movement up and down the hierarchy destroys a class system. But physical mobility can be destructive to the old order, too, if it enables those stuck in a rigid society to leave and seek their fortunes elsewhere. And the mobility of symbols—the mass media—may show people images of quite different social orders, or lead them to develop a greater admiration for distant movie stars than for their local aristocrats. All forms of mobility tend away from class, toward status.

Status is what comes after class, and I'm not really prepared to say it's much of an improvement. Status seems to work reasonably well in some ways for the selves of people who have it, as long as they have it. It helps them believe they exist. It can in some cases—see Ronald Reagan—advance an individual political career. But it does not serve as a determinant of political loyalties and alliances. The classic labels of "identity politics" such as race or the modern era's preeminent political invention, nationality, do a much better job, although they are in some ways losing their grip as well.

In and Out of the Melting Pot

American identity politics is instructive for other countries that are also becoming nations of immigrants. It illustrates the basic political agendas that tend to emerge in mixed societies—assimilationist, exclusionist, and pluralist—and it gives us a glimpse of what a post-identity society looks like when people begin to lose confidence in all those paths.

In the early years of the twentieth century, Americans were infatu-

ated with the assimilationist "melting pot" metaphor that originated
in Israel Zangwill's play of that name. It was a wonderful piece of
feel-good symbolism of the sort that went well in grammar-school
textbooks and political speeches; its general idea was that America
was "God's crucible" in which all races and cultures would be
improved by coming together, making of the whole a stronger metal
like those that were being forged in the great smoking mills of
Pittsburgh. The metaphor had an egalitarian spirit, at least in its
original form, but what it really meant for most Americans was that
immigrants should get rid of their more conspicuously "foreign"
behaviors and become more like Anglo Protestants. That was the *de
facto* policy of the U.S. government, which established a Director of
Americanization within the Department of Interior and launched a
variety of educational programs designed to help new immigrants (in
the words of a Bureau of Americanization publication) "renounce
allegiance to their old and prepare to live or die for the glory of the
new—America."[8]

The much more hard-nosed agendas of exclusion—based on the
conviction that assimilation couldn't do the job of protecting American society from being fatally polluted by foreign influences—had
many supporters throughout the peak years of immigration. They
gained a certain intellectual legitimacy from the eugenics movement,
with its pseudoscientific scare doctrines about how foreigners were
corrupting not only American society but also the national gene pool.
Eugenicists tended to equate national origin with race and attributed
all kinds of criminality to varius "races" as matters of genetic inheri-
tance. William Davenport, one of the leading American eugenicists,
believed it to be scientific fact that Italians were incurably predisposed
to crimes of personal violence, Jews prone to thievery, and Hungarians
given to "larceny, kidnapping, assault, murder, rape, and sex-
immorality." He was also a bit on the sexist side—he once wrote that
love for the sea was a sex-linked recessive trait, since it showed up only
in the male side of seagoing families—and he dismissed the melting-
pot myth as an unscientific relic of a "pre-Mendelian age" because, he
said, the various unsavory characteristics of foreigners would not be

diluted by interbreeding but would persist in the society as recessive genes.[9]

Ideas about the genetically based shortcomings of foreigners played their part in the passage of restrictive new federal immigration laws and also in state laws that permitted the sterilization of criminals and prohibited intermarriage between people of different races.

The idea of "pluralism" first surfaced early in the twentieth century as a kinder, gentler alternative to both assimilation and exclusion. Pluralist writers advocated an America made up of many different cultural groups, each retaining its customs, language, arts and music, and religions, not sacrificing them to white-bread respectability. This view of happily coexisting cultures was reflected in some of the popular entertainment media: in romantic comedies such as *Abie's Irish Rose*; in World War II movies about groups of American soldiers, each with his distinct ethnic identity, shoulder to shoulder against the foe.[10] This idealistic pluralism had its supporters among some leftist intellectuals and activists, but most liberal reformers preferred breaking down the barriers among racial and ethnic groups to celebrating their differentness.

Then, appearing first in the 1950s and peaking in the 1960s amid the explosion of civil-rights activism that marked that stormy decade, a new attitude emerged. People of all sorts who had accepted their identities as marks of inferiority now aggressively flaunted them. The role models for this new attitude were the radicals of color who spoke for black power, black nationalism, who coined the powerful slogan "Black is beautiful." But the same style was soon adopted by some Asian-Americans, Latinos, Native Americans, women, gays and lesbians, handicapped persons, mental patients, the elderly, even descendants of European immigrants. I knew people who readopted old family names—Polish ones, for example—that had been Americanized by their parents or grandparents; if the names were hard to pronounce, so much the better. Once-shameful labels like "queer," "crip," and "crazy" became proud slogans—at least when used by the right people. This new identity politics was a healthy thing in many ways, but of course it was divisive. It gave opposing groups of whites, males, and others a justification for proclaiming their own identities and defending what they saw as their threatened rights. And it led to a new polarization (in Gary Peller's description): "an intense cultural clash between black nationalists on one side, and integrationists (white and black) on the other."[11]

Identity politics is still with us, but it is no longer on the cutting edge. Its moment has passed; it is the victim of its own internal contradictions. It failed to recognize that identities are products of construction and choice. It empowered people to choose new descriptions of themselves and did not foresee that once people had learned they could make choices, they would continue making them, sometimes in ways that suited their own life purposes better than the agendas of their leaders.

The Centers Do Not Hold

Identity politics gave rise to a huge body of theoretical work among intellectuals in the universities and think tanks. Now another intellectual movement has emerged, calling itself "post-identity scholarship." Some of its leading proponents claim (in a recent book entitled *After Identity*) that the discourses of identity politics tended to "obscure the differences among women, among gays, among blacks and others, and to ignore the significance of multiple allegiances, communities and experiences. . . ."[12]

Identity politics assumed that since everybody naturally and obviously belongs to some group that claims his loyalty and shapes her identity, then racial or other labels can be reliably used to mark off real and distinct social entities the way national boundaries marked real and distinct polities. Post-identity politics is based on the recognition that the center doesn't always hold within the labeled groups. It is a search for a different vision, less inclined to shove people into any of the pigeonholes that organized our understanding in the past—race, for example.

Although most people now see class as socially constructed, race still looks like a *real* reality. For racist conservatives it is the God-given order of things, just as class once was; for good-guy liberals it is the supreme social evil to be overcome by tolerance and civil rights laws; and for many blacks it is a reality that needs to be transformed— endowed with pride rather than shame—and yet maintained. But it begins to appear now that if we get past racism it will not be through the triumph of antiracist political strategies—although they may have done much good along the way—but because of a widespread emperor's-new-clothes discovery that race, too, was a social construction.

Many biologists are already there, saying that, scientifically speaking, race scarcely exists. According to Jonathan Marks of Yale, "Race has no basic biological reality. The human species simply doesn't come packaged that way"; to Luigi Cavalli-Sforza of Stanford, one of the world's leading geneticists, "The characteristics that we see with the naked eye that help us to distinguish individuals from different continents are, in reality, skin-deep. Whenever we look under the veneer, we find that the differences that seem so conspicuous to us are really trivial."[13] These statements are controversial—some scholars still insist on distinct racial differences in intelligence and other qualities—but they now represent the majority view, which is precisely the opposite of the official reality we all were taught in school.

Some people of color are also growing skeptical of the labels, including the ones they had hung on themselves. The idea of the "black community" to which all African-Americans somehow magically belong has been one of the staples of political discourse for decades, but Regina Austin says it is now "more of an idea, or an ideal, than a reality. . . . 'The black community' . . . is partly the manifestation of a nostalgic longing for a time when blacks were clearly distinguishable from whites and concern about the welfare of the poor was more natural than our hairdos."[14]

You can see the breakdown of the black-community myth in the fracturing of African-American consensus about affirmative action. The majority of blacks still support such programs, but the absence of unanimity is conspicuous in California, where the leading crusader against them is Ward Connerly, a black Republican businessman. There are still black communities, but no black community.

Racial solidarity is further weakened as people do what comes naturally when different races coexist in the same geographic area—mate and reproduce. "Race is over," declared Stanley Crouch in *The New York Times*—a little prematurely, I think, but undeniably correct in that the boundaries become less and less clear as people intermarry. "Americans of the future will find themselves surrounded in every direction by people who are part Asian, part Latin, part African, part European, part American Indian. What such people will look like is beyond my imagination, but the sweep of body types, combinations of facial features, hair textures, eye colors and what are now unexpected skin tones will be far more common, primarily because the current paranoia over mixed marriages should by then be largely a superstition of the past."[15] His case is dramatically supported by the photographs that accompany his article—facial shots of children of mixed race: kids like Katja Frazier, who is Finnish and African-American; Daniel Cohen-Cruz, who is Russian, Polish-Jewish, and Puerto Rican; Lauren Oti, African-American and Pennsylvania Dutch; and Neri Edmond, African-American, Filipino, American Indian, and French Canadian.

When people move beyond identity politics, they don't necessarily give up their ethnic, racial, or cultural identities. They might fold those into a more complex and shifting multicommunity sense of self. As the cultural historian David Hollinger described:

> A postethnic perspective recognizes that most individuals live in many circles simultaneously and that the actual living of any individual life entails a shifting division of labor between the several "we's" of which the individual is a part. How much weight at what particular moments is assigned to the fact that one is Pennsylvania Dutch or Navajo relative to the weight assigned to the fact that one is also an American, a lawyer, a woman, a Republican, a Baptist, and a resident of Minneapolis?[16]

Most of the daily choices that people make, the ones that express this "postethnic" or "post-identity" way of life, have no ideological agenda, no conscious aim at being "post" anything. People merely want to be more ethnic at certain times than they do at others, and sometimes they don't want to be particularly ethnic at all. Sociologist Mary Waters, who made a study of these kinds of choices, said that "ethnicity has become a subjective identity, invoked at will by the individual."[17] She pointed out that over time, people may give different answers to a survey question about their ethnic identities. They may emphasize one at one stage of their lives, another later. Or it may depend on the time of year—Irishness seems to increase around St. Patrick's day—or the particular community in which the respondent happens to be. They make choices. If you're African-American, Filipino, American Indian, and French Canadian, you can do that. You really can't help doing that.

Ethnicity is closely linked to that other great social construction: nationality. We still tend to accept ethnic nationality as a "real" description of some true and deep personal characteristic, but how meaningful is the French component of the kid who is African-American, Filipino, American Indian, and French Canadian? That "French" stands there as though it were some solid building block, but it quickly crumbles when scrutinized. Which one of the ancient Gallic races were the French ancestors? Breton? Burgundian? Basque? How about the Filipino segment—which part of that Filipino ancestry is mountain tribesman, which part Chinese, which part Spanish? How about the Spanish? Were they Aragonese? Galician? Descended from the Romans who once occupied Spain; from the Vandals and Visigoths, who occupied it later; or from the Moors, who occupied it later still?

If you want to believe in nationality, never look closely at it.

Nationality is the most transparently fictitious of identity markers, yet the one that has been most important in the modern world—and may continue to be for some time, although perhaps in quite different ways. The histories of nationalism and of the nation-state are full of surprises.

Surprises of Nationalism

How could any "realistic" student of politics, present in 1648 when the modern system of states was being legitimized in the Peace of Westphalia, have guessed that it would take only a bit more than a century until the proclamation in France of the "Rights of Man"? Such a development would have been both repugnant and unthinkable to the monarchs, who were happily building a new order in which the only right that counted—as they saw it—was the divine right of kings.

How would any wise observer of history, seeing Europe in the early twentieth century—the Europe of the Maginot Line, obsessed with boundaries, preparing to drag the world into two huge wars over its national vanities—imagine that at the end of the same century, Europe's most contentious issue would be how to go about creating a common currency?

Who would have guessed that nation-states would evolve into open systems, as they are now doing? The European nations were created as closed systems: bounded, defended against one another and against meddling by outside influences such as the Roman Church. Well before Westphalia, the French philosopher Jean Bodin had articulated the principles of sovereignty: the "absolute and perpetual power" contained in a state and embodied in its king, whose authority within the nation's boundaries could not be limited by any force, internal or external. In the state the people were bound to their sovereign, to the national territory, to their religion (according to the principle of "to each region, its own religion"), and to one another. They were also bound to their history, which told mighty tales of good deeds done by their heroes, and evil deeds done against them by other nations, and which they were taught to regard as a record of their common experience. Nationalism created a sense of a *people*, of a national *self*, which had never existed in the days of feudal loyalties. David Jacobson, in his study of nationhood, noted that according to the Oxford English Dictionary, "the use of the word self as a prefix, as in 'self-determination' or in 'self-realization,' first appears in English in the sixteenth century, and multiplies rapidly in use in the seventeenth century. Self-determination as a specific term first appears in the seventeenth century."[18]

One surprise was that nationalism proved to be just as energizing to people without a monarch as to those with one, that the principle of sovereignty could outlive sovereigns. This was dramatically demonstrated by countries such as France and the United States, which gave people a proud sense of their national identity as *citizens* rather than as subjects of the king. Citizenship, patriotism, shared history, the sense of "us" against "them"—all of these helped to make nationalism such a vibrant ideology and political force.

Nationalism was a formidable identity project which came close to reorganizing not only Europe but the whole world, as the European model was imitated by (and imposed upon) other peoples. It was the view of political reality that made possible the creation of maps with neat lines dividing different countries—images we all have seen and carry in our minds. Nationality became the great human label, the token by which you could attribute all manner of psychological characteristics to citizens of this or that country. Thus Leo Tolstoy, in one of the classic expressions of that sort of character analysis, wrote in *War and Peace* about the shadings of conceit:

> The Frenchman is conceited from supposing himself mentally and physically to be inordinately fascinating both to men and to women. An Englishman is conceited on the ground of being a citizen of the best-constituted state in the world, and also because he as an Englishman always knows what is the thing to do. . . . An Italian is conceited from being excitable and easily forgetting himself and other people. A Russian is conceited precisely because he knows nothing and cares to know nothing, since he does not believe it possible to know anything fully. A conceited German is the worst of them all . . . for he imagines that he possesses the truth in a

science of his own invention, which is to him absolute truth.[19]

Today it would be risky business to attribute such characteristics to people of any nationality—especially any European one, as European countries become societies of immigrants on the American model. In France, for example, immigration has accounted for 40 percent of the population growth since World War II. It's no longer possible to get away with any sweeping statement concerning what a Frenchman is conceited about—or even what a Frenchman *is*.

Yet ethnic nationalism is built deeply into the modern mind and the modern world. We may disapprove of its excesses, and many people may be drifting into multiphrenic postmodern lifestyles that flow through and around its rigid structures, but it is still the official reality. Israel exists because of ethnic nationalism, and Palestine is trying to exist because of it as well. Ethnic cleansing in the former Yugoslavia is an expression of it. Canada may yet implode because of it. Ethnic nationalism is the dream of community, the urge to be surrounded by people like oneself—and it is not only a dream, but a formidable chunk of law and public policy.

At the end of World War II, political leaders agreed on a principle—the self-determination of peoples—which promised to be a foundation for permanent world order. It hasn't succeeded, and there are many reasons why. One reason is that it assumed nationality to be an identity that all people naturally "had," and that was more important than their various other labels. The trouble with the idea of self-determination is that it fudges the question of self. In places where national identity still has not been secured, it seems to work as a prime identifier. In other places—such as the industrialized nations of the West, where people are moving into the uncharted terrain of post-identity politics—it doesn't work so well. The new question becomes: What self? Why not self-determination for gays? Women? Scientologists? In Canada, the Native American tribes within Quebec logically ask why, if Quebec becomes separate from Canada, they can't become separate from Quebec.

The political leaders of the modern era tried desperately hard to make a world that conformed to their two-dimensional maps of it, but that project was never a complete success. There were always opportunists who wanted to redraw the lines, minorities on one side who thought they should be on the other, international people like the Jews and Gypsies who didn't quite fit into the system at all. We fought two world wars in the service of that mapmaking project, managed to kill millions in the process, and still didn't complete the job. And it begins to appear now that we never will. There are still parts of the world trying desperately to establish their nationhood, to catch up to the modern era. But meanwhile growing numbers of people are becoming, in various ways, postmodern—they are immigrants, legal or illegal; global citizens; members of global communities based on profession, gender, sexual orientation, pastime, or favorite rock group; they are people who have their national identities (sometimes two or three), and are not had by them.

The Rights of Postmodern Man (and Woman)

Issues of identity frequently become issues of rights—matters to be disputed by the political theorists, adjudicated in the courts, and sometimes fought over on the battlefields and in the streets. Although rights were an invention of the modern era, historically inseparable from the invention of the individual self and the nation-state, they are metamorphosing in the postmodern era. In some ways they seem to be moving in opposite directions—being used as tools in the creation of a post-national global order, and also being used in the defense of premodern cultures. In the contemporary world, as people and societies everywhere strive to choose, define, and in some cases protect their identities, there has grown up a lively debate about individual rights versus group rights.

The communitarians, cultural preservationists, and defenders of indigenous peoples believe that thinking about rights has placed too much emphasis on individual freedoms that may be eroding the values and institutions of traditional societies. They argue instead for a "politics of the common good," a legal order recognizing "the group's right to protect its identity," even when that limits certain individual rights.[20] This proposition has some advantages and some dangerous shortcomings: A system of group rights can foster a certain kind of tolerance, a working pluralism, but when different communities have the right to organize as they see fit, they may use this right to enforce religious or cultural orthodoxy and thus to override the rights of personal choice. Political philosopher Will Kymlicka gave a historical example of such a social order, the millet system of the Ottoman Empire:

> Under the millet system, Christians, Jews and Muslims were all self-governing, and each imposed religious orthodoxy on its own members. So while the Muslims did not try to suppress the Jews, or vice versa, they did suppress heretics within their own community. Heresy (questioning the orthodox interpretation of Muslim doctrine) and apostasy (abandoning one's religious faith) were punishable crimes within the Muslim community. Restrictions on individual freedom of conscience also existed in the Jewish and Christian communities.
>
> The millet system was, in effect, a federation of theocracies. It was a deeply conservative and patriarchal society, antithetical to the ideals of personal liberty endorsed by liberals from Locke to Kant and Mill. The Ottomans accepted the principle of religious tolerance, where that meant the willingness of a dominant religion to coexist with others, but did not accept the quite separate principle of individual freedom of conscience.[21]

Some group rights seem to be workable even in countries that have legal systems based heavily on individual rights, such as the

United States. It's a matter of degree. Most communitarian advocates of group rights recognize that "essential" personal rights like *habeas corpus* should be protected. Coming from the other side, American defenders of civil liberties are generally willing to concede that some group rights go with self-governance of Indian tribes. There is room for compromise as long as people share a worldview in which a given group is "real" and legitimate. That's the tough part, the identity issue again. Sociologist Todd Gitlin raised the key question:

> Just what is a "group" anyway? Exactly who authenticates an authentic identity? Who is entitled to issue membership cards? Boundaries shift in time and space. Resemblance is relative to the culture and the purpose of classification. To a passerby or a census-taker, I am white. To an anti-Semite, I am simply a Jew. To a German Jew, I may be one of the *Ostjuden*; to Sephardim, an Ashkenazi Jew; to an Israeli Jew, American; to a religious Jew, secular; to a right-wing Zionist, an apostate, or no Jew at all. Advocates of identity politics will insist that the issue is not simply the elusiveness of categories or the American tradition of self-naming, but oppression and persecution. . . .
>
> But what follows from these categories once they are imposed? Identity is no guide to accuracy, to good judgment or political strategy. Race [or gender, or sexual preference, or disability] is far from an adequate, let alone complete, guide to the world, since all identity is a blindness as well as a way of seeing.[22]

Although it can be hard to agree on what a group is, the cause of group rights promises to be a part of global politics for some time to come. But expect to see much more action—both progress and conflict—around individual rights. This is the thrust of the "human rights" activity of nongovernmental organizations, including women's groups, and it is also the direction of policy in most Western nations.

The nation-state is quietly taking another unexpected turn in its surprise-filled history, uncoupling rights from nationality and laying the basis for a true global citizenship. David Jacobson of Arizona State University, in his study of this development in international post-identity politics, wrote:

> Transnational migration is steadily eroding the traditional basis of nation-state membership, namely citizenship. As rights have come to be predicated on residency, not citizen status, the distinction between "citizen" and "alien" has eroded. The devaluation of citizenship has contributed to the increasing importance of international human rights codes, with its premise of universal "personhood." The growing ability of individuals and nongovernmental organizations (NGOs) to make claims on the basis of international human rights instruments has implications well beyond the boundaries of the individual states such that the contours of the international, as well as the domestic, order are likely to change significantly.[23]

The legal foundation for this change is international human-rights law, which has been advancing steadily since the end of World War II. The United Nations's 1948 Universal Declaration of Human Rights affirmed a number of personal liberties, including freedom from slavery, freedom from arbitrary arrest, freedom of religion, and the right to own property. That was only a declaration, but its provisions became international law in the 1960s and 1970s as the International Covenant on Civil and Political Rights and the International Covenant on Economic, Social and Cultural Rights were signed and ratified.

This marks an important shift. The carrier of human rights, now, is not the citizen but the person (regardless of citizenship). Human rights are universal and not merely the privilege of any particular nationality or group. The next step, of course, is putting them into practice, and that step is being taken far more vigorously in some places than it is in others. But it is being taken. Human-rights claims are being made by people and by NGOs, and international law is being enforced—to a far greater extent than most people suspect—by many national governments. This is, as one scholar puts it, "a sea change in international law," by which the nation-states take on a new role as enforcers of international human rights.[24]

Other parts of the sea change are taking place within nations as they recognize the rights of people who are not citizens. European countries, although still clinging to their national cultures and ethnic identities, are moving progressively toward a concept of "denizenship" for their sizable populations of workers and refugees. The distinction between citizen and resident noncitizen becomes less and less significant. In most countries noncitizen residents have full protection of rights and freedoms, access to social services, and legal property ownership. In several countries they can vote in local elections, and some political parties in the Netherlands and Sweden advocate conferring national voting rights as well.[25]

After Nations

Human institutions, like people, are shape-shifters: They often change behind the words we use to describe them. That was certainly the case with that venerable institution called the Holy Roman Empire, which changed shape so much that Voltaire pointed out that in his time it was neither holy, nor Roman, nor an empire. Something of the same sort seems to be happening to the nation-states, since most of them are no longer nations (uniformly populated by people who share a common ethnic identity), nor states (sovereign governments of clearly defined territories). It is often said now that we are entering into a "postnational" era, but there's no great consensus about what that means.

Francis Fukuyama, in his much-quoted "end of history" writings, said that all societies are becoming capitalist liberal democracies, and that as this is finalized it will be the "end state" of the historical process—the end of ideology and of the national aspirations that most of history has been about. He sees nationalism becoming fat around the middle in its European place of origin, and ceasing to pose much of a threat to world peace: "Modern Europe has been moving rapidly to shed sovereignty and to enjoy national identity in the soft glow of private life. Like religion, nationalism is in no danger of disappearing, but like religion, it appears to have lost its ability to stimulate Europeans to risk their comfortable lives in great acts of imperialism."[26]

Political scientist Samuel Huntington of Harvard also has peered over into the future, which to him looks much more perilous. He proposes that we are now edging into a new stage of global politics—new in some ways, old in others. The new part will be the emergence of what he calls the different "civilizations" as powerful supercommunities with which people will identify—and which will dangerously divide the world:

> It is my hypothesis that the fundamental source of conflict in this new world will not be primarily ideological or primarily economic. The great divisions among humankind and the dominating source of conflict will be cultural. Nation states will remain the most powerful actors in world affairs, but the principal conflicts of global politics will occur between nations and groups of different civilizations. The clash of civilizations will dominate global politics. The fault lines between civilizations will be the battle lines of the future.[27]

He sees this world as made up of seven or eight civilizations: Western, Eastern Orthodox, Latin American, Islamic, Japanese, Chinese, Hindu, and possibly African. It's an interesting scenario, but it is more identity politics—that's the old part. It assumes that people will be, and will remain, deeply attached to those civilizations. It assumes also—and this may be the weakest part of Huntington's argument—that the civilizations will have some recognizable *territorial* identity.

The French diplomat Jean-Marie Guehenno (currently France's ambassador to the European Union) has written a book entitled *The*

End of the Nation-State, arguing that the increasing mobility of people, of the economy, and of information make territoriality increasingly irrelevant as an organizing principle. He foresees the end not only of the nation-state as we have known it, but also of politics as we have known it: "From the beginning, since the Greek city (*polis*), politics has been the art of governing a collectivity of people defined by their rootedness in a location, city or nation. If solidarity can no longer be locked into geography, if there is no longer a city, if there is no longer a nation, can there still be politics?"[28] In place of politics as we have known it—the great global leviathans playing the dangerous games of national interest, the parties and pressure groups playing "capture the flag" in the national capitals—we will have other kinds of interaction, calling for different skills and understandings:

> We are entering into the age of open systems, whether at the level of states or enterprises, and the criteria of success are diametrically different from those of the institutional age and its closed systems. The value of an organization is no longer measured by the equilibrium that it attempts to establish between its different parts, or by the clarity of its frontiers, but in the number of openings, of points of articulation that it can organize with everything external to it.[29]

These visions are similar in some ways, radically different in others. All assume that nationalism is running out of gas, yet some see a continuing role for the nation-state. I think Guehenno's scenario is the most perceptive, even though he does not note the nation-state's new role as custodian of transnational human rights. And I think we are going to see a lot of politics for some time to come—definitely including the kinds that are going out of style.

The Shapelessness of Things to Come

The shape of identity politics in the years ahead—and indeed of all politics—will be determined in large part by the decisions people and societies make concerning primary identifiers. "Primary identifier" isn't a very elegant term, but it points toward something that is central to all political power, all political conflict, and all political progress. It signifies the definition of self that transcends all the others, that proclaims in a final and unquestionable way—to you and to everyone else—exactly what you are.

Nationality has generally enjoyed that spot in the modern world, but its primacy has often been in question. Today, in our complex premodern-modern-postmodern world, we have all kinds of primary identifiers and candidates for primacy. For many people, tribal identity is still paramount—it has been so for Hutus and Tutsis in Africa, and is probably so for many groups of indigenous peoples in the world who are not much attached to their nationalities. Some leaders of the worldwide women's movement hope to get women to place their solidarity with one another above their loyalty to oppressively male-dominated traditional cultures. Samuel Huntington claims that civilizations are going to take precedence in the hearts and minds of twenty-first-century humanity.

For an identity to attain and maintain primacy, it really needs to be regarded as primordial, not socially constructed, not imagined into being by some intellectual or prophet, but rather representing some great and eternal reality.

You really can't have an orderly world—I mean orderly in the way moderns have imagined such a world to be, with clear boundaries that can be shown on a two-dimensional map—without primary identities. Everybody has to have one. Furthermore, everybody has to have the same kind. As long as people insist on placing other kinds of identities—tribe, civilization, gender, generation, religion, class, e-mail address, whatever—above their national identities, the world is not going to be easy to put onto a map.

Yet I expect that identity politics will be for some time to come a powerful force in the world, made even more powerful by becoming obsolete. It may well be, as historian Eric Hobsbawm believes, that much of the strength of racism, nationalism, and other current manifestations of identity politics is a reaction against the confusing conditions of the postmodern world:

> Young American Jews searched for their 'roots' when the things which stamped them indelibly as Jews were no longer effective markers of Jewry; not least the segregation and discrimination of the years before the Second World War. Though Quebec nationalism insisted on separation because it claimed to be a 'distinct society,' it actually emerged as a significant force precisely when Quebec ceased to be the 'distinct society' it had so patently and unmistakably been until the 1960s. . . . The very fluidity of ethnicity in urban societies made its choice as the only criterion of the group arbitrary and artificial. In the USA, except for Blacks, Hispanics, and those of English and German origins, at least 60 per cent of American-born women of *all* ethnic origins married outside their group. . . . Increasingly one's identity had to be constructed by insisting on the non-identity of others. How otherwise could the neo-Nazi skinheads in Germany, wearing the uniforms, hair-styles and musical tastes of the cosmopolitan youth culture, establish their essential Germanness, except by beating up local Turks and Albanians? How, except by eliminating those who did not 'belong' could the 'essentially' Croat or Serb character of some region be established in which, for most of history, a variety of ethnicities and religions had lived as neighbours?[30]

The appeal of having a good, clear identity—national, racial, whatever—is strongest for those who don't have much of anything else. Yet it would be a disastrous mistake to assume that multiple identities, shifting identities, postmodern concepts of self, are coming into the lives only of cosmopolitan sophisticates. It is also happening for refugees, migratory workers, immigrants to new lands, people who marry into other cultures. Ordinary people. Ordinary postmodern, post-national, global people.

PART 4

Maps
of an
Undiscovered
Land

The universe is at root a magical illusion and a fabulous game, and . . . there is no separate "you" to get something out of it, as if life were a bank to be robbed.

ALAN WATTS [1]

See that you are not what you believe yourself to be. Fight with all the strength at your disposal against the idea that you are namable and describable.

SRI NISARGADATTA MAHARAJ [2]

13

Liberation from the Self: Where East Meets West

If you put together all the scattered pieces, all the discourses and dialogues and debates about self and identity that are currently under way in the worlds of psychology, cognitive science, medicine, computer communications, economics, politics—the whole global identity crisis—you begin to see something absolutely unprecedented. Never before has such a fundamental theme of human existence been discussed on such a scale, within the context of a global civilization. Yet there is an older discourse, stretching back at least to the time of Heraclitus and his Asian contemporary known as the Buddha, to ages long before the particular kind of consciousness we call the modern self was invented. It is global, too, in the sense that it has turned up at many different times and places and been heard in many languages, but most people in the West have managed either to ignore it or to misunderstand it completely. Usually it has been safely pigeonholed in the category of mysticism or Oriental religion and thus kept separate from the realm of practical, ordinary life.

This other discourse revolves around the proposition that self is an illusion. Has no existence except as an abstract concept and an ongoing act of description. Is merely kind of a mental glitch that can be cleared up, leaving the mind vastly expanded—not to mention somewhat relieved. It is a subversive, often secret discourse, undermining the received truths of ancient and modern societies with complete impartiality.

Now, I know that this older dialogue is also something of a literary movement that has, over the millennia, produced a mountain of books—Buddhist sutras and commentaries, Sufi tales, works by Western philosophers such as Meister Eckhardt, books by contemporary interpreters of Oriental thought such as D. T. Suzuki and Alan Watts, a good portion of the ever-growing library of New Age spirituality—and that many of those writings are both eloquent and useful. And yet I propose that it is time to take another look at the concept of enlightenment or liberation, to see it in a fresh way. The present situation—all the things that we have been exploring in the previous chapters—creates a necessity for doing that, and also offers a priceless opportunity. The subject of the self is on the table in a way that it has never been before, and I don't think it is going to be possible in the long run, maybe even the short run, to entertain such concepts as the multiple self, the protean self, the decentered self, the self-in-relation, without proceeding from there to the even scarier idea of no self at all.

The Trouble with Words

The time has come to take the subject of liberation (which I think is the best word available for what we're talking about) and make it accessible and understandable to people who are not inclined toward mysticism, spirituality, Oriental culture, or any of the several varieties of New Age woo-woo. The condition called liberation is not a radical and only rarely achieved deviation from natural human consciousness, but rather *is* natural human consciousness. Thus it is possible for anyone to understand liberation and experience it, to rethink the self and reorganize personal consciousness in a way that leads to the "no-self" perspective—yet it is definitely not easy, because the doing involves the use of language, and our language is the language of self. We can't really get around that, but we can make the rethinking effort a lot more manageable if we recognize it.

I first came across that phrase "language of self" about thirty years ago, in a remarkable essay by Herbert Fingarette of the University of California at Santa Barbara. His essay was entitled "The Ego and Mystic Selflessness," and it was based on a study of psychoanalysis and the insights achieved by psychoanalytic patients. Fingarette had discovered a surprising similarity between the experiences described by people who had successfully completed psychotherapy, and the writings of Oriental mystics. I had not previously read anything about bridging the gap between Western psychology and Eastern religion (or even much about Eastern religion at all), and the essay gave me a powerful jolt—my first glimpse into that state of mind, my first sweet taste of how it felt to be there. It also set me off on a lifelong exploration of what lay on both sides of the gap.

Previously it had seemed to me most unlikely that there could be any similarities between the two, since everything I had understood about them seemed to indicate that they were as different from each other as a steak dinner from a bowl of rice. Fingarette noted:

> In the great mystical writings of East and West it is said that the mystic insight results ideally in egolessness, selflessness, absence of desire and of striving, passivity instead of control, cessation of logic, thought, and discrimination, a life beyond morality, beyond sensation, and perception. The psychoanalyst, however, aims [ideally] at using insight to strengthen the ego, and to develop a self—a self with a rich variety of goals and with substantial ability to gratify desires, with reasonable self-control and mastery of the environment, and with the ability to perceive realistically, discriminate clearly, and act with some sense of the appropriate values.
>
> The way of psychoanalytic therapy aims at minimal disruption of everyday life. The mystic way notoriously involves unusual practices and symptoms . . .[3]

Yet despite having started out with this presumption of irreconcilable difference, Fingarette found great congruence between the end products of the two—and found also that the similarities were terribly hard to describe in unambiguous and final terms. The language he and his research subjects were using seemed to have a devilish capacity to say quite different things in the same words.

One of the more striking similarities between the ex-patients and the mystics was a certain detachment. That's a linguistic snare in itself, because the word "detachment" easily connotes uncaring, emotionless apathy. But such listlessness wasn't at all what came through in the statement one former patient, Katherine, made about her feelings concerning another woman, Alice, with whom she once had had strong conflicts—strong enough to have played an important part in her sessions with her psychoanalyst. Asked about her present desires in connection with Alice, she said, "Well, I don't have any desires now. I used to want Alice to be shown up in her true colors, to have people see how wrong she was. Now I just don't think about it. I just act. I get along." Asked if her way of relating to Alice had become one of total passivity and self-abnegation, she replied, "Well, of course, I still may think that what she's doing is wrong at times, but it doesn't matter much. That is, well, I would defend myself if she did anything wrong to me . . . but, well, I wouldn't *dwell* on its being wrong. I'm just not involved. It doesn't matter *in the same way*." Katherine also mentioned that she had become much less hungry for praise from others, but still felt satisfaction when praised for something that she personally considered well-done. She mentioned "not trying so hard"—although with no sense of accomplishing less. She referred once to having "exploded" in anger, even though, somehow, she didn't get worked up about it even when it was happening. Asked about that, she replied in some confusion, "No! . . . well . . . yes, that is . . . I'm angry at the thing and not in general. It's hard to explain."[4]

Yes, it's hard to explain what happens when the feeling of life changes radically, yet life continues to be, well, life. We can still describe it with only the usual words, the language of self, the language that centers around statements of an "I" that is presumed to be at the center of all our experiences—which is why a psychotherapist can't simply explain to a patient how to stop being anxious or obsessive, and also why a spiritual teacher can't simply explain to a student how to go about becoming enlightened. Fingarette suggested that the mystic "is trying to distinguish between two important but different kinds of experience, both naturally expressed by the same introspective self-language. He wants us to achieve one kind of experience and to guide us away from another mode of experience which, as it happens, is expressed by the same sort of language."[5]

The quality of experience that Fingarette discovered among some of his research subjects, and compared to liberation, was best described as a sort of absence—but not an absence of emotion, cognition, motivation, or awareness. Not an absence, either, of the feeling of being a particular person with a name and a social identity. Rather, an absence of a conscious sense of *self*, "an unselfconsciousness akin to the normal unawareness of our breathing."[6] An absence of a needy, vain, driven "I" constantly shadowed by intrapsychic conflict. All the ordinary perceptions were there, yet somehow everything was different. And he found this state similar to those described in the writings of mystics: "Desire flows into the mind of the seer, but he is never disturbed"[7]; "Ignorant ones . . . imagine that Nirvana consists in the future annihilation of the senses and the sense-minds. This is not so with the genuinely enlightened."[8]

Citing several Western commentators on mysticism, he emphasized that liberation does not involve any radical departure from what would appear to others to be ordinary life or psychological functioning. The self which is lost, they agree, "*is not the self essential to the practical carrying on of one's ordinary daily activities; nor is it the ego in the psychoanalytic sense.*"[9] What he was getting at was an understanding of a way of being that is both ordinary and extraordinary, accessible along at least two paths (therapy and spiritual practice), and capable of being described—but with the sneaky little problem that the same words used to describe the enlightened way of being could just as easily be used to describe the opposite:

We should not be surprised that, partly as a result of the ambiguity of the language of self, many persons fail in one degree or another to distinguish these two different forms of subjective experience. This is true even though the difference, once perceived, is profound. Certain anxiety symptoms (for example, "nervousness," faintness) are easy to distinguish. But most often the anxiety-motivation of behavior is masked, the behavior frequently being rationalized. Thus the man who has always worked compulsively at his job is likely to be unable to distinguish his behavior from that of an industrious and enthusiastic but anxiety-free worker. The attempts of others to use language to suggest to him the subtle but profound difference in the "feel" of the two experiences will most likely be met by him either with incomprehension or defensive scorn, or both. When he asks them to describe in "plain" language how *they* approach their work, victory is his—for they have to use the very same language forms he does. If someone says that anxiety-free work has a kind of absorbed and devoted character, the compulsive replies that those are just the words that describe his work! And he is right.[10]

Alan Watts and the 1960s Model

Another bridger of the East-West gap, whose work I began to become acquainted with a few years later, was Alan Watts. Watts arrived at very similar conclusions about liberation, but his message came in a different and much more raffish cultural package. Where Fingarette was merely a philosophy professor—previously unknown to me—whose essay I happened to find in a collection of writings on psychology, Watts was a famous—if not notorious—character about whom I had been hearing for years. In the 1950s he had been the Zen priest of the Beat writers—he appears as Arthur Whane in Jack Kerouac's novel *The Dharma Bums*—and was becoming, in the mid-1960s, one of the high priests of LSD. Where Fingarette had relied heavily on Freudian psychoanalysis as his main psychological reference point, Watts drew on the whole pantheon of thinkers whose works were then becoming hot on the West Coast—R. D. Laing, Norman O. Brown, Gregory Bateson, and Fritz Perls, among others—to help him in his search for commonalities between the Eastern quest for liberation and the Western quest for psychological development.

In his book *Psychotherapy East and West*, Watts argued that it would be useful for Westerners to remove the various Eastern paths such as Buddhism from the category of philosophy or religion, and to think of them instead as something more nearly resembling psychotherapy:

> The main resemblance between these Eastern ways of life and Western psychotherapy is in the concern of both with bringing about changes of consciousness, changes of feeling in our own existence and our relation to human society and the natural world. The psychotherapist has, for the most part, been interested in changing the consciousness of peculiarly disturbed individuals. The disciples of Buddhism and Taoism are, however, concerned with changing the consciousness of normal, socially adjusted people. But it is increasingly apparent to psychotherapists that the normal state of consciousness in our culture is both the context and the breeding ground of mental disease.[11]

The deeper core problem for Watts was what he called egocentric consciousness, a "limited and impoverished consciousness without foundation in reality."[12] That consciousness—the one which we ordinarily think of as "I" and take to be our true identity—is "confined to a very small and mainly fictitious part of our being."[13] The point of liberation is to awaken to a larger sense of who and what we are. In a later work, entitled *The Book: On the Taboo Against Knowing Who You Are*, he argued that "the prevalent sensation of oneself as a separate ego enclosed in a bag of skin is a hallucination which accords neither with Western science nor with the experimental philosophy-religions of the East. . . ."[14]

So the idea that I am exploring here—let's call it the secular view of liberation—is not an entirely new one. Not only Fingarette and Watts, but also Erich Fromm, Gardner Murphy, and many other writers were discovering, in the 1960s, the similarities and differences between mysticism and psychotherapy, and looking for ways to make the concept of liberation accessible and available to people in the Western world. But Watts's personal contribution to this effort was significant in many ways. He was, for one thing, a first-rate scholar. Trained as a theologian, ordained as an Anglican minister before he became a bit too bohemian even for that tolerant branch of Christianity, he had made extensive studies of the various teachings he drew on in his work. He was also a productive writer and eloquent speaker whose ideas reached many people; he probably did more than any one person to popularize Buddhism in the West. And he was one of the small group of people—Aldous Huxley having been the first—to put forth to Westerners the audacious idea that psychedelic drugs could be an entry to genuine spiritual experience, to a deeper and truer perception of the real world.[15] His most important contribution of all, I think, was his insistence that you really didn't need to put yourself through the equivalent of a religious conversion to draw on the wisdom of the East. People were doing that all around him, rushing to become Buddhists or Taoists or yogis, to follow in the footsteps of this or that guru, and he suspected most such pursuits would lead nowhere—at worst, might lead to a whole new set of top-heavy institutionalized religions. He cautioned against "excessive reverence," which, he said, had already caused the ossification in the East of the very teachings that were now being so enthusiastically discovered in the West:

> Whenever a tradition becomes venerable with the passage of time, the ancient masters and sages are elevated to pedestals of sanctity and wisdom which lift them far above the human level. The way of liberation becomes confused with a popular cult; the ancient teachers become gods and supermen, and thus the ideal of libera-

tion or Buddhahood becomes ever more remote. No one believes that it can be reached except by the most unusually gifted and heroic prodigies. Consequently the medicine of the disciplines becomes a diet, the cure an addiction, and the raft a houseboat. In this manner, a way of liberation turns into just another social institution and dies of respectability.[16]

Watts thus laid the foundation for two propositions central to my argument here. They are (1) that the state of mind called spiritual enlightenment or liberation is not abnormal, inaccessible, or even particularly unusual, and (2) that the understanding of it is not the exclusive province of any sect, school, culture, teacher, or geographic region.

But a lot has happened since the '60s and '70s, when Watts was spreading his countercultural version of Zen. We have seen the development and dissemination of postmodern psychology and cognitive science, rapid globalization, the leap into cyberspace, and various other developments that create new opportunities for understanding the no-self experience. They establish a different context within which Western, more or less secular, people can think about such matters. We'll return to that postmodern context, but first let's take a closer look at older forms of mysticism that have been, in some ways, postmodern all along.

The Soul (and Non-Soul) of Eastern Religion

Two points about the Eastern spiritual traditions are especially useful in getting to the core of what they have to say about the self. These are, first, the difference between exoteric and esoteric religions, and second, the difference between religions that believe in the soul and those that don't.

The exoteric religions that most of us think of when we think of religion—the ones with temples, holy scriptures, hierarchies, and all that—aren't really the same as the esoteric traditions such as Zen Buddhism and Sufism. In the first, religion is belief in God—usually one God—and the chief problems to overcome are lack of faith in this God, and sins against His laws. In the second, religion is about liberation or enlightenment, and the chief problems to be overcome are attachments and illusions about the nature of the self. In the first kind of religion, you make spiritual progress by remaining true to your beliefs; in the second, you make spiritual progress by examining your beliefs closely and, when necessary, letting go of them. Nothing is more highly valued in the esoteric traditions than walking away from dogmas. If you don't do that, say the esoteric teachers, you are in danger of starting another religion. Because the esoteric traditions are so different from what we in the West commonly envision when we talk about religion, it's not surprising that people like Watts think it's better not to call them religions at all.

Every official religion seems to have its esoteric undercurrent. Zen is an esoteric version of Buddhism (quite possibly in danger of turning into another official religion, but that's another story for another book); Sufism is a rough designation for many esoteric schools of Islam; there is esoteric Christianity—which says that the kingdom of heaven spoken of by Christ is a state of liberated consciousness in your present life, not someplace you go after you die; and so forth. The esoteric movements are sometimes rebellious, sometimes subject to stern disapproval from the religious higher-ups, often deliberately irreverent. I have heard of Zen monasteries where the ancient Buddhist scriptures were used as toilet paper.

The second fundamental point we should keep in mind is that Buddhism brought to the East a radical message about the soul. Now, the idea of a personal and immortal soul, a "divine self," is, as we noted in chapter 1, a common feature in many religions, East and West. It is the faith of Socratic philosophy, Christianity, Islam, Hinduism. And it's one of the all-time theological booby-traps. It offers a beguiling assurance of connection to the Divine, coupled with a downside message of separateness, because the soul has a personal identity and a personal career—a potential for gaining great rewards in the Beyond or getting into cosmic trouble big-time for wrong thoughts or actions on the part of its human caretaker. The Hindu version is the *atman*, the indestructible personal soul that is held to be the core of human existence.

The Buddha taught the radical doctrine of *anatman*—no *atman*, no soul, and for that matter, no fixed "I," no self other than the illusion of self. Human consciousness has no core, but is rather a flow of events, mental activities called *dharmas* in the Sanskrit texts, and the aim of spiritual practice is to awaken to this reality. This radical message of the Buddha's teaching tends to get lost in much of Buddhism, which has in many parts of the world turned into a rather stodgy business of studying the ancient scriptures and preaching the Buddhist version of the Ten Commandments.

So the student of esoteric spirituality sets out upon a course of practice radically different from—in some ways the opposite of—that of the believer who is concerned about the salvation of his or her immortal soul. The goal instead is to get comfortable with having no soul and no self in the usual meaning of those words, to discover that such an understanding, once attained and assimilated, feels somehow as though it were always there. The advice of the late Sri Nisargadatta Maharaj was: "Find what you have never lost . . ."[17]

There is, I have heard, an exercise that spiritual teachers in the East often employ as a way of guiding their students toward higher wisdom. It consists simply in asking the question "Who are you?"—not once, but over and over again. Each time the student answers, the teacher, instead of saying, "Oh, so that's who you are," merely repeats the question. Sooner or later, if the exercise is successful, the student sees through the emptiness of all such self-definitions, recognizes that they all are in a sense correct and in another sense irrelevant. The practice of meditation, in which the practitioner patiently observes the endless churning of her own interior conversations, is aimed toward the same kind of realization. So are the mind-bending *koans* of Zen, which confront the student with demands such as: "Show me the true face that was yours before your mother and father were born."

These teachings are still popularly identified with the East, but it has been a long time since they were to be found only there. Indeed, since Buddhism has now spread around the globe, the teachings may at the present time be a greater force in Europe and America than they are in Asia. They all have become part of the global meme pool.

Since they *are* available, it seems sensible to me that we turn to them for some occasional guidance—and go about it by borrowing whatever is useful and not feeling that it is necessary to become a card-carrying Buddhist, Taoist, Hindu, Sufi, or whatever in the process. I know that a lot of Westerners are doing that, and I don't see anything wrong with it if you happen to want to add one more identity to the baggage you are already carrying. But you don't have to. All the various teachings and techniques can best be seen as sufficient but not necessary.

The Logic of Liberation

I am going to proceed from here with the assumption that the state of consciousness commonly described as enlightenment or liberation *makes sense*, and furthermore that it makes more sense to Westerners today than it did a few decades ago. To say that it makes sense doesn't mean that the existence of such a state can be irrefutably proven to the dedicated skeptic. Neither can the state itself be transmitted from one person to another with a simple, straight-on explanation, any more than a state of happiness can be transmitted to someone who is depressed. But it is achievable through rational thought, and it is within the realm of reality as we know it.

There is nothing alien to Western psychology about the idea of mental states that are different from what we might call normal consciousness, but which we understand only from the outside. Most of us don't really *know* what a schizophrenic or dissociated person experiences; we know only what we assume on the basis of our various beliefs and preconceptions, and perhaps from what we are told by the person with the problem. In the absence of what might be considered objective information about such states, it's possible for some psychiatrists to contend—as many do—that there is no such thing as schizophrenia and that nobody really has multiple personalities. Personally I don't find it hard to believe that human consciousness covers an enormous spectrum of possibilities beyond what we call "normality"—the reverse proposition strikes me as far more improbable—but in the last analysis all you ever really know about experience is what you experience yourself. So there's nothing I can say in these pages that will overwhelm the person who refuses to believe that there is any such thing as liberation in either its Eastern or Western variations. Probably the best I can do is persuade you that the idea isn't nearly as far-out as you may have suspected, and that our present postmodern situation presents an interesting new approach to it.

The state called liberation is in a very real sense the most natural way of being conscious and human, but it's also the result of a process of cognitive development—a kind of learning. It is something that people come to understand about themselves. Some traditions (such as Zen) stress the instant flashes when the understanding breaks through all at once, and others incline more toward a slow deepening of understanding that goes on through a lifetime. But the understanding is, whatever its timetable, the product of an investigation. The raw material is always personal experience, the events of real life as they happen, which you keep *studying*, questioning, against which you test all you have been told about who and what you are and how everything works. The investigation may go on for many years, and it may (or may not) involve any or all of the techniques that are commonly employed in this connection—conversing with a teacher, reading books, using psychedelic drugs, meditating—but it is still a cognitive process. It is something that the human mind is inclined to do and is equipped to do.

I think that when Watts began to talk glowingly about LSD—and wrote a book about it, *The Joyous Cosmology*—he misled a lot of people into thinking that it or any other drug can be a shortcut to liberation, a quick hit that requires no more understanding than taking a couple of aspirins. I don't doubt that the right chemicals can provide a hearty nudge in the right direction under certain conditions, but Watts did not always make it clear that he came to his own psychedelic adventures with a lot of advance preparation. He did his exploring in middle age, and he had been a serious student of Eastern mysticism (he published his first book, *The Way of Zen*, at age twenty-one) and a practitioner of meditation for many years. He had absorbed a tremendous amount of information that is not available to the average person who dabbles in drugs, however spiritual might be the intent. He had, in short, a story he could tell himself (and others) about his experience.

Liberation involves understanding—actually at least three different kinds of understanding: the understanding involved in the liberation experience itself (whether it's a one-time thing or an ongoing process); the understanding involved in the person's description of that experience *to himself*; and the understanding that *others* may have, the public philosophy concerning such matters.

The first kind is a matter of discovering the erroneous nature of what you have been experiencing as the "I" and taking to be your complete consciousness, which involves a reorganization of consciousness, with certain recognizable features. One of those features is a sense that things happen but don't necessarily happen to any central processor. This kind of experience is described in various Zen writings that speak of thoughts without a thinker, things seen and heard yet no one who sees and hears them. I have read of a Zen Buddhist nun who avoids using any personal pronouns that express a self. Instead of saying, "I'm hungry," she will say, "There's hunger here."[18] These locutions may seem mighty strange—the language of no-self isn't much better than the language of self—but they are simply attempts to describe a way of being conscious without routing all thought and sensation through a Cartesian central processor. Another common experience is an enormous feeling of connectedness, or, to put it in negative terms, an absence of a feeling of being separate from the environment.

For most people who begin to understand themselves in this way, the emotional side of the experience can be a delightful sense of discovery accompanied by feelings of profound peace and joy. But others find it quite disturbing—an uncomfortable sense of emptiness, loss, vertigo. These feelings seem to have to do with not being able to place the experience in any context—which leads me to the second kind of understanding.

This is what I would call meta-understanding, your need to figure out what it is that you have figured out. We are never entirely free from description, and most people who have liberation experiences need a story to tell themselves, a way to explain the changes that are occurring as they reorganize their own consciousness. Fingarette's psychoanalytic patients seem to have been inclined to describe their changes as freedom from neurotic attachments and modes of behavior. Students of Zen naturally define them with such words as "enlightenment" or "liberation," or the Japanese "*satori*" or "*kensho*". Religious people speak of achieving unity with God. Good scientific-rationalists achieve unity with the universe or with the evolutionary process. The follower of postmodern thought moves beyond the restrictions of the single modern self, or becomes comfortable in a world of socially constructed realities. You might simply describe such understanding as a matter of growing older and wiser and letting go of a lot of self-centered foolishness. I suspect quite a bit of that kind of liberation goes on.

The third kind of understanding is the social or cultural understanding. What do people think about somebody who has had a liberation experience? Do they think she's crazy? Do they think he has suddenly turned into some sort of wise man or saint? Either is possible, and neither is much help. We need much better public resources of comprehension and assistance for the person who is either in the process of figuring something out or who has figured something out and is looking around for some understanding of what has happened.

Notice that I said "*better* resources," not *more*. The cultural inventory is enormous, virtually infinite, and that very richness can be its own problem. The postmodern turn-of-the-century global civilization is so symbolically varied and complex, so crowded with different ideas and realities—some of them totally opposed to one another, others saying more or less the same thing in different words—that it can be a bewildering place for a person who is seriously trying to figure out something about psychological growth.

For most people who have liberation experiences—and in fact for all the people I have talked to who have had such—the job is never done. There is further understanding to be achieved, and there is always the possibility of slipping back from a moment of profound insight. The Zen literature speaks of "big mind" and "little mind," and of the human tendency to commute between the two. I personally have backslid many times from what seemed to be clear, pristine, and irreversible insights. The experience has been rather like what you have when you look at one of those gestalt drawings—the facing profiles that turn into a vase, or vice versa—and find that you can switch back and forth between the two ways of understanding what you see. But I suppose that if Martin Marty can commute between religious and secular modes of thought, I can communicate between ego and liberation. Actually, there's a bit more to it than that. A better metaphor might be living all your life within a house and looking at the world through a single window and then discovering, one day, that you are outside the house. That may seem like an enormous and final liberation—but then later you find that you are back in again, looking out through the old window. That can easily happen, but you always know there is an outdoors. It helps if other people know it also, and if your society knows it.

The traditional esoteric schools are wise about this, understand both the need for advancement and the possibilities of regression. They take care to surround the seeker with people who are on the same path, speaking the same language. In the Zen tradition, much emphasis is placed on the *sangha*, the spiritual community, and on the authority of the teacher who will reinforce the seekers' discoveries. Relatively few people today live in such social contexts, and must try to get their reinforcement by fishing in the global meme pool. This pool, this postmodern global culture, is changing rapidly and provides a new cultural context within which people go through the mysterious business of growing up in adulthood.

Self Happens

The various spiritual and psychological writings that try to deal with liberation talk about the self or the ego as the problem to be overcome, and you can easily get the impression that it is a thing, an entity that you somehow have to find, kill, and bury. And you can easily get the impression also that the self, once killed and buried, stays dead. But it doesn't seem to work that way.

It's much more productive—and much closer to our present understanding of how the human mind works—to think of self as process. Self (or, if you prefer, ego in the Eastern sense) consists of various patterns of thought that arise in certain occasions and that have the effect of unliberating you. Some spiritual teachers often talk of attachments—unhealthy fixations on things, people, or ideas—in that way. Others tell you to be on guard against becoming excessively judgmental. Some systems maintain that each of us has certain passions—vanity, fear, sloth, the desire for vengeance—that take over our lives, color our views of the world, cause us to build fictitious barricades against discovering what we are. So the prescription for the person in search of enlightenment is in some ways similar to the Christian exhortation to avoid the occasions of sin—except it is to look out for the occasions of ego.

To develop some sensitivity to those kinds of thought patterns—to become liberated—is definitely not to lose personal identity or any of the outward manifestations of selfhood. You are still you.

I have heard legends of mystics who simply retired from their identities upon attaining enlightenment, wandered anonymously through the world or withdrew to meditate forever in a cave. So I suppose you could do that. You can also do as many other people do, which is go about the business of being whoever you were before, continue to live that self while knowing that you are a human being, something larger and more mysterious and ultimately undefinable.

So the Dalai Lama, who I imagine has a pretty good view of that wider terrain, goes about the business of having a public identity. He makes speeches, travels about the world, gets his picture taken, and, as far as I can tell, thoroughly enjoys it all. I read somewhere that he enjoys going shopping, especially for electronic goods and cat food. Alan Watts remained Alan Watts, and a number of people I have met, and whom I would call liberated, still have their credit cards—and, for that matter, occasional bouts of ego.

The Postmodern Place, and Postmodern Possibilities

"Postmodern" is the best word for describing our present situation, but I say that with full awareness that language is an imperfect tool and that no such term is without its shortcomings. Certainly I don't mean, in defending the term, that everything so labeled is worth pursuing. I can't think of anything I would more happily counsel ignoring than everything under the heading of deconstruction, the complete works of Derrida and all his followers. But the word "postmodern" does mean something, and there are profound differences between the worlds of the mid-twentieth century—the apex of modernity—and the present era. Today we—and here I mean, literally, everybody—are being propelled headlong into different experiences and understandings. Some of these experiences may lead the individual in the direction of the kinds of understanding that have traditionally been called liberation, and some of the understandings may help us toward a deep and radical reorganization of our own sense of who and what we are.

I use the word "some" in all its wonderful vagueness to indicate my profound uncertainty about how hopeful to be about the various things now unfolding in the world. Are the multiphrenic, protean people described in the research of psychologists such as Gergen and Lifton out there on a growth curve, headed toward a Zen-like liberation from the illusion of self? Are brain research and psychoactive drugs helping to construct a radically new understanding of how we think and feel? Are advances in medicine helping to break down the traditional boundaries of the physical self? Is cyberspace an entirely new medium with virtually infinite possibilities for the creation of new social selves? Are developments in economics and politics helping to create entirely new senses of personal identity? As the reader who has stayed with me this far will have seen, I clearly think all these possibilities need to be taken seriously—a lot more seriously than I see most people taking them—but am also cautious about the power of back-lash, the unknown psychological and social and political pitfalls that may lie ahead as we travel farther beyond the era of the modern self. I am uncertain about those matters, yet quite certain about something else: We have not yet achieved anything that might conceivably be described as a culture of liberation.

But in identifying what isn't, we also identify a goal, an image of what might yet be achieved and is certainly worthy of being aspired to. A culture of liberation would be one in which the continued psychological growth of adults were understood and supported, and in which there were many resources available for such support. Postmodern psychology has much to contribute to this, but certainly isn't the final answer. Much of postmodern thought is what Robert Kegan aptly terms "anti-modernist," chiefly engaged in waving an intellectual finger at the fallacies of modernism without offering any constructive concepts about personal progress beyond those fallacies.

Nor is a mere adoption of Eastern religion by the West the final answer either. Those religions are a part of global culture now; we have passed beyond the bridge-building stage. The modernist project—Fingarette's and Watts's—of making linkages between what was regarded as two whole and distinct categories, Eastern religion and Western psychology, has done its work. What we need to do now is recognize that those categories are social constructions that served their purposes in their times and are ready to be discarded or at least drastically redescribed. The issue now is not East or West, religion or psychology, but human consciousness and its possibilities. We need—and may be beginning to have—a culture in which all the accumulated wisdom of the East is simply part of the public domain, and in which the leaders of those schools are involved not only in teaching, but also in learning and changing.

The liberated human mind is not in the keeping of any religion, culture, sect, school, or guru. It is nobody's property, and nobody's secret. If it is a secret at all, it's because people keep it from themselves—and that may be getting harder to do.

Imagine there's no countries . . .
And no religion too.

JOHN LENNON[1]

It's not given to mortals to see the future.
All one can do is analyze the present,
especially those parts that do not fit what
everybody knows and takes for granted.

PETER DRUCKER[2]

14

Futures of the Self

I used to watch reruns of *Star Trek* with my son, and I often mused, as I followed those stirring adventures in outer space, that although we have brilliant powers of imagination regarding technological and even political changes, we seem to wax wimpy when it comes to imagining any fundamental *psychological* changes. There on the screen were all those gallant men and women of the far-distant future, acting in pretty much the same way as the characters in World War II movies. All stuck in their single roles, their limited ranges of thought and behavior, and their rigidly defined places along the chain of command. The starship itself seemed to be a metaphor of the modern self, with Captain Kirk sitting in the command center like a well-dressed Cartesian pineal gland, observing everything and steering a steady course into the great unknown.

But psychological changes *have* taken place over the course of history, and are taking place now. It's not too difficult to recognize that this is happening; the difficult part is knowing where it all may lead. It is so much easier to comprehend the stunning imaginary futures given us by the science-fiction writers—the creation of humanlike robots,

245

the conversion of Mars into a green and fertile planet, the pursuit of modern warfare and premodern political intrigue out across enormous galactic empires—than it is to imagine a world in which people are really much different from, say, Harry and Bess Truman. Can we do that? Can we conceive of a future in which experiences of self and ideas about identity continue to change, perhaps change even more rapidly and dramatically than they have in recent years, and in which those changes are widely recognized and understood?

In this closing chapter we will take a few small steps in that direction, by examining some scenarios—descriptions of possible worlds of the early twenty-first century.

Scenarios are inventions of the twentieth century, born of our wisdom and our ignorance. We live now in a universe that is immensely larger than the one our ancestors inhabited a few centuries past. It has expanded in the dimensions of time, also, as scientists peer backward toward the origins of the universe and speculate about the distant future. Unlike people who lived in more stable eras, we can't expect the future to be like the present. We know it will be different, but we really don't know how different or in what ways. The more I think about the future, the more I believe it is as unknowable as God; in fact I was most intrigued some time ago when I happened to come across the work of an innovative theologian who wrote that the future *is* God—the mysterious creative spirit, always beyond us, leading us on, preparing surprises.[3] There is such enormous complexity in life, so little understanding of why things happen as they do, that it is folly to believe we are able to know what is about to happen.

Yet even after we have confessed to our inability to know what lies ahead, we find that we are still obligated to think hard about it anyway, because you can't handle today without some concept of tomorrow. According to John Holland, the dean of complexity theorists, all living organisms, from the simplest single-celled creatures to you and me, operate by anticipating the future.[4]

Future-thinking is as fundamental to life as reproduction. What human beings do now—as we try to turn anticipation into something resembling a science or an art, or both—is tell stories. We call them scenarios, but they're just stories constructed in certain ways for certain purposes. Usually scenarios come in sets, and a set focuses on some specific issue or question—population growth, for example—or looks at the possible futures of a specific organization. Scenarios provide ways of moving beyond the linear "predict-and-control" approaches by which countries and companies used to base planning on a single set of expectations about the future, and then be taken completely by surprise if something radically different from the "official future" came along—which, all too regularly, it did. Frequently corporate scenarios focus on the externals: the world in which the business will operate, the possible changes in supply and demand, the political conditions. When a number of scenarios of the future have been developed, any group within the company that is developing a strategy, plan, or long-term project will test it against each scenario. The object of such an exercise is not to decide which scenario is "right," but to think about how different conditions might affect the project and what steps would need to be taken. "In this way," wrote one specialist of the genre, "the first objective of scenario planning became the generation of projects and decisions that are more robust under a variety of alternative futures."[5]

Scenario planning was first developed by the military, then applied to corporate decision making by Shell and other companies after World War II, and more recently has come into general use by all kinds of people who feel the need to think seriously and creatively about what might lie ahead. In one scenario exercise, a group of South Africans from all across the political spectrum collaborated in 1991 and 1992 on a set of stories about how the country might succeed or fail in becoming a peaceful democracy; the four scenarios were published in the newspapers and became a common theme, a kind of reference point in the public dialogue. Later in the same decade, a group of Canadians participated in a similar exercise to look at ways their country might come together—or fall apart. So scenarios, when taken out of the corporate boardrooms, become tools of democracy, thought exercises that ordinary people can use not only to imagine the future but also—as the authors of *The Futures of Women* put it—to "illuminate the present."

The stories in this chapter will be about different ways the world might evolve through the present turn-of-the-century identity crisis.

This set will include two scenarios in which the postmodern human being is coming into his/her/its own—thinkable worlds of the not-very-distant future in which a different sense of identity has become an explicit part of our personal, political, social, economic, and spiritual lives. It will also include two scenarios in which the resistance to this kind of psychological change proves to be as strong as, if not stronger than, the impulses to move beyond the boundaries of the modern self.

Global Inevitables, Global Unpredictables

Scenarios, creative expeditions into the unknowable future, begin with predictions—not of specific events, but of current forces that show every indication of sweeping onward for some time to come. Here we will work with two such forces, one having to do with individual people, the other having to do with the global system as a whole. The first is the erosion of the modern self, and its replacement by a self-concept variously described as multiple, protean, decentered, relational. The other is the kind of systemic change that has characterized the world of the late-twentieth century: economic growth, technological progress, and globalization. The first changes personal boundaries and identities. The second changes organizational boundaries and identities: the authority of nations, the domains of businesses, the scope of action of nongovernmental organizations, the autonomy of communities. These are really just facets of the same process, but it's useful to look at them separately.

The erosion of the modern self, the global identity crisis, is not about to go away quietly: When you have people changing sex and gender, identity games in society and cyberspace, psychologists arguing about self, psychiatrists arguing about multiple personalities, cognitive scientists arguing about memory, a new dialogue about mystic selflessness—all that and more—you are not going to get a peaceful retreat to the days when the boundaries of the self were believed to be clear and self-evident. You might conceivably get a *forced* retreat to some such situation—all the challenges to the modern self are being disputed, and I don't underestimate the strength of those reactions at all—but the issue will not disappear. Self has (to use Robert Kegan's terminology) gone from being subject to object. It is out there in the open now, no longer an invisible part of the background of consciousness, and we all have to make a decision about it—in fact many decisions, as we go about the business of running our daily lives.

The growth of a global economy—accompanied by rapid technological changes and an increase in linkages among all the world's cultures, governments, and ecosystems—is a modern story, yet also one that has been unfolding for tens of thousands, perhaps hundreds of thousands, of years. Globalization really began when our ancestors began migrating out of Africa. Over the course of that incredible diaspora, people became more open systems in some ways, more closed in others. They showed a stunning capacity to move across geographic boundaries, to explore, to adapt to new environments, and in some ways to adapt environments to themselves. They showed great creative abilities as they invented tools, cultures, languages, rituals, religions, social orders. They also, in many cases, shut down as they settled into the various regions that became their homes, and decided they were distinct and unique. Many tribes and societies chose names for themselves that translate roughly as "the people," with the implicit—and sometimes explicit—understanding of other peoples as deeply different and somehow less than human. But even the most tightly closed societies were affected sooner or later by movement, trade, technological change, population growth—forces that pushed toward globalization and are pushing now with a momentum unequaled in human history. The global economy and its new technologies penetrate and change ancient cultures, local communities, regional economies, traditional lifestyles; in some places they generate opposition, backlash, stress, and conflict. We now have a truly global civilization, and globalization itself is its most explosive and divisive issue. In the years just ahead, local and regional systems of all kinds—

communities and economies and subcultures—will still exist. But they all will operate within a global context and will define themselves differently because of it. And the people involved in them will argue over how globalization should be managed. And our personal selfhood—or no-selfhood—will be defined in that context as well.

These are not particularly risky predictions, only declarations that large-scale processes currently under way will continue. They don't deal with the specific forms these large-scale processes may take, nor do they reckon how strong may be the resistance to them. To do that we have to turn to the scenarios, and remember that they are fictitious.

Scenarios: Two Kinds of Progress

A scenario, in the jargon of the professional futurists, is a thinkable future, an internally consistent story assembling data and imagined events to draw a picture of a world that might conceivably come into being. The following four scenarios tell stories about two different kinds of progress.

The first kind of progress is the kind most people think of today when they use the word: continued expansion of the world economy with increasing output of goods and services, rapid development of all kinds of new high-tech wonders (food products and medical advances from biotechnology, new materials for industrial uses, efficient and nonpolluting energy, rapid low-cost transportation systems, among others), and high mobility—lots of business travel, lots of tourism, lots of immigration. We'll call this P-1 for short. The low P-1 scenarios represent rejection of this sort of progress, or failure to achieve it.

The second kind of progress, which we'll call P-2, is progress along the psychological lines we have explored in this book— movement beyond the modern self toward more multifaceted, change-able, or decentralized identities and personalities, or even toward the no-self consciousness sometimes called enlightenment or liberation. In the high P-2 scenarios, individuals have little attachment to personal identifiers such as race, nationality, ideology, or occupation. People and organizations tend to become open systems. In the low P-2 scenarios, most people retain strong modern or traditional identity structures, and organizations both reflect this and encourage it.

So let's see what we might get if we look at the four possible combinations.

ONE WORLD, MANY UNIVERSES: *High economic growth, technological progress, and globalization combined with high psychological development.*

This is, in many ways, a world without boundaries. Most of the standard identifiers that people have known throughout the modern and early postmodern eras no longer play major parts in their personal or political lives. Most people have many identities and social roles, but no particular attachment to any one of them as the primary definer of who and what they are. There is a global civilization and an ever-changing system of global governance—actually a system of systems including governments; intergovernmental organizations; nongovernmental organizations; and many different kinds of networks, markets, and communities. Nation-states are important elements in this global system as enforcers of universal human rights and as participants in intergovernmental organizations, but nationalism has lost its emotional force. Being a citizen of a particular nation means about as much as being a resident of a particular county or province; the old national passions revive only around the Olympic games and other international sporting events. The freedom of people to move gradually increases with the relaxation of immigration laws. Most countries have fairly simple requirements for obtaining citizenship or legal "denizenship" and voting rights, and human-rights advocates now propose that people should have the same complete freedom of movement internationally that they have within the boundaries of their own countries.

Boundaries of class and caste that once shaped most societies continue to fade in the global civilization. Marxism is withering away too, along with other rigid ideologies that once served as props of personal identity. All of the major organized religions—including Christianity, Judaism, Buddhism, Hinduism, and Islam—are alive and reasonably well in the twenty-first century, but they change in many ways. They all are becoming truly "world religions," with members in all parts of the world, and are no longer clearly and exclusively identified with specific cultures and geographic regions. People everywhere feel free to convert to other religions, and many people identify with more than one religion.

Yet there is tremendous diversity, as people choose different lifestyles and continually create new cultural forms—sometimes improvising on the old ones, and sometimes striking off in entirely new directions. Governance, society, religion, and ecology all are now recognized as art forms. Active human life spans have been lengthened through various advances in health maintenance and medicine—including organ transplants—and this allows more people to develop to higher levels of psychological maturity.

Many people live much of their lives in cyberspace, which has become a rich and realistic realm of experience. One of the activities to be found there is the No-Self Network. Simply known as The Network to the countless numbers of people in all parts of the world who participate in its discussions, its subject matter is the ancient one of liberation from the self. The Network bears little or no resemblance to any spiritual school or movement. It has no formal organizational structures, no leaders, no dues, no disciples. It is more an adult educational project, an ongoing conversation. The Network began as an interdisciplinary dialogue among psychologists and students of Oriental philosophy, intellectuals who were interested in developing an understanding of enlightenment more appropriate to the lives of people in the twenty-first century. But it was an open conversation, and as the number of participants grew, it evolved into several different conversations and soon added thousands of participants all around the world. Many of these arranged local meetings, ongoing groups, scientific conferences. Among the members of The Network, liberation is regarded as a more or less ordinary human achievement, roughly comparable to having learned to play the piano, and not as a superhuman or divine status.

THE DYSFUNCTIONAL FAMILY: *High economic growth, technological progress, and globalization, but little psychological development.*

Economic globalization proceeds rapidly, with the spread of consumerism and popular culture based on movies, television, music, and other forms of mass entertainment. Technological progress makes it possible for people to extend human life spans, conquer diseases, change appearances through plastic surgery, manipulate moods with psychoactive chemicals. But most of these benefits are expensive and available only to those who can afford them; there are enormous inequities. There has long been a growing wealth gap in the world, and inseparable from it is the "health gap": People in the wealthier parts of the world live longer, eat better, are better protected against disease. With new life-extending and performance-boosting enhancements, that gap grows even wider, to the point that the rich and the poor are hardly the same species.

This world is no longer divided between two great power blocs and two great ideologies, as it was in the mid-twentieth century. It is, rather, a world divided along countless fault lines—economic, geographic, cultural, religious. It is a world of postmodern people happily doing their things; of modern people still obsessed with progress, economic gain, and organizational bigness; and of premodern people getting trampled and getting angry.

The globalization of Western-influenced popular culture is opposed by fundamentalists and other groups who prefer to retain their traditions, languages, rituals, and power structures. Enduring conflicts over human rights strain relations between states seeking to extend the enforcement of them and other countries—notably East Asian and Muslim—that view those attempts as violations of their sovereignty and culture. Major non-governmental forces, such as religious groups and women's organizations, are involved in this huge and seemingly unsolvable global dispute. Within religions and other groups that still retain some cultural identity, the "culture wars" rage on, dividing traditionalists from advocates of change. People move by the millions—and some of the movement is forced migration caused by ecological and political chaos—but migrants often become homeless refugees, having been refused entry into the more prosperous nations.

LIVING LIGHTLY: *High levels of psychological development all around the world; low economic growth, technological progress, and globalization.*

A worldwide economic depression sets in early in the twenty-first century, and a series of ecological disasters—including global climate change, massive pollution of air and water, and plagues caused by antibiotic-resistant bacteria—are widely regarded as having been caused by technology. A new global consensus gradually builds around the feeling that the twentieth century's preoccupation with economic and technological growth was a kind of mass delusion. The new ethic is based on the twin values of living lightly on the planet and living lightly within the values and beliefs and institutions inherited from the past—respecting them, even preserving them in some ways, but not being too tightly bound by them. Distinctions of nationality, race, tribe, ethnicity, class, and gender have ceased to have much meaning, and there is a general willingness among people to cooperate and manage the wealth that is available. Although technological change is no longer galloping ahead as it did in the late-twentieth century, telephone service is extending to most of the world, and people everywhere are able to communicate and share information. But there is much less migration and travel than there was in the past, and tourism is no longer the world's major industry.

All around the world there is an enormous interest in traditional and premodern cultures, yet this is linked with a general understanding that there is no real return to the past and that all cultures change over time. People enjoy re-creating ancient rituals and art and adopting those as parts of their lives. There is a great deal of spiritual exploration, and most is done by perpetuating the practices and teachings of the classical traditions such as Buddhism.

BACK TO BASICS: *Low economic growth, technological progress, and globalization; low psychological development.*

This historical process, which unfolds quickly in a spread of conflicts around the world, is a classic of Hegelian dialectic, one historical force giving rise to its exact opposite. In this case it is globalization that creates the conditions many people find repugnant—and also creates the conditions for a revolt against globalization. Communications and mobility provide an environment in which an antiglobalist movement is able to emerge, spread worldwide, and eventually become a more powerful (and ultimately far more successful) force than Marxism had been in the twentieth century.

The global ideology of "devolution" races through international popular culture early in the twenty-first century. It is embraced by Hollywood, where high-budget movies with major stars dramatize revolutions against big institutions and the creation of idyllic independent communities. "Devo" Web sites are enormously popular and make possible discussion of beliefs and the spread of devolutionist literature in a way that no other political movement in the past had ever achieved. And when the devolutionist movement turns violent, the global arms trade is right there to make it possible.

The original theoreticians of devolution were mainly Western intellectuals of a neo-Romantic bent who, in their works, painted a picture of a utopian return to communities, ancient ethnic identities, local economies, and traditional spirituality. This vision was enthusiastically received by Green parties and other radical ecological groups, who believed that "bioregional" communities would be the surest guarantors of environmental responsibility.

But then, to the surprise and great dismay of the idealistic devolutionists, their ideology is seized upon with even greater enthusiasm by religious fundamentalists, political conservatives, ethnic nationalists, racists, and neo-Fascist paramilitary groups. Young men in many parts of the world, caught in the grip of poverty and chronically high unemployment, choose to fight for the cause of independence and self-government.

Devolution proves to be highly contagious. In Spain, for example, the Basque separatists succeed in breaking away—after a long war as debilitating to the government in Madrid as the Chechen separatist war had been to the government in Moscow—and establish the new nation of Euskadi. Neighboring Catalans proceed to declare the independence of Catalonia. The rest of Spain soon falls apart as well into various small states such as Aragon, Castille, Galicia, and the Balearic Islands. A similar process ensues in Italy after the northern regions proclaim the independent republic of Padania. Other armed movements create new nations of Scots, Tamils, Kurds, Palestinians. Some of these movements succeed in establishing viable nation-states, but others find themselves continually harassed by their own internal separatist movements based on tribal or regional identities. Different regions become bastions of fundamentalist Christianity, fundamentalist Islam; some become Marxist communities. Each group maintains its traditions and lifestyles with minimal change, dilution, or outside interference. Authority structures are strong—group rights prevail over individual rights everywhere—and they prove to be quite capable of resisting deviations such as feminist movements. The intrusion of mass-media systems and global popular culture is successfully resisted in many areas. There is still some international trade, but most countries have high tariffs and import-substitution policies, and many local economies are fiercely independent and suspicious of anything made by outsiders. The collapse of global communications systems drastically slows the progress of scientific research and the diffusion of technologies.

Which Future?

Some of the professionals who help construct scenarios for businesses and governments insist that in order for a set of scenarios to work, all of them must be regarded as equally likely. No playing favorites. Only in this way, they say, will planners really open their minds to other possibilities besides the official future. That's undoubtedly a good rule, and we don't have to follow it. The scenarios above are thought experiments rather than strategy-planning devices, and we are free to use them to clarify our own visions and agendas, hopes and fears. Sometimes, when scenarios are constructed by a group of people working together over a period of time, only one result seems desirable, and two or more do not. Or several scenarios will have attractive features, and people will take sides about which looks best.

This set has two that seem desirable to me: "Living Lightly" and "One World, Many Universes." Many readers will incline toward "Living Lightly," which has most of the features of the utopian—and Ecotopian—futures that are cherished by people committed to environmentalism, voluntary simplicity, and reverence for traditional societies. One feature this scenario does not include, however, is the sort of deep connection to a single place championed by the bioregionalists. I know bioregional loyalty is regarded as the height of humble wisdom to many people, but to me it looks like just another ego attachment; I really can't equate it with psychological growth. I don't consider this scenario to be a likely one, since it is based on the premise of a slowdown or virtual halt to both economic growth and technological advancement. I can easily conceive of a global economic collapse, but I think continued rapid scientific and technological change is a virtual certainty.

"One World, Many Universes" is, for me, the most persuasive mix of idealism and realism. Some readers may see in it a resemblance to the future described by Francis Fukuyama in his much-cited essay (and later book) "The End of History?"[6] But personally I don't expect to see the end of anything. In fact this particular future is likely to be the most fast-changing one, rapidly evolving beyond what I have described here.

The "Dysfunctional Family" bears the closest resemblance to the world we're living in now, with its enormous disparities of wealth and opportunity, its global tensions between postmodern forces and the custodians of modern and traditional worldviews. It has much in common with the dystopias described by Samuel Huntington and Ben Barber, and by Robert Kaplan in his visions of large regions of the world slipping into anarchy.[7] A strong case can be made—and a lot of people are busily engaged in making it—that this is our most likely future. Not a cheerful thought—but remember that scenarios are meant to be fast-shutter-speed snapshots of history on the run, not sitting portraits of a world at rest. This world, explosive and unstable, could change dramatically—could, in fact, easily evolve into something resembling any of the other three scenarios.

"Back to Basics" strikes me as a world defeated, but it is, of course, the agenda of many people—some of whom are prepared to die to achieve it. As described here it is not simply a world of communities, but also a world in which those communities are for the most part organized around strong authority structures. It comes close to the ideal future of the conservative sociologist Robert Nisbet, who insisted—to the dismay of more softhearted idealists—that real communities, if they are to preserve their identities and their unique cultural values, would have to be based on hierarchy and authority. In this scenario the culture wars are over and the postmodern revisionists are subjugated people.

The Progress of Evolution, the Evolution of Progress

All this talk of progress may seem out of place in a book about the postmodern world. After all, one of the most commonly cited definitions of the postmodern era is David Harvey's view that we are living in the aftermath of the collapse of the "Enlightenment project," which got under way in the eighteenth century. That project (as Harvey described it) was an attempt to get all people to think together rationally, to recognize that there was only one possible right answer to every question. Its belief was that as people everywhere became more adept at clear scientific and mathematical thought, they would be able to manage everything—from nature to society to personal life—more effectively. The Enlightenment in this view was not just a philosophical movement but also an ideology and an agenda based on belief in "linear progress, absolute truths, and rational planning of ideal social orders."[8] For some it was virtually a religion, its faith expressed by prophets such as the young French philosopher Turgot, who delivered a memorable lecture at the Sorbonne declaring that humankind "advances ever, though slowly, towards greater perfection."[9] Many intellectuals picked up this idea with great enthusiasm and often played down the "slowly" part. It was a powerful driving force behind the great revolutions, which many people regarded as leaps of progress, vaulting forward into civilizations based on ideals of right, equality, and justice for all.

There were always stern dissenters from such bedazzled, onward-and-upward visions of progress, but the visions had a powerful appeal, and some people still cling to them. There isn't much social consensus about progress these days, though—not even an "official future." Your view of progress (or its absence) is likely to be a function of your lifestyle or social role: The environmentalists think everything is going down the drain; the economists champion economic growth; the techies see science solving all our problems; the New Agers cheer for a spiritual transformation; and so it goes—in all directions. The prevailing mood, both in intellectual circles and on the streets, seems to me now to be a good deal more doubtful about the human prospect than it was a few decades ago. This was the subject of a recent book entitled *The Idea of Decline in Western History*, which argues that pessimism has now become downright trendy.[10]

We can still speak of progress—in fact we have to—but it needs to be done in a much more careful way, as when, for example, we speak of sustainable development instead of simply development. There was a time when development alone was good enough; it was progress. But now we need to think of it with a greater awareness of such troubling downside matters as pollution, depletion of nonrenewable resources, destruction of ecosystems, impacts on the global climate, and disruption of local cultures and economies.

The best framework we have for talking about progress is evolution—progress toward increasing levels of complexity of organization. In the evolution of life on Earth, we can see progress from single-celled life forms to sexual reproduction, and other advances such as the appearance of speech and then writing; the emergence of increasingly sophisticated technologies and institutions; the globalization of culture, politics, finance, and trade; the invention of the individualistic, enterprising, modern self.

It is fashionable among postmodern thinkers to speak of the death of the self, but that is putting the matter in negative, simply antimodernist terms. It is not just that the self is dying, but that our concepts of the human brain and the person are changing, becoming more complex and multidimensional. Something else is being born—or, I will argue here, being invented.

Posting Toward the Future

Although I am far from enthusiastic about all the things that fly the flag of postmodernism, I have made it and other "post" words—such as post-identity—central to the vocabulary of this book. And done it quite deliberately, because "post" means "after." It means something has ended, and there is no going back, even if we don't know what lies ahead or even, exactly, what lies around us now. We use the word "postmodern," as Stephen Toulmin once memorably put it, to describe a world that "has not yet discovered how to define itself in terms of what it is, but only in terms of what it has just-now-ceased to be."[11]

Now, when the "post" prefix is used this way, as when Peter

Drucker speaks of postindustrial society, it doesn't mean that something has completely gone away. Industry, obviously, is still with us. But it means that the modes of thought and organization that accompanied industry's dominant period are now obsolete, that industrial production has been superseded by a knowledge economy that calls for new modes of thought and organization. Industry exists in an entirely new context, and we do not return to that context even if we continue to have factories, even if we turn the factories into historical landmarks, even if we wax nostalgic for the primitive grandeur of the Industrial Age and have periodic festivals in which we dress in grimy working clothes and cook up pots of molten steel. Similarly, when political theorists speak of the present era as "post-national," they don't mean that nations have gone away—only that, again, nations exist in a different context and no longer can claim a monopoly on governance. We have definitely moved into a "post-sovereignty" political context, even though that word still stirs the blood of old-fashioned nationalists.

In the postmodern era the institutions and worldviews of modernity survive, and so does the modern self; everywhere we can find people who remain deeply attached to their identities, to their boundaries, to their personal continuity, to their sense of themselves as single entities seeing the world from someplace just behind the eyes. We can also find many people who don't experience life this way but believe they *should*, because they think it represents normalcy and sanity. But the context is changing, and the change is a step—a giant, difficult step—in human evolution.

One of the most amazing developments in the evolution of the human species was the invention of language. It must have taken an enormously long time; it required learning to use certain organs in a new way, for different purposes than those for which they originally had evolved, and it required larger brains with language-processing capacity. And with language invented, the human species turned around and reinvented itself—many times over, in fact. People created cultures, created social orders with complicated structures of belief, and created selves. Language, according to Lewis Mumford, was the first technology—but like other technologies, not fully understood. People thought it was merely a tool for describing the world, and didn't know it was a tool for creating it.

The great discovery of the postmodern era—indeed, the one that defines postmodernity—has been the discovery of this other function of language. It is the discovery that language does not merely represent reality, but constitutes it. Our social orders, for example—the ones we identify with, such as nation-states, ethnic groups, races, tribes— could not exist without their words and visual systems. Our personal identities would be hard to locate without the network of symbols within which we are defined and the internal monologue with which we continually remind ourselves who we think we are.

This discovery can be terribly frightening, but it is ultimately liberating. It is liberating because people begin to use their symbolic tools instead of being used by them, begin to have their identities without being had by them. We are no longer hopelessly in the grip of what William Blake aptly called "mind-forged manacles."

So identities continue to exist in the post-identity society, just as industries and nations do—but in a different context.

It would be nice to be able to say, in these closing pages, that we are making an evolutionary transition beyond the self, but that isn't quite the case—not yet, anyway. What we are doing is catching a glimpse of the self, recognizing it as a fiction, yet continuing to have selves, identities, public personas, internal "I" narratives, and, yes, egos. You will note that I have switched from the singular to the plural, because that is what we all do as we become multilocality, multicommunity, flexible, changeable beings. We move in and out of different symbolic universes, defining ourselves and experiencing ourselves differently as we do.

A postmodern person is being invented, but not out of any clear design, nor in one place, nor by a single creative genius. The modern self was not invented by a single individual either—not even Descartes in his Bavarian bungalow. The postmodern person is in part the product of other inventions—such as the personal computer—that were not conceived as agents of psychological change. He is in part the product of research in fields such as cognitive science that give us a new understanding of our own thought processes. She is in part the result of improvised, often difficult adjustments to new conditions, when she finds it no longer possible to be as she was.

The postmodern person is by no means a finished product; we are evolutionary work in progress. We all are being required by the changes in the world around us to become more open systems—taking in new information, making new connections, moving our boundaries, and even reexamining our ideas of what a human being is. As we do, we become in some ways less than the modern self—less permanent, less centered, less separate—and in some ways much more: Each of us is more than a self, and also more than a postmodern progression of multiple selves; each of us is also a marvelously complex, highly evolved, and somewhat confused apparatus through which the universe becomes aware of *it*self, admires itself, and tries to figure out what it is.

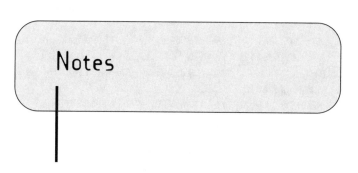

Notes

Introduction

1. W. R. Ashby, "Self-Regulation and Requisite Variety," in F. E. Emery (ed.), *Systems Thinking* (New York: Penguin, 1983).

Chapter One

1. Charles Taylor, *Sources of the Self: The Making of the Modern Identity* (Cambridge, MA: Harvard University Press, 1989), p. 112.
2. Clifford Geertz, *Local Knowledge: Further Essays in Interpretive Anthropology* (New York: Basic Books, 1983), p. 59.
3. Saul Bellow, *Mr. Sammler's Planet* (New York: Viking, 1969), p. 111.
4. Geertz, p. 59.
5. Taylor, pp. 112–13.
6. Bruno Snell, *The Discovery of the Mind* (Cambridge, MA: Harvard University Press, 1953), ch. 1.
7. Julian Jaynes, *The Origins of Consciousness in the Breakdown of the Bicameral Mind* (Boston: Houghton Mifflin, 1976), p. 72.
8. Ibid., p. 73.

9. William Ernest Henley, *Echoes. IV* (1888), *In Memoriam R. T. Hamilton Bruce* (*"Invictus"*), stanza 4.

10. Milton C. Nahm (ed.), *Selections from Early Greek Philosophy* (New York: Appleton-Century-Crofts, 1947), p. 93.

11. Edward Hussey, *The Presocratics* (New York: Scribner's, 1972), p. 55. The anecdote about Cratylus is mentioned in Aristotle's *Metaphysics* (1010: 10–15).

12. Richard Tarnas, *The Passion of the Western Mind* (New York: Harmony Books, 1991), p. 33.

13. A. J. Lyon, "Problems of Personal Identity," in G. H. R. Parkinson (ed.), *The Handbook of Western Philosophy* (New York: Macmillan, 1988), p. 442.

14. Isaiah Berlin, *The Crooked Timber of Humanity: Chapters in the History of Ideas* (New York: Knopf, 1991), p. 53.

15. Marcel Mauss, "A Category of the Human Mind: The Notion of Person, the Notion of 'Self,' " in *Sociology and Psychology: Essays*, trans. Ben Brewster (London: Routledge & Kegan Paul, 1979), p. 81.

16. Augustine, *De Vera Religione*, XXXIX, 72, quoted in Taylor, p. 129.

17. Roy F. Baumeister, *Identity: Cultural Change and the Struggle for Self* (New York: Oxford University Press, 1986), p. 30.

18. Georges Duby, "Solitude: Eleventh to Thirteenth Century," in Philippe Aries and Georges Duby (eds.), *A History of Private Life*, vol. 2, *Revelations of the Medieval World* (Cambridge, MA: Harvard University Press, 1987–1991), p. 509.

19. Philippe Aries, *Centuries of Childhood: A Social History of Family Life*, trans. R. Baldick (New York: Random House, 1962).

20. L. Stone, *The Family, Sex and Marriage in England 1500–1800* (New York: Harper & Row, 1977).

21. K. J. Weintraub, *The Value of the Individual: Self and Circumstance in Autobiography* (Chicago: University of Chicago Press, 1978).

22. Theodore Zeldin, *An Intimate History of Humanity* (New York: HarperCollins, 1994), p. 65.

23. Baumeister, p. 36.

24. Lionel Trilling, *Sincerity and Authenticity* (Cambridge, MA: Harvard University Press, 1971), p. 13.

25. Tarnas, p. 280.

26. David Hume, *A Treatise of Human Nature* (1738), quoted in Baumeister, p. 12.

Chapter Two

1. Anthony Giddens, *Modernity and Self-Identity: Self and Society in the Late Modern Age* (Stanford, CA: Stanford University Press, 1991), p. 14.

2. David Reisman, in collaboration with Reuel Denney and Nathan Glazer, *The Lonely Crowd: A Study of the Changing American Character* (New Haven: Yale University Press, 1950), p. 26.

3. Ibid., p. 22 (italics in original).

4. Ibid., p. 26.

5. Ibid.

6. Rollo May, *The Meaning of Anxiety* (New York: Ronald Press, 1950), p. *v*.

7. In T. S. Eliot, *Selected Poems* (New York: Penguin, 1951), pp. 9–14.

8. See my essay "Four Different Ways to Be Absolutely Right," in *The Truth About the Truth* (New York: Tarcher/Putnam, 1995).

9. Bruce Wilshire, *Romanticism and Evolution: The Nineteenth Century* (New York: Putnam, 1968), p. 11.

10. Abraham H. Maslow, *Toward a Psychology of Being* (New York: Van Nostrand, 1962), p. 3.

11. Phyllis Schlafly, *The Power of the Positive Woman* (New Rochelle, NY: Arlington House, 1977), p. 49.

12. Sheila McNamee, "Therapy and Identity Construction in a Postmodern World," in Debra Grodin and Thomas R. Lindlof (eds.), *Constructing the Self in a Mediated World* (Thousand Oaks, CA: Sage, 1996), p. 145.

Chapter Three

1. Kenneth J. Gergen, *The Saturated Self: Dilemmas of Identity in Contemporary Life* (New York: Basic Books, 1990), p. 228.

2. Robert Jay Lifton, *The Protean Self: Human Resilience in an Age of Fragmentation* (New York: Basic Books, 1993), p. 2.

3. Paul Kugler, "The 'Subject' of Dreams," *Dreaming* 3, no. 2 (1993): 125.

4. C. G. Jung, *Tavistock Lectures, Lecture 3* (London: Routledge & Kegan Paul, 1935), p. 81.

5. Roberto Assagioli, *Psychosynthesis: A Manual of Principles and Techniques* (New York: Hobbs, Dorman, 1965), p. 26.

6. Kenneth J. Gergen, "The Healthy, Happy Human Being Wears Many Masks," *Psychology Today* (1972). Reprinted in Walter Truett Anderson (ed.), *The Truth About the Truth* (New York: Tarcher/Putnam, 1976).

7. Steinar Kvale, "From the Archaeology of the Psyche to the Architecture of Cultural Landscapes," introduction to Kvale (ed.), *Psychology and Postmodernism* (Newbury Park, CA: Sage, 1992), p. 1.

8. Peter Berger, Brigitte Berger, and Hansfried Kellner, *The Homeless Mind: Modernization and Consciousness* (New York: Vintage, 1974), p. 63.

9. *The New Yorker Twenty-Fifth Anniversary Album* (New York: Harper, 1951).

10. This briefly summarizes the historical overview I have presented in two previous works: *Reality Isn't What It Used to Be* (New York: HarperCollins, 1990), and *The Truth About the Truth* (New York: Tarcher/Putnam, 1995). The reader may want to consult the various works on postmodernism and related themes that are cited in those books.

11. Gergen, *The Saturated Self*, p. 69.

12. Karl Mannheim, *Ideology and Utopia* (New York: Harcourt, Brace, 1936), p. 7.

13. Gergen, *The Saturated Self*, p. 46.

14. Ibid., p. 151, citing, among others, Mark L. Snyder, "Self-Monitoring Processes," in Leonard Berkowitz (ed.), *Advances in Experimental Social Psychology*, vol. 12 (New York: Academic Press, 1979).

15. Robert J. Lifton, *Thought Reform and the Psychology of Totalism: A Study of "Brainwashing" in China* (New York: W. W. Norton, 1963).

16. Robert J. Lifton, *Boundaries: Psychological Man in Revolution* (New York: Vintage, 1970).

17. Lifton, *The Protean Self*, p. 8.

18. Ibid., pp. 8–9.

19. Kugler, p. 125.

20. Ernest Becker, *The Denial of Death* (New York: The Free Press, 1973), p. *ix*.

21. Brewster Smith, "Selfhood at Risk: Postmodern Perils and the Perils of Postmodernism," *American Psychologist*, May 1994, p. 405.

22. Kenneth J. Gergen, "Exploring the Postmodern: Perils or Potentials," *American Psychologist*, May 1994, p. 414.

23. Robert N. Bellah et al., *Habits of the Heart: Individualism and Commitment in American Life* (Berkeley: University of California Press, 1985).

24. Amitai Etzioni, *Spirit of Community: Rights, Responsibilities, and the Communitarian Agenda* (New York: Crown, 1993).

25. Gergen, *The Saturated Self*, p. 150.

Chapter Four

1. Jean Baker Miller, "The Development of Women's Sense of Self," in Judith V. Jordan et al. (eds.), *Women's Growth in Connection: Writings from the Stone Center* (New York: The Guilford Press, 1991), p. 11.

2. Pamela McCorduck and Nancy Ramsey, *The Futures of Women: Scenarios for the 21st Century* (Reading, MA: Addison-Wesley, 1996), pp. 3–4.

3. Mary Catherine Bateson, *Composing a Life* (New York: Atlantic Monthly Press, 1989), p. 13.

4. Daniel Levinson, *The Seasons of a Man's Life* (New York: Alfred A. Knopf, 1978).

5. Janet L. Surrey, "The Self-in-Relation: A Theory of Women's Development," in Judith V. Jordan et al. (eds.), *Women's Growth in Connection*.

6. Harry Stack Sullivan, *The Interpersonal Theory of Psychiatry* (New York: W. W. Norton, 1953), p. 10.

7. Dorinne Kondo, *Crafting Selves: Power, Gender and Discourses of Identity in a Japanese Workplace* (Chicago: University of Chicago Press, 1990), p. 14.

8. Thomas Alan Parry, "Without a Net: Preparations for Postmodern Living," in Steven Friedman (ed.), *The New Language of Change: Constructive Collaboration in Psychotherapy* (New York: The Guilford Press, 1993), p. 429.

9. Bateson, *Composing a Life*, p. 9.

10. Mary Field Belenky, Blythe McVicker Clincy, Nancy Rule Goldberger, and Jill Mattuck Tarule, *Women's Ways of Knowing: The Development of Self, Voice, and Mind*

(New York: Basic Books, 1986), p. 15. The conceptual scheme is based on the research of William Perry; see his *Forms of Intellectual and Ethical Development in the College Years* (New York: Holt, Rinehart & Winston, 1970).

11. R. Klatch, "Coalition and Conflict Among Women of the New Right," *Signs: Journal of Women in Culture and Society* 13 (1988): 676–77.

12. Anne Fausto-Sterling, *Myths of Gender: Biological Theories About Women and Men* (New York: Basic Books, 1992).

Chapter Five

1. Michael S. Gazzaniga, *The Social Brain: Discovering the Networks of the Mind* (New York: Basic Books, 1985), p. x.

2. Francis Crick, *The Astonishing Hypothesis: The Scientific Search for the Soul* (New York: Scribner's, 1994), p. 3.

3. Alan Watts, *The Book: On the Taboo Against Knowing Who You Are* (New York: Random House, 1966), p. ix.

4. Sigmund Freud, *An Outline of Psychoanalysis* (1940), trans. James Strachey (New York: Norton, 1949), p. 14.

5. Ibid., p. 110.

6. Sigmund Freud, *Moses and Monotheism*, trans. Katherine Jones (New York: Knopf, 1939), p. 152.

7. Sigmund Freud, *Introductory Lectures to Psychoanalysis* (1915–1917), trans. James Strachey, in Strachey (ed.), *The Standard Edition of the Complete Works of Sigmund Freud*, vol. 16 (London: Hogarth Press, 1953–1974), pp. 284–85.

8. Sigmund Freud, *New Introductory Lectures on Psycho-Analysis* (New York: Norton, 1933), p. 112.

9. Sigmund Freud (with Josef Breuer), *Studies on Hysteria* (1893), trans. James Strachey (London: Hogarth Press, 1961), p. 305.

10. Sigmund Freud, *Civilization and Its Discontents* (1930), trans. James Strachey (New York: W. W. Norton, 1951), p. 80.

11. Israel Rosenfield, *The Invention of Memory: A New View of the Brain* (New York: Basic Books, 1988), p. 13.

12. Howard Gardner, *The Mind's New Science: A History of the Cognitive Revolution* (New York: Basic Books, 1987), p. 271.

13. Robert E. Ornstein, *The Psychology of Consciousness* (San Francisco: W. H. Freeman, 1972), p. 50.

14. Gazzaniga, p. 48.

15. Gardner, p. 11.

16. Daniel C. Dennett, *Consciousness Explained* (Boston: Little, Brown, 1991), p. 106.

17. Francis H. C. Crick, "Thinking About the Brain," *Scientific American*, Sept. 1979.

18. Marvin Minsky, *The Society of Mind* (New York: Simon & Schuster, 1985), p. 51.

19. Gazzaniga, p. 4.

20. Dennett, p. 113.

21. Quoted in Douglas R. Hofstadter and Daniel C. Dennett, *The Mind's I: Fantasies and Reflections on Self & Soul* (New York: Basic Books, 1981), p. 13.

22. Rosenfield, p. 5.

Chapter Six

1. Lewis Thomas, *The Lives of a Cell: Notes of a Biology Watcher* (New York: Bantam, 1974), pp. 84–85.

2. Charles Siebert, "The Cuts That Go Deeper," *The New York Times Magazine*, July 7, 1996, p. 40.

3. Thomas, pp. 85–86.

4. Walter Truett Anderson, *Evolution Isn't What It Used to Be: The Augmented Animal and the Whole Wired World* (New York: W. H. Freeman, 1996), p. 95.

5. Dr. Donald Laub, quoted in Amy Bloom, "A Reporter at Large: The Body Lies," *The New Yorker*, July 18, 1994, p. 47.

6. Philip Reilly, *Genetics, Law and Social Policy* (Cambridge, MA: Harvard University Press, 1977), p. 199. For further discussion of this subject, see Walter Truett Anderson, *To Govern Evolution: Further Adventures of the Political Animal* (Boston: Harcourt Brace Jovanovich, 1987).

7. Youssef M. Ibrahim, "Ethical Furor Erupts in Britain: Should Unclaimed Embryos Die?" *The New York Times*, Aug. 1, 1996, p. 1.

8. "British Clinics, Obeying Law, End Embryos by Thousands" (AP), *The New York Times*, Aug. 2, 1996, p. A3.

9. Barbara Koenig and Sara Tobin, "Should Cloning Be Banned? Think about what we know," *San Francisco Chronicle*, March 21, 1997, p. A29.

10. Siebert, pp. 20–22.

11. "Surgeon Is Convicted of Disguising a Fugitive," *The New York Times*, Feb. 28, 1997, p. A9.

12. Michael Murphy, *The Future of the Body: Explorations Into the Further Evolution of Human Nature* (Los Angeles: Jeremy P. Tarcher, Inc., 1992).

13. Siebert, p. 25.

14. B. D. Colen, "Organ Concert," *Time*, Fall 1996, pp. 70–74.

15. Yumiko Ono and Craig S. Smith, "Mane Attraction: When It Comes to Hair, Extensions Stretch Clear Across the Globe," *The Wall Street Journal*, Oct. 4, 1996, p. 1.

Chapter Seven

1. Michael Ryan, *Secret Life: An Autobiography* (New York: Pantheon, 1995), p. 4.

2. Frank Putnam, *Diagnosis and Treatment of Multiple Personality Disorder* (New York: The Guilford Press, 1989), p. 53.

3. Theodore Zeldin, *An Intimate History of Humanity* (New York: HarperCollins, 1994), p. 311.

4. Quoted in Egon Larsen, *The Deceivers: Lives of the Great Impostors* (New York: Roy Publishers, 1966), p. 16.

5. Ibid., p. 70.

6. Ibid., p. 119.

7. Ryan, pp. 6–7.

8. Allan Janik and Stephen Toulmin, *Wittgenstein's Vienna* (New York: Simon & Schuster, 1973), p. 61.

9. Amity Pierce Buxton, *The Other Side of the Closet: The Coming-Out Crisis for Straight Spouses and Families* (New York: Wiley, 1991).

10. M. Boor, "The Multiple Personality Epidemic: Additional Cases and Inferences Regarding Diagnosis, Dynamics and Cure," *Journal of Nervous and Mental Disease* 170 (1982): 302–4.

11. Ian Hacking, *Rewriting the Soul: Multiple Personality and the Sciences of Memory* (Princeton, NJ: Princeton University Press, 1995), p. 8.

12. Ibid., p. 79.

13. Stanley Krippner, "Cross-Cultural Treatment Perspectives on Dissociative Disorders," in Steven Jay Lynn and Judith W. Rhue (eds.), *Dissociation: Clinical and Theoretical Perspectives* (New York: Guilford, 1994), p. 351.

Chapter Eight

1. William James, *The Varieties of Religious Experience* (New York: Mentor, 1958), p. 298.

2. Jerome Kagan, quoted in David Concar, "Design your own personality," *New Scientist*, March 12, 1994, p. 22.

3. Geoffrey Cowley et al., "The Promise of Prozac," *Newsweek*, March 26, 1990, pp. 38–41.

4. Peter D. Kramer, *Listening to Prozac: A Psychiatrist Explores Antidepressant Drugs and the Remaking of the Self* (New York: Penguin, 1993), p. xvi.

5. Ibid., p. 15.

6. Gerald L. Klerman, "Psychotropic Hedonism vs. Pharmacological Calvinism," *Hastings Center Report* 2 (4): 1–3.

7. Kramer, p. 10.

8. Ibid., p. 14.

9. Ibid., p. 29.

10. Walker Percy, *The Thanatos Syndrome* (New York: Farrar, Straus & Giroux, 1987), p. 21.

11. Kramer, p. 299.

12. Humphry Osmond, quoted in Bernard Aaronson and Humphry Osmond, *Psychedelics: The Uses and Implications of Hallucinogenic Drugs* (New York: Anchor, 1970), p. 478.
13. Sidney Cohen, *The Beyond Within: The LSD Story* (New York: Athaneum, 1964).
14. Walter N. Pahnke, "Drugs and Mysticism," in Aaronson and Osmond, p. 148.
15. See Pahnke and William A. Richards, "Implications of LSD and Experimental Mysticism," in Charles T. Tart (ed.), *Altered States of Consciousness: A Book of Readings* (New York: John Wiley & Sons, 1969), pp. 399–428.
16. Concar, p. 22.
17. Christopher S. Wren, "Keeping Cocaine Resilient: Low Cost and High Profit," *The New York Times*, March 4, 1997, p. 1.

Chapter Nine

1. Elizabeth M. Reid, "Electropolis: Communication and Community on Internet Relay Chat" (adapted from Honours thesis, University of Melbourne, Australia, 1991), p. 8.
2. Robert Rossney, "America Online's Multi-Identity Crisis," *San Francisco Chronicle*, Sept. 21, 1995, p. E7.
3. Victor Grey, *Web Without a Weaver: The Meaning of the Internet* (unpublished manuscript), p. 1.
4. David Tomas, "Old Rituals for New Space: Rites de Passage and William Gibson's Cultural Model of Cyberspace," in Michael Benedikt, *Cyberspace: First Steps* (Cambridge, MA: MIT Press, 1991), pp. 45–46.
5. Sherry Turkle, *Life on the Screen: Identity in the Age of the Internet* (New York: Simon & Schuster, 1995), pp. 12–13.
6. Howard Rheingold, *The Virtual Community: Homesteading on the Electronic Frontier* (Reading, MA: Addison-Wesley, 1993), p. 10.
7. Turkle, p. 13.
8. Ibid., p. 14.
9. Amy Bruckman, "Identity Workshops: Emergent Social and Psychological Phenomena in Text-Based Virtual Reality" (Master's thesis, Massachusetts Institute of Technology Media Laboratory, 1992).
10. Rheingold, p. 164.
11. Allucquere Rosanne Stone, "Will the Real Body Please Stand Up?: Boundary Stories about Virtual Cultures," in Michael Benedikt (ed.), *Cyberspace: First Steps* (Cambridge, MA: MIT Press, 1991), p. 84.
12. Turkle, p. 191.
13. Lindsay Van Gelder, "The Strange Case of the Electronic Lover," *Ms*, Oct. 1985, pp. 94–134. Stone gives a somewhat different version in the article cited above. Also see Turkle, pp. 228–30.
14. Van Gelder, p. 99.

15. Barbara Fitzsimmons, "Dangerous Liaisons: Encounters on-line prove hot enough to melt some marriages," *San Diego Union Tribune*, March 23, 1996, p. E-1.
16. James Gleick, "Big Brother Is Us," *The New York Times Magazine*, Sept. 29, 1996, pp. 131–32.
17. Emerald Yeh and Christine McMurry, "Having Your Identity Stolen Out from Under You," *San Francisco Chronicle*, May 26, 1996, p. 6.
18. Amitai Etzioni, "Why fear data rape?: As computers peer deeper into our lives, we can live better with less privacy," *USA Today*, May 20, 1996, p. 14A.
19. Neal Stephenson, *Snow Crash* (New York: Bantam, 1992).
20. Robert Rossney, "Metaworlds," *Wired*, June 1996, p. 212.

Chapter Ten

1. Robert Wright, *The Moral Animal: Evolutionary Psychology and Everyday Life* (New York: Pantheon, 1994), p. 328.
2. Robert Kegan, *In Over Our Heads: The Mental Demands of Modern Life* (Cambridge, MA: Harvard University Press, 1994), p. 34.
3. Kevin Fagan, "Condemned Killer a Different Man, Lawyers Say," *San Francisco Chronicle*, May 1, 1996, p. 1.
4. Alasdair MacIntyre, *After Virtue* (Notre Dame, IN: University of Notre Dame Press, 1981), p. 38.
5. Ibid., p. 12.
6. Ibid., p. 31.
7. Ibid., p. 33.
8. James Davison Hunter, *Culture Wars: The Struggle to Define America* (New York: Basic Books, 1991), p. 44 (italics in original).
9. Martin Marty, "Religio-Secular Society," *New Perspectives Quarterly* 10 (3): 57.
10. William Perry, quoted in Kegan, p. 29.
11. Lawrence Kohlberg, *Essays on Moral Development*, vol. 1, *The Philosophy of Moral Development* (New York: Harper & Row, 1981), p. 18.
12. Carol Gilligan, *In a Different Voice: Psychological Theory and Women's Development* (Cambridge, MA: Harvard University Press, 1982).
13. Kegan, p. 32.
14. Ibid., pp. 198–99.
15. Ibid., p. 112.
16. Ibid., p. 130.
17. Ibid., p. 270.
18. Ibid., p. 345.
19. Ibid., p. 320.
20. Ibid., p. 313.
21. Ibid., p. 350.
22. Ibid., p. 344.

23. Steve Jones, "Our Genetic Future: The Evolution of Utopia," *The (London) Independent*, Dec. 19, 1991, p. 12.

Chapter Eleven

1. Paul Leinberger and Bruce Tucker, *The New Individualists: The Generation After the Organization Man* (New York: HarperCollins, 1991), p. 418.
2. Ernest Sternberg, *The Economy of Icons*, work in progress.
3. William Bridges, *JobShift: How to Prosper in a Workplace Without Jobs* (Reading, MA: Addison-Wesley, 1994).
4. Arthur M. Louis, "No Place to Call Home: Verifone is a 'virtual workplace,' " *San Francisco Chronicle*, Oct. 22, 1996, p. C1.
5. Charles Perrottet (The Futures Group, Glastonbury, CT), "Traditional Firm's Death Means Change for Consumers," *San Francisco Chronicle*, Jan. 24, 1994, p. C3.
6. Steven L. Goldman, "Agile Competition and Virtual Corporations: The Next 'American Century'?" *Phi Kappa Phi Journal*, Spring 1994, pp. 43–47.
7. International Commission on Peace and Food, *Uncommon Opportunities: An Agenda for Peace and Equitable Development* (London: Zed Books, 1994).
8. Don Smyth, "Achievements, new directions from 1994 ILO conference," *Monthly Labor Review*, Sept. 1994, pp. 46–51.
9. William H. Whyte, Jr., *The Organization Man* (New York: Simon & Schuster, 1956), p. 3.
10. Leinberger and Tucker, pp. 11–12.
11. Ibid., p. 15.
12. Ibid., p. 16.
13. Ibid., p. 17.
14. Richard Rorty, *Contingency, Irony, and Solidarity* (Cambridge and New York: Cambridge University Press, 1989), pp. 73–74.
15. Gerald F. Seib, "Capital Journal," *The Wall Street Journal*, July 24, 1996, p. A20.
16. Leinberger and Tucker, p. 196.
17. Ibid., p. 419.
18. Charles Mackay, *Extraordinary Popular Delusions and the Madness of Crowds* (New York: Farrar, Straus & Giroux, 1932, 1841).
19. Thomas F. Mandel, "American Social and Consumer Trends in the 1990s," Values and Lifestyles Program, SRI International, Menlo Park, California.
20. Jim Collins, *Uncommon Cultures: Popular Culture and Post-Modernism* (New York: Routledge, 1989), p. *xiii*.
21. Shawn Tully, "Teens: The Most Global Market of All," *Fortune*, May 16, 1994, p. 90.

Chapter Twelve

1. Eric Hobsbawm, *Age of Extremes: The Short Twentieth Century, 1914–1991* (New York: Viking Penguin, 1994).

2. Leon Wieseltier, "Against Identity," *The New Republic*, Nov. 28, 1994, p. 30.

3. Jean Baudrillard, *America*, trans. Chris Turner (London and New York: Verso, 1988).

4. Wieseltier, p. 30.

5. Alastair Roderick Ewins, *Tradition, Politics, and Change in Contemporary Fiji and Tonga* (Ph.D. thesis, The Australian National University, 1995), p. 148.

6. Ibid., pp. 239–40.

7. Charles Dickens, *The Chimes, Second Quarter*.

8. F. C. Butler, *Community Americanization* (Washington, DC: Government Printing Office, 1920), p. 14.

9. Quoted in Daniel Kevles, *In the Name of Eugenics* (New York: Knopf, 1985), pp. 102–4.

10. David A. Hollinger, *Postethnic America: Beyond Multiculturalism* (New York: Basic Books, 1995), p. 95.

11. Gary Peller, "Race Consciousness," in Dan Danielsen and Karen Engle (eds.), *After Identity: A Reader in Law and Culture* (New York: Routledge, 1995), p. 67.

12. Introduction to Danielsen and Engle, p. *xiii*.

13. Robert S. Boyd, "Race has no basic biologic reality," *The Buffalo News*, Oct. 27, 1966, p. H-6.

14. Regina Austin, " 'The Black Community,' Its Lawbreakers, and a Politics of Identification," in Danielsen and Engle, p. 143.

15. Stanley Crouch, "Race Is Over," *The New York Times Magazine*, Sept. 29, 1996, p. 170.

16. Hollinger, p. 106.

17. Mary C. Waters, *Ethnic Options: Choosing Identities in America* (Berkeley: University of California Press, 1990), p. 7.

18. David Jacobson, *Rights Across Borders: Immigration and the Decline of Citizenship* (Baltimore: Johns Hopkins University Press, 1996), p. 128.

19. Leo Tolstoy, *War and Peace*, part IX, chapter 10, trans. Constance Garnett (New York: Modern Library, 1994), p. 932.

20. See, for example, Charles Taylor, "The Politics of Recognition," in Amy Gutmann (ed.), *Multiculturalism and the Politics of Recognition* (Princeton: Princeton University Press, 1992).

21. Will Kymlicka, "Interpreting Group Rights," *The Good Society* 6 (2): 9.

22. Todd Gitlin, *The Twilight of Common Dreams: Why America Is Wracked by Culture Wars* (New York: Metropolitan, 1995), pp. 37–38.

23. Jacobson, pp. 8–9.

24. Thomas M. Franck, "The Emerging Right to Democratic Governance," *American Journal of International Law* 86 (46): 50.

25. Jacobson, pp. 38–39.
26. Francis Fukuyama, *The End of History and the Last Man* (New York: The Free Press, 1992), p. 272.
27. Samuel P. Huntington, "The Clash of Civilizations?" *Foreign Affairs*, Summer 1993, p. 22.
28. Jean-Marie Guehenno, *The End of the Nation-State*, trans. Victoria Elliott (Minneapolis: University of Minnesota Press, 1995), p. 17.
29. Ibid., p. 49.
30. Hobsbawm, p. 429.

Chapter Thirteen

1. Alan Watts, *The Book: On the Taboo Against Knowing Who You Are* (New York: Vintage, 1989), p. 130.
2. Sri Nisargadatta Maharaj, *I Am That*, trans. Maurice Frydman (Durham, NC: The Acorn Press, 1973), p. 204.
3. Herbert Fingarette, "The Ego and Mystic Selflessness," in Maurice Stein, Arthur J. Vidich, and David Manning White (eds.), *Identity and Anxiety: Survival of the Person in Mass Society* (Glencoe, IL: The Free Press, 1960), p. 553.
4. Ibid., pp. 554–55.
5. Ibid., p. 557.
6. Ibid., p. 581.
7. *The Bhagavad-Gita*, trans. Prabhavananda and Christopher Isherwood (New York: New American Library, 1954), p. 84.
8. D. Goddard, *A Buddhist Bible* (New York: E. P. Dutton, 1938), pp. 352–54.
9. Fingarette, p. 560 (italics in original).
10. Ibid., pp. 563–64.
11. Alan W. Watts, *Psychotherapy East and West* (New York: Mentor, 1963), p. 11.
12. Ibid., p. 53.
13. Ibid., p. 77.
14. Watts, *The Book*, p. *ix*.
15. See Aldous Huxley, *The Doors of Perception* (New York: Harper, 1954).
16. Watts, *Psychotherapy East and West*, p. 73.
17. Nisargadatta, p. 96.
18. S. E. Braude, *First Person Plural: Multiple Personality and the Philosophy of Mind* (Lanham, MD: Rowman and Littlefield, 1995).

Chapter Fourteen

1. John Lennon, "Imagine."
2. Peter Drucker, quoted in "A cantankerous interview with Peter Schwartz and Kevin Kelly," *Wired*, August 1996, p. 182.

3. Wolfhart Pannenberg, *The Kingdom of God and Theology* (Philadelphia: The Westminster Press, 1969).

4. See John H. Holland, *Hidden Order: How Adaptation Builds Complexity* (Reading, MA: Addison-Wesley, 1995), pp. 31–34.

5. Kees van der Heijden, *Scenarios: The Art of Strategic Conversation* (New York: Wiley, 1996), p. 17.

6. Published first as Francis Fukuyama, "The End of History?" *The National Interest*, no. 16 (Summer 1989), pp. 3–18; then expanded to book size as *The End of History and The Last Man* (New York: Free Press, 1992).

7. See Robert D. Kaplan, *The Ends of the Earth: A Journey at the Dawn of the 21st Century* (New York: Random House, 1996).

8. David Harvey, *The Condition of Postmodernity: An Enquiry into the Origins of Cultural Change* (Cambridge, MA: Basil Blackwell, 1989), p. 27.

9. See Robert Nisbet, *History of the Idea of Progress* (New York: Basic Books, 1980).

10. Arthur Herman, *The Idea of Decline in Western History* (New York: The Free Press, 1997).

11. Stephen Toulmin, *The Return to Cosmology: Postmodern Science and the Theology of Nature* (Berkeley: University of California Press, 1982), p. 254.

Index

About the Author

Walter Truett Anderson is currently fellow and vice president of the Meridian International Institute; president, American Division of World Academy of Art and Science; and associate editor and columnist for Pacific News Service. He lives in northern California.